Voice over IP: Strategies for the Converged Network

Voice over IP: Strategies for the Converged Network

Mark A. Miller, P.E.

M&T Books
An imprint of IDG Books Worldwide, Inc.

Foster City, CA ◆ Chicago, IL ◆ Indianapolis, IN ◆ New York, NY

Voice over IP: Strategies for the
Converged Network

Published by
M&T Books
An imprint of IDG Books Worldwide, Inc.
919 E. Hillsdale Blvd., Suite 400
Foster City, CA 94404
www.idgbooks.com (IDG Books Worldwide Web site)

ISBN: 0-7645-4617-1

Printed in the United States of America

10 9 8 7 6 5 4 3 2

1W/TR/RQ/QQ/FC

Distributed in the United States by IDG Books Worldwide, Inc.

Distributed by CDG Books Canada Inc. for Canada; by Transworld Publishers Limited in the United Kingdom; by IDG Norge Books for Norway; by IDG Sweden Books for Sweden; by IDG Books Australia Publishing Corporation Pty. Ltd. for Australia and New Zealand; by TransQuest Publishers Pte Ltd. for Singapore, Malaysia, Thailand, Indonesia, and Hong Kong; by Gotop Information Inc. for Taiwan; by ICG Muse, Inc. for Japan; by Intersoft for South Africa; by Eyrolles for France; by International Thomson Publishing for Germany, Austria and Switzerland; by Distribuidora Cuspide for Argentina; by LR International for Brazil; by Galileo Libros for Chile; by Ediciones ZETA S.C.R. Ltda. for Peru; by WS Computer Publishing Corporation, Inc., for the Philippines; by Contemporanea de Ediciones for Venezuela; by Express Computer Distributors for the Caribbean and West Indies; by Micronesia Media Distributor, Inc. for Micronesia; by Chips Computadoras S.A. de C.V. for Mexico; by Editorial Norma de Panama S.A. for Panama; by American Bookshops for Finland.

For general information on IDG Books Worldwide's books in the U.S., please call our Consumer Customer Service department at 800-762-2974. For reseller information, including discounts and premium sales, please call our Reseller Customer Service department at 800-434-3422.

For information on where to purchase IDG Books Worldwide's books outside the U.S., please contact our International Sales department at 317-596-5530 or fax 317-596-5692.

For consumer information on foreign language translations, please contact our Customer Service department at 800-434-3422, fax 317-596-5692, or e-mail rights@idgbooks.com.

For information on licensing foreign or domestic rights, please phone +1-650-655-3109.

For sales inquiries and special prices for bulk quantities, please contact our Sales department at 650-655-3200 or write to the address above.

For information on using IDG Books Worldwide's books in the classroom or for ordering examination copies, please contact our Educational Sales department at 800-434-2086 or fax 317-596-5499.

For press review copies, author interviews, or other publicity information, please contact our Public Relations department at 650-655-3000 or fax 650-655-3299.

Library of Congress Cataloging-in-Publication Data
Miller, Mark, 1955-
    Voice over IP : strategies for the converged network / Mark A. Miller.
        p. cm.
    Includes bibliographical references and index.
    ISBN 0-7645-4617-1 (alk. paper)
    1. Internet telephony. 2. TCP/IP (Computer network protocol)
    I. Title.
TK5105.8865. M55   2000
621.382'1--dc21
                                                    99-462380

 is a registered trademark or trademark under exclusive license to IDG Books Worldwide, Inc. from International Data Group, Inc. in the United States and/or other countries.

 is a trademark of IDG Books Worldwide, Inc.

ABOUT IDG BOOKS WORLDWIDE

Welcome to the world of IDG Books Worldwide.

IDG Books Worldwide, Inc., is a subsidiary of International Data Group, the world's largest publisher of computer-related information and the leading global provider of information services on information technology. IDG was founded more than 30 years ago by Patrick J. McGovern and now employs more than 9,000 people worldwide. IDG publishes more than 290 computer publications in over 75 countries. More than 90 million people read one or more IDG publications each month.

Launched in 1990, IDG Books Worldwide is today the #1 publisher of best-selling computer books in the United States. We are proud to have received eight awards from the Computer Press Association in recognition of editorial excellence and three from Computer Currents' First Annual Readers' Choice Awards. Our best-selling ...For Dummies® series has more than 50 million copies in print with translations in 31 languages. IDG Books Worldwide, through a joint venture with IDG's Hi-Tech Beijing, became the first U.S. publisher to publish a computer book in the People's Republic of China. In record time, IDG Books Worldwide has become the first choice for millions of readers around the world who want to learn how to better manage their businesses.

Our mission is simple: Every one of our books is designed to bring extra value and skill-building instructions to the reader. Our books are written by experts who understand and care about our readers. The knowledge base of our editorial staff comes from years of experience in publishing, education, and journalism — experience we use to produce books to carry us into the new millennium. In short, we care about books, so we attract the best people. We devote special attention to details such as audience, interior design, use of icons, and illustrations. And because we use an efficient process of authoring, editing, and desktop publishing our books electronically, we can spend more time ensuring superior content and less time on the technicalities of making books.

You can count on our commitment to deliver high-quality books at competitive prices on topics you want to read about. At IDG Books Worldwide, we continue in the IDG tradition of delivering quality for more than 30 years. You'll find no better book on a subject than one from IDG Books Worldwide.

John Kilcullen
Chairman and CEO
IDG Books Worldwide, Inc.

Steven Berkowitz
President and Publisher
IDG Books Worldwide, Inc.

WINNER
Eighth Annual Computer Press Awards ≥1992

WINNER
Ninth Annual Computer Press Awards ≥1993

WINNER
Tenth Annual Computer Press Awards ≥1994

WINNER
Eleventh Annual Computer Press Awards ≥1995

Credits

ACQUISITIONS EDITORS
Michelle Baxter
Jim Sumser

PROJECT EDITOR
Robert MacSweeney

TECHNICAL EDITOR
Dr. John Thompson

COPY EDITORS
Annette S. Devlin
Julie M. Smith

PROJECT COORDINATOR
Linda Marousek
Marcos Vergara

QUALITY CONTROL SPECIALISTS
Laura Taflinger
Chris Weisbart

GRAPHICS AND PRODUCTION SPECIALISTS
Jude Levinson
Michael Lewis
Ramses Ramirez
Victor Pérez-Varela
Dina F Quan

BOOK DESIGNER
Jim Donohue

ILLUSTRATOR
Donna Mullen

PROOFREADING AND INDEXING
York Production Services

About the Author

Mark A. Miller, P.E. is the author of *The Network Troubleshooting Library* and The IP Technologies Library, both published by M&T Books. Other titles include: LAN Troubleshooting Handbook, 2nd Edition, LAN Protocol Handbook, Internetworking, 2nd Edition, Troubleshooting Internetworks, Troubleshooting TCP/IP, 3rd Edition, Managing Internetworks with SNMP, 2nd Edition, and Implementing IPv6, 2nd Edition. He is President of DigiNet Corporation, a Denver-based data communications engineering firm specializing in the design of local area and wide area networks. Mr. Miller is a frequent speaker at industry events, and has taught numerous tutorials on internetwork design and analysis at ComNet, Comdex, Networld+Interop, Next Generation Networks, and other conferences. He is a member of the IEEE and NSPE and a registered professional engineer in four states. For information on his many tutorials, including one that is based upon this text, contact him via mark@diginet.com.

To Holly, for her steadfast support

Preface

Technology (and for that matter, life in general) seems to be moving at an ever-increasing pace. The classic technical example is the Internet, where terms such as *multimedia* and *electronic commerce* were not widely used just a few years ago. (I will leave the classic *life* example up to your own research!) While we used to debate whether IBM's SNA, Digital Equipment Corporation's (now part of Compaq Computer Corporation) DECnet, or Novell's NetWare was the strongest networking architecture, there is now a clear and indisputable winner – the Internet Protocol or IP – which is supported in virtually all network operating systems, including SNA, DECnet, and NetWare. And of the various elements of the Internet protocol suite, the Hypertext Transport Protocol, or HTTP, which is used to transfer information on the World Wide Web, is now the most frequently used application on many networks.

Part of the buzz surrounding IP, and its emergence as the primary networking alternative of choice, is the term *network convergence*. Simply put, convergence means that all networking applications – voice, data, fax, image, or various combinations – should employ a single, cohesive networking infrastructure.

However, *convergence* is one of those terms that differs in theory and practice. In theory, voice traffic, which can be converted into a digital format, can coexist along with LAN traffic on a packet network. In practice, however, a voice application is quite unique, *primarily because the voice application must occur in real time.* And that challenge – the transport of real-time information via an IP-based network infrastructure – is the topic of this, the fourth volume in the *IP Library* series.

Who Should Read This Book

This book is written for network designers, managers, and engineers who are exploring converged network technologies and thinking about combining their voice, data, video, or other information into a single system. It is assumed that readers have some degree of experience with both voice and data communication systems, such as Private Branch Exchanges (PBXs) and routers, respectively. It is also assumed that readers have had some exposure to both local and wide area networks, and to how TCP/IP and other Internet protocols operate on these networks. Readers needing details regarding TCP/IP may find two other volumes of this series to be helpful: *Troubleshooting TCP/IP*, 3rd Edition, or *Implementing IPv6*, 2nd Edition.

How This Book is Organized

This book is organized into three major sections: text chapters, reference appendices, and a CD-ROM.

The text chapters fall into four main categories: converged network principles and applications (Chapters 1 and 2), converged network business issues (Chapter 3), converged network technologies for protocols, wide area transport, and premises equipment (Chapters 4, 5, and 6), and converged network implementation (Chapter 7).

The appendices provide a number of ready references for the reader, including lists of relevant standards, contact information for standards organizations, trade organizations, and IETF working groups, acronyms, abbreviations, and more.

The CD contains four main categories: Request for Comments (RFC) documents from the Internet Engineering Task Force (IETF) that relate to converged network technologies, a sample voice over IP client implementation, a sample fax over IP client implementation, and some sample traffic analysis calculators.

I trust that the information in this book will assist you in converging your networks for the next networking millennium!

mark@diginet.com
January 2000

Acknowledgments

Many individuals made contributions to this work. The management and staff at IDG Books Worldwide, Inc., including Michelle Baxter, Robert MacSweeney, Kevin Shafer, and Julie Smith, provided editorial support. My technical editor, Dr. John Thompson, made numerous suggestions for improvement, and my copy editor, Annette Devlin, made sure that no grammatical rules were violated. Donna Mullen did most of the research on the appendices and produced all of the figures.

A number of individuals assisted with the case studies, examples, and figures given in this text. In alphabetical order, they are: Rod Anderson, Dane Andon, Berge Ayvazian, Yasmin Bendror, Woody Bode, David Bonner, Peter Broughton, John Gallant, Glen Gerhard, Emily Hierstein, Tim Hood, Joel Hughes, Ted Jackson, Eldon Mast, Sanjay Mewada, Chris Miller, Ed Morgan, Frank Ohrtman, John Peters, Birgit Reipe, Robyn Roberts, Lee Tune, Scott Wilson, Beth Winkowski, and David Yuan.

Joe Covey, Tom Howard, and Luc St-Arnaud provided the client software that is included on the CD-ROM that accompanies this text.

Contents at a Glance

Contents

Table of Illustrations

Chapter 1

Principles of Converged Networks

The concepts of network convergence – using one network to transmit both voice and data information – are not new. We can trace the evolution of these technologies back several decades to the birth of the Integrated Services Digital Network (ISDN) developments. This work, which was standardized by the International Telecommunication Union – Telecommunications Standards Sector (ITU-T), or formerly the Consultative Committee for International Telephony and Telegraphy (CCITT), was the subject of much discussion and interest in the 1980s. We will begin with a brief history lesson.

1.1 The Promise of Network Convergence

In the 1980s, the term *convergence* was rarely used. Instead, telephone providers and subscribers used the term *integrated* to describe their vision of using a single telephone line to their home or business, and then being able to use that multifunction line for a variety of applications. These included voice communications (one or possibly two conversations over that single line), data applications for remote host access (stay-at-home shopping, remote electric meter reading, and so on), and even video applications (à la the famed Picturephone developed by Bell Telephone Laboratories in the 1950s). At that time, ISDN proponents envisioned that these new technologies would displace the currently deployed analog Public Switched Telephone Network (PSTN) within a few years.

Unfortunately, the implementation of ISDN was more of a challenge than the architects of the technology envisioned. When the telephone companies began to deploy ISDN, it was discovered that a large number of the local loops, or, in other words, the physical circuits from the telephone company central office to the end users' premises (home or small business), would not support this high speed data transmission. In particular, some of the loops were too long, and some included systems to optimize the network for voice transmission, which would not support the transmission of high speed data.

As a result, ISDN deployments were primarily focused on the requirements for new construction. For example, if a new housing development was under construction, and new telephone service was required, then making that new service compatible with ISDN technology made sense. On the other hand, retrofitting existing outside plant systems to support ISDN was much more expensive, and was often not undertaken. As an end result, there are still large parts of the United States that do not have ISDN service available. So in that respect, we could say that the promise of converged networks based on ISDN technologies met with limited success. The North American ISDN Users' Forum (NIUF) is a good resource for those interested in ISDN technologies [1-1].

But before dismissing the concepts of converged voice and data networks as just one more carrier offering, we need to look at another significant trend – this time coming from the data side of telecommunications – the emerging ubiquity of the Internet Protocol, or IP. This protocol was originally designed in support of U.S. military and higher education data networks, and was migrated into general business usage in the 1990s. The predecessor network to the current Internet was named the ARPANET, an acronym for the Advanced Research Projects Agency Network, which was funded in part by the U. S. Government. The ARPA architecture divided the computer communication functions into four different layers as shown in Figure 1-1: the Network Interface or Local Network Layer, the Internet Layer, the Host-to-Host Layer, and the Process/Application Layer.

OSI Layer	ARPA Architecture
Application	Process / Application Layer
Presentation	Process / Application Layer
Session	Process / Application Layer
Transport	Host-to-Host Layer
Network	Internet Layer
Data Link	Network Interface or Local Network Layer
Physical	Network Interface or Local Network Layer

Figure 1-1 Comparing OSI and ARPA Models

Figure 1-1 also compares the ARPA architecture, originally developed in 1969, with the more familiar Open Systems Interconnection (OSI) Reference Model, originally published by the International Organization for Standardization (ISO) in 1978 [1-2].

The ARPA Network Interface or Local Network Layer corresponds with the OSI Physical and Data Link Layers and comprises the hardware elements of the networking infrastructure. The ARPA Internet Layer corresponds with the OSI Network Layer and is responsible for routing and switching the information (typically divided into packets) through that networking infrastructure; as such, it must deal with issues such as packet delivery, routing tables, addressing schemes, and so on. The Internet Protocol (IP) resides at the ARPA Internet Layer. The ARPA Host-to-Host Layer corresponds with the OSI Transport Layer and is responsible for the reliable end-to-end delivery of those packets. The Transmission Control Protocol (TCP) resides at the ARPA Host-to-Host Layer. Finally, the ARPA Process/Application Layer deals with the functions in support of the end user's application, such as the logical connection (OSI Session Layer), data formats (OSI Presentation Layer), and application-specific support (OSI Application Layer).

At the present time, it would be very difficult to find any type of computing platform, from the smallest laptop to the largest mainframe computer, that does not support IP. In most cases, IP is used in conjunction with other protocols, such as the Transmission Control Protocol, or TCP. The term TCP/IP actually refers to a suite of protocols, which in most cases are incorporated into the host's operating system. A companion text, *Troubleshooting TCP/IP* [1-3], provides details on this widespread support for TCP/IP.

Two trends have emerged thus far. Looking at the voice networking side first, the idea of some type of combined voice/data network is not new. Unfortunately the early implementations, such as ISDN, were somewhat problematic, and as a result, most of the voice networking infrastructure within the PSTN of today is much like it was several decades ago (albeit with allowances for improvements in network technologies and capacities). Looking at the data networking side second, IP has become the common denominator infrastructure of choice, widely implemented around the world. Thus, addressing the needs for combined voice/data networks, with technologies that are now more implementable than those of decades past, has some definite appeal [1-4]. Reference [1-5] discusses the widespread acceptance that IP-based technologies have currently achieved.

Our study of Voice over IP systems (VoIP) will begin with a look at the principles of network convergence – the concepts that allow voice, data, and video signals to share a common networking infrastructure. We will start this journey by looking at some of the principles – and caveats – that are driving this area of technology, as discussed in References [1-6] through [1-12].

1.2 Connectionless vs. Connection-Oriented Network Architectures

In general, communications networks can provide one of two different types of network services: connectionless (CLS) network service and connection-oriented (CO) network service. More specifically, an individual layer within that network architecture can also be defined by the service that it provides to the adjacent layer above: either CO or CLS service. Taken as a whole, the communication architecture may incorporate some combination of these services in support of a particular application.

The typical model for a connection-oriented network service is the Public Switched Telephone Network (PSTN). When the end user takes the telephone off-hook, they notify the network that service is requested. The network then returns dial tone, and the end user dials the destination number. When the destination party answers, the end-to-end connection is confirmed through the various switching offices along that path. A conversation (or more typically a voice mail message) can then ensue, and when the conversation is completed, the parties say goodbye and hang up. The network then disconnects the call, terminates the billing process, and makes the network resources available for another conversation.

For the duration of the connection (or conversation), the communication path may be modeled like a very long pipeline: information is inserted into one end of the pipeline and taken out at the other end of the pipeline. During the time that the connection is active, certain statements can be made about that pipeline. For example, the data should arrive in the order in which it was sent (sequentiality). The data should follow the same path (either a physical or logical path, depending on the network architecture in use) from the source to the destination. Finally, the relative delay of the data should be constant along that path. That is, if there is a 20 millisecond delay on the first word that is transmitted through the telephone network, there should be the same relative delay for the second word, the third word, and so on. Since these characteristics, such as sequentiality, delay, and so on, positively impact the quality and reliability of the transmission, a connection-oriented network is often referred to as a *reliable* network. The Transmission Control Protocol (TCP) is an example of a connection-oriented protocol.

In contrast, a connectionless network could be modeled by the postal system. A full source and destination address is attached to the packet (or envelope), and then that information is dropped into the network (or post office box). Each of these packets is routed independently through the network, and through the miracles of packet delivery protocols, delivery to the ultimate destination occurs – we hope. But like the postal system, connectionless network delivery is on a "best efforts" basis, which means that they will do all they can to get your information through the network, but there are no guarantees. In other words, there are no guarantees of packet sequentiality, delay, or for that matter, delivery at all. (At least, no guarantees for the price of a first class stamp. If you want more reliable package delivery, you can call FedEx, but it will cost you considerably more. Similarly, if a connectionless network does not meet your needs, you can always go with a CO system, but the overhead will generally be higher.) The Internet Protocol (IP) and the User Datagram Protocol are examples of connectionless protocols.

1.3 Voice and Data Network Characteristics

Most enterprise networks are really a "network of networks," with distinct infra-structures that address specific requirements. For example, there may be a separate network for circuit switched voice and fax, a private tie-line network for intra-company voice and fax, a centralized processing data network, such as one based on IBM's System Network Architecture (SNA), a distributed processing data network supporting client/server applications, a private internet or intranet for communication between employees, a public internet or extranet for communica-tion with customers and/or suppliers, and systems and networks supporting other remote access configurations.

In general, voice networking infrastructures are connection-oriented, while data networking infrastructures are connectionless. But in order to determine which network type will be most prevalent in the years to come, let's consider some specifics of each technology.

1.3.1 Voice Network Characteristics

Traditional voice networks, such as the PSTN, are connection-oriented. To initiate a call, the end user takes their telephone off-hook, which signals the telephone com-pany Central Office (C.O.) that service is requested (Figure 1-2). The end user then enters the destination telephone number via the numeric keypad (or rotary dial, if you are into antiques!). The destination telephone number becomes input to the signaling system between the various C.O. switches to set up the call along the path from the source to the destination. The last C.O. in the chain signals the destination user's telephone that an incoming call is in process by sending ringing current through the line, thus creating an audible signal. When the end user (or that person's answering machine) takes the phone off-hook, the circuit is completed and communication can proceed.

One of the key elements that makes the PSTN so effective is its ubiquity, or universal service — the premise that states that basic telephone service should be an affordable commodity to anyone who wants it. As a result, reaching (almost) any end user via the PSTN should be possible.

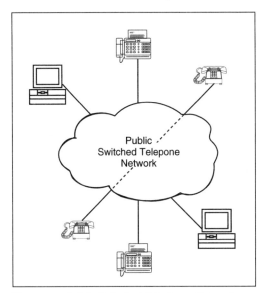

Figure 1-2 Public Switched Telephone Network

This circuit provides a bandwidth of 64 Kbps, an element that is known as a Digital Signal Level 0 (or DS0) channel. We will explore the characteristics of DS0 channels in greater detail in subsequent chapters. For now, suffice it to say that the 64 Kbps of bandwidth that is provided with a DS0 (which dates back several decades) is much more than is required with current voice and fax technologies. For example, a fax transmission uses only 9.6 or 14.4 Kbps of bandwidth, while the balance goes unused. We will see how this "leftover" bandwidth can be used for other conversations with voice compression technologies, thus providing some of the economies of scale that help justify the investment in VoIP and FoIP equipment.

In some cases, switched network connections, which provide 64 Kbps per channel, are not adequate for the amount of information that needs to traverse the connection. For example, two PBXs may have a required number of simultaneous connections between two locations. For those applications, a private voice network can be configured, with trunk circuits provisioned according to the bandwidth requirements (Figure 1-3). As an example, if a dozen or so simultaneous conversations were expected between two locations, a Digital Signal Level 1 (or DS1) circuit would likely be employed, which provides 24 of the DS0 (64 Kbps) channels. As one might expect, the bandwidth of the trunk circuit is primarily limited by the depth of your checkbook – the carrier is quite content to provide more bandwidth as long as you are willing to pay for it. For example, the next step in the multiplexing hierarchy is known as DS3, which operates at 44.736 Mbps and provides the equivalent of 672 DS0 channels between two locations. Not too many organizations need this amount of bandwidth just for voice, but when other media, such as data, fax, and video are considered, then that amount of bandwidth is much easier to justify.

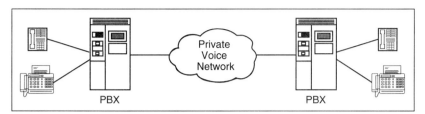

Figure 1-3 Private Voice Network

For the duration of a particular call, however, resources along the path of the circuit have been reserved on behalf of the communicating parties, and, as a result, the parties will pay for the network services for the time that these resources have been reserved. The reservation of resources provides some predictable characteristics of that connection, including a constant delay for that unique path and sequential delivery of the information (the first word that I speak is the first word that you hear, and so on).

But if we were to summarize the characteristics of the telephone network, the term *reliable* would have to be used. Since the PSTN is considered a national resource, regulatory bodies such as the Federal Communications Commission (FCC) and state Public Utility Commissions (PUCs) monitor a number of PSTN operational characteristics. These include: the number and duration of service outages, the time it takes to repair and restore service in the event of an outage, prices the carriers charge for their services, and so on. The term "five nines of reliability" comes from an industry standard for central office switches, which are designed for 2 hours of downtime in a period of forty years of service. If all goes according to design, the network downtime would be calculated as:

2 hours of downtime/40 years * 365 days/year * 24 hours/day = 2/350,400 or 0.00000571

If this number is converted to availability (or uptime) by subtracting it from 1, you have

Network availability = 1 - 0.00000571 = 0.99999429

Converting this to a percentage yields:

99.999429 percent availability (or reliability)

Hence, the term "five nines of reliability".

As we will explore throughout this book, the ultra-reliable performance of the PSTN can be both a blessing and a curse. It is a blessing in that it rarely fails. (For example, when was the last time you went to a payphone to make a call, and the payphone was out of order?) It is a curse in that the end users know how reliable the telephone network is, and will expect that same level of service from a VoIP network.

1.3.2 Data Network Characteristics

In contrast to voice networks, which are generally connection-oriented, data network infrastructures are typically connectionless. Note that a distinction needs to be made between the networking infrastructure and the applications that run over that infrastructure. The applications may require a connection orientation, which would be typically handled by the ARPA Host-to-Host Layer (or OSI Transport Layer). For example, the File Transfer Protocol requires some degree of reliability and synchronization between the sending and receiving file transfer processes. Those functions are handled by TCP, which runs at the ARPA Host-to-Host Layer. IP, which is a connectionless protocol and runs at the (next lower) ARPA Internet Layer, would be considered the defining infrastructure protocol.

The origins of data networking are frequently traced to the development of packet switching and the X.25 protocol in the late 1960s. Packet switching technologies were developed, in part, in response to U.S. Government requirements for secure military communication. The premise was to divide a large message into a number of smaller elements (called packets), and to then send these packets via different routes. The diverse routing made it much harder for an adversary to eavesdrop on the message (thus yielding some degree of network security) when that message was broken up into smaller pieces and transmitted via different paths. Other benefits were also derived from this concept, such as load balancing between these different routes.

Early data networks relied heavily on leased line and packet switched (using X.25) connections, migrating to Internet connections as that transmission medium became more prevalent (Figure 1-4). From the host-to-host applications that were prevalent in the 1960s and 1970s, local area networks (LANs) became the data network of choice in the 1980s. Private data networks that comprised both the local network infrastructure (such as Ethernet LANs) and the wide area connections became the next step in the evolutionary process (Figure 1-5).

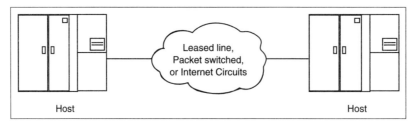

Figure 1-4 Public Data Network

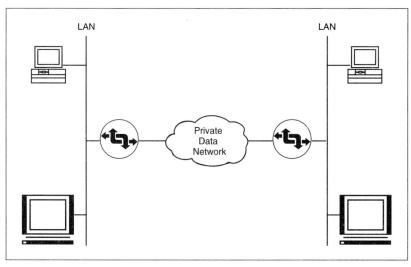

Figure 1-5 Private Data Network

In contrast to the ultra-reliable, ubiquitous PSTN, data networks offer what is called "best-efforts" service. In other words, if your transmission on the Ethernet collides with mine, both are destroyed. But that's the way it goes – the Ethernet undertook its "best efforts" to get the transmission through. This translates to quite a bit less than 99.999 percent reliability; 70–80 percent reliability is a number that is typically quoted. (If you doubt this, ask your end users if they can remember the last time that a payphone failed. Then ask them if they can remember the last time their local network failed. Compare the results, and I think you will get the point.) But when the transmission is successful, you have access to a huge amount of network bandwidth – perhaps megabits per second of bandwidth – not limited to the 64 Kbps channels that are typically provisioned in voice networks.

As a similar contrast, data networks are typically priced based on consumption. If you migrate from 10 Mbps Ethernet to Fast Ethernet to Gigabit Ethernet, you will pay more per port. In a similar fashion, if your WAN connections migrate from a DS1 circuit to a DS3, you also pay more. In contrast, PSTN pricing tends to be relatively flat, because the bandwidth consumed is a consistent 64 Kbps. For example, your PSTN rate may be $0.10 per minute anytime of the day, to any destination in the United States.

Finally, there is a big difference in the speed at which innovation is required within data networks. These technologies move very quickly. The sales, marketing, engineering, customer support, and other departments within data networking organizations must be prepared to move quickly as well, as the end users of this service demand higher and higher data transmission rates, amounts of memory and information storage, and so on. Contrast this with the innovation that is required in the PSTN. The process of making a telephone call today, and one several decades ago, is about the same. The PSTN infrastructure, such as the internal signaling systems, has markedly improved. However, since many of these improvements are not readily visible to the end user, the service presented to those end users may appear to be quiescent.

Which brings us back to the subject of network convergence, and the implementation of an integrated voice/data network, such as that shown in Figure 1-6. Note that elements from both public and private voice and data networks will be present. Our objective, however, will be to take the most favorable characteristics of each network type, and design the new system to optimally handle both voice and data transport with equal facility. Our network infrastructure of choice will be based on IP.

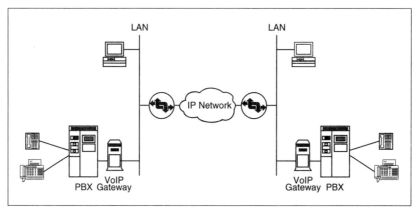

Figure 1-6 Integrated Voice/Data Network

1.4 Voice and Data Network Growth Factors

This section will present some market growth and sizing information that relates to the Internet and other IP-based networks. We will also contrast traffic characteristics of voice and data networks. As with most research of this nature, the observations of the general *trends* become much more important than the finite *details* of the projections themselves, as it is unlikely that any of us can claim a high degree of success in predicting the future. Keep that premise in mind as you study this section, and look for the information that can guide you toward an informed decision regarding network convergence plans for *your* infrastructure.

In most organizations, the *growth* of voice traffic has been relatively flat in the past few years, while the *growth* of data traffic has increased much more aggressively, as shown in Figure 1-7. Note that at this point in our discussion, we are considering growth patterns, not actual traffic volumes. You will also notice that the exact point of crossover on the time axis has been omitted, as this would be a network-specific characteristic so it varies from enterprise to enterprise.

For example, a high technology research center with an ATM switched infrastructure and fiber optic trunk connections may have seen its growth in data traffic exceed that of voice traffic some time ago. In contrast, a call center or service operations center may continue to have more voice than data, and may not have an equivalent amount of voice and data traffic growth (the crossover point) for some time to come. And when you consider that most voice traffic today is still 64 Kbps traffic – not compressed, as the technologies of this text will discuss – then the amount of traffic (measured in bits per second) that leaves your office may be greater in the voice case (today) than in the data case. In any event, however, consider that your data traffic growth should exceed that of your voice network at some time in the future, hence your interest in a converged network infrastructure.

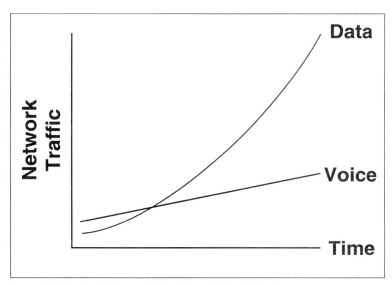

Figure 1-7 Typical Voice and Data Network Growth Patterns

To evaluate this premise, consider the following generalizations. The aggregate voice network (considering the PSTN, private networks, and so on) supports one primary application (voice) and a few data applications (such as modem traffic) that consume relatively small amounts of bandwidth (typically 64 Kbps per channel or less). The aggregate data network (including the Internet, private internetworks, virtual private networks, and application-specific networks, such as SNA backbones) supports many data applications. Much of this is heavily influenced by the large growth in the number of users that are attached to the Internet, as illustrated in Figure 1-8, taken from Reference [1-13]. The most prominent of this Internet traffic is World Wide Web information, which is clearly growing at exponential rates, fueled by electronic commerce and other interactive applications. (For an interesting look at how fast the number of Internet-connected hosts is growing on a daily basis, consult Reference [1-14]). It would not be an exaggeration to depict the generalized growth in voice traffic as being relatively flat (or linear), while the growth in data traffic has some positive slope (and possibly an exponential slope), as depicted in Figure 1-7.

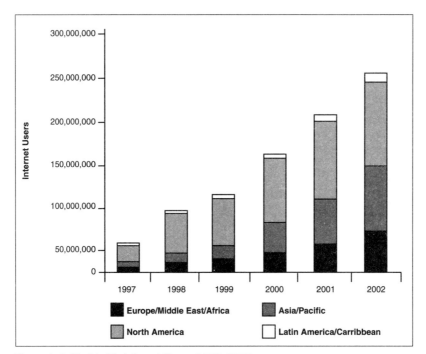

Figure 1-8 Worldwide Internet Users: 1997–2002
(Courtesy of Probe Research, Inc.)

With respect to wide area networks, measurement of the *volume* of traffic can also be informative. A study by the Yankee Group (Boston, Massachusetts) revealed the following information regarding relative volumes of voice and data traffic [1-15].

Year	Voice Traffic Volume	Data Traffic Volume
1996	98	2
1997	96	4
1998	93	7
1999	87	13
2000	78	22
2001	65	35
2002	51	49
2003	41	59

From Figure 1-9, note that the overwhelming majority of WAN traffic volume in 1996 was voice traffic (98 percent), while only a minority of the WAN traffic was data traffic (2 percent). Also note that the WAN traffic volume for data is projected to exceed the volume of voice traffic in the 2002 timeframe (for comparison purposes, the numbers on this graph have been normalized to 1996 values).

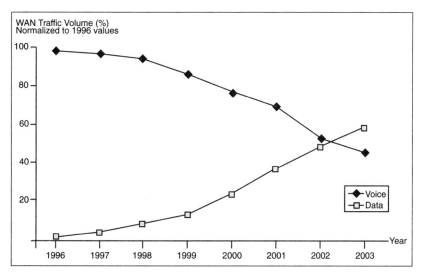

Figure 1-9 Voice vs. Data WAN Traffic Growth: 1996–2003
(Courtesy of The Yankee Group)

An interesting paradigm shift is occurring. In the last several decades, data has been treated as a special application to be sent over voice circuits, with dial-up modem traffic the most prevalent example. In today's environment, with packet-oriented data traffic being the area of highest growth, treating the voice traffic as a special application of data transport garners some appeal.

This can also be illustrated when the mix of global network traffic is segmented by both public (PSTN) and private networks (Figure 1-10). As we have discussed, the PSTN voice traffic has relatively flat growth (the lower portion of Figure 1-10). When packet and private voice traffic is considered, network traffic is only slightly higher (the next highest, or second portion of Figure 1-10). PSTN data traffic has a higher rate of growth than either of the voice cases (the next highest, or third portion of Figure 1-10), while the packet and private data traffic has the highest growth (the top portion of Figure 1-10).

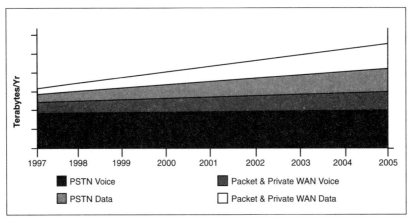

Figure 1-10 Global Network Traffic
(Courtesy of Probe Research, Inc.)

New public network infrastructures are being designed and built to handle these consolidated networks, such as those being designed by Quest Communications International, Inc., Level 3 Communications, Inc., and others. In building these new infrastructures, these firms are leveraging some of the significant increases in technology that have occurred in the last few years, such as high capacity fiber optic backbones and routers that can handle aggregate throughputs in the gigabit per second range. These increases in technology provide one key ingredient necessary for the success of converged networks – favorable economies of scale that promise to reduce the overall costs of the enterprise infrastructure.

But determining the sources of this growth is essential for understanding the rate at which this growth will occur. Probe Research has identified five different market drivers for the Voice over IP (VoIP) and Fax over IP (FoIP) market

(Figure 1-11). The Hobbyist phase (1996–1997) allowed two PC users equipped with compatible software and sound cards to send voice over the Internet. The Tariff Arbitrage phase (1998–1999) afforded the end user an opportunity to lower their long distance telephone costs, which became especially important for international connections. Parity with existing public and private voice systems will drive the market in the next phase (2000). For example, IP telephony gateways will move toward interoperable, not proprietary solutions, and compatibility with existing voice switching systems, such as private branch exchanges (PBXs) and central office (C.O.) switches, will become a higher priority of the vendor community. New applications will drive the market during the following phase (2001–2002), as both end users and network managers realize the benefits of unified messaging, multimedia conferencing, enhanced call centers, and other key applications. The final phase (2003–2005) will provide cost parity between packet-based voice services and the existing circuit-switched voice services. In other words, the costs of the new technologies must present some advantage over the existing, well-established technologies, in order to convince network managers of the long-term viability of voice and fax over IP solutions.

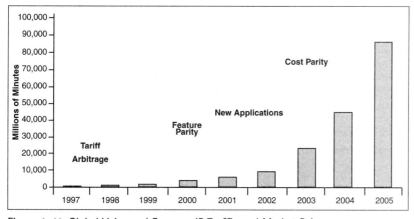

Figure 1-11 Global Voice and Fax over IP Traffic and Market Drivers
(Courtesy of Probe Research, Inc.)

During these five phases, the end users of this technology can be segmented into several categories. Probe Research divides the IP telephony market into three general areas: wholesalers of telephony services, consumer/small business users, and enterprise/institutional customers (Figure 1-12). The wholesalers are those who are reselling telephone service via calling cards purchased at discount stores, convenience stores, gas stations, and so on. The calling card purchaser (or end user) is interested in low-cost telephone service, and the more technical issues regarding quality of that service, delays, and so on, are of lesser concern (assuming, of course, that some minimum threshold of acceptable service has been met or exceeded). The consumers and small business users are possibly the most price-sensitive, but are also the earliest adopters (note their presence in the 1997–1999 timeframe). Enterprise and institutional customers are slower to adopt this technology (the 2000–2001 timeframe), but after that have a high rate of growth as the technology is further implemented and tested. One might speculate that concerns over quality make for a more cautious entry into this technology for these organizations.

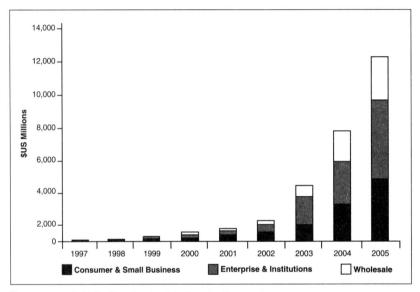

Figure 1-12 IP Voice/Fax Service Markets by Segment
(Courtesy of Probe Research, Inc.)

Financial research firm U.S. Bancorp Piper Jaffray, Inc. (Minneapolis, Minnesota) has looked at the voice and fax over IP market from the perspective of equity investments, and has published a very comprehensive guide to these technologies: *IP Telephony: Driving the Open Communications Revolution* [1-16].

For the purposes of their research, Piper Jaffray segments the IP telephony market into five different categories. The Core Enabling Technology Platforms are the hardware and software components that enable IP telephony functions, and would include various network interfaces, call processing and digital signal processing capabilities, switching systems, and so on. The Enterprise Solutions category would include voice gateways, client software, and other telephony applications. The Carrier-Class Solutions are systems that are implemented within a carrier's network to include large-scale servers and routers, gatekeepers, billing systems, and applications. The Internet Telephony Service Providers (ITSPs) are the carriers that provide IP telephony services to subscribers. End-to-End Services are those organizations that are integrating voice and data equipment sales, installation, and other consulting-related services to other organizations.

Piper Jaffray estimates that by the year 2003, the aggregate IP telephony market will total $14.7 billion in revenues. This is segmented somewhat differently, and broken down as follows: 6 percent for the core enabling platforms, 27 percent from gateway equipment, 8 percent from applications, and 59 percent from services. Specifics regarding the growth divided by the five segments noted above is shown in Figure 1-13.

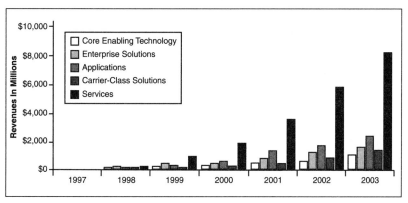

Figure 1-13 Market Growth Forecast 1997–2003 by Segment
(Courtesy of U.S. Bancorp Piper Jaffray, Inc.)

This market can be further segmented by geography – detailing the mix of product revenues that will come from international or domestic (U.S.) sources (Figure 1-14a). Note the shift from the 1997 conditions (20 percent domestic and 80 percent international) to the 2003 projections (55 percent domestic and 45 percent international), as more domestic carriers and firms adopt these technologies.

A similar change is noted in in Figure 14-b, which shows the mix of services revenues, from the 1997 conditions (5 percent domestic-to-domestic, 20 percent international-to-international, and 75 percent domestic-to-international) to the 2003 projections (30 percent domestic-to-domestic, 28 percent international-to-international, and 42 percent domestic-to-international). As with the previous case, the domestic traffic will increase at the expense of the international traffic.

The market growth by number of minutes of use for VoIP and FoIP services is also a key indicator of the anticipated popularity of the service (Figure 1-15). IP Telephony traffic in 1998 was estimated at 476 million minutes, with 57 percent for VoIP and 43 percent for FoIP. By 2003 the total is projected to be 81.7 billion minutes, with 77 percent from VoIP, 17 percent from FoIP, and 6 percent from video over IP services.

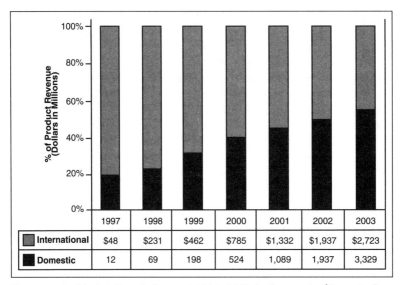

Figure 1-14a Market Growth Forecast 1997–2003 by Geography (Percent of Product Revenue) (Courtesy of U.S. Bancorp Piper Jaffray, Inc.)

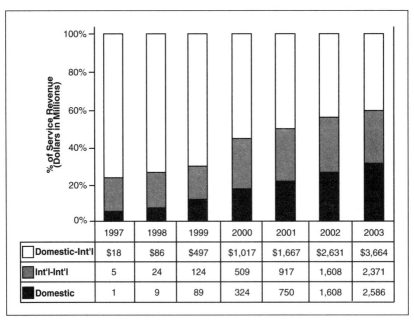

Figure 1-14b Market Growth Forecast 1997–2003 by Geography (percent of Services Revenue) (Courtesy of U.S. Bancorp Piper Jaffray, Inc.)

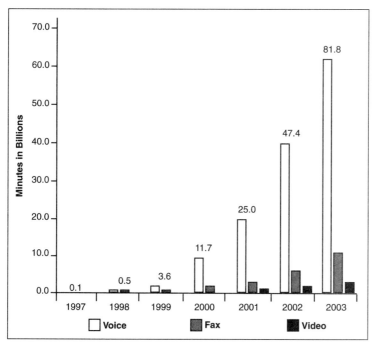

Figure 1-15 Market Growth Forecast 1997–2003 by Minutes Used
(Courtesy of U.S. Bancorp Piper Jaffray, Inc.)

The current market for telecommunication services is very large, dominated by carriers such as AT&T (United States), NTT (Japan), Deutsche Telekom (Germany), and British Telecom (United Kingdom), which primarily offer traditional dial up and leased line solutions [1-16]. As VoIP and FoIP solutions become more commonplace, it is anticipated that a significant number of the minutes of use (MOUs) will migrate to IP-centric carriers (Figure 1-16). By 2003, it is estimated that this will represent over 81 billion MOUs, and $8.6 billion in revenues (Figure 1-17). Reviewing Figure 1-16, note that as a percentage of the total PSTN MOUs, those that represent IP telephony services is a relatively small number. However, 6 percent of the total aggregate of worldwide telephony usage still produces some very large revenue numbers! This may be one reason that the more traditional carriers (such as AT&T) are developing IP-centric services to compete with the start-up Internet Telephony Service Providers (ITSPs) such as Level 3 and Qwest. Reviewing Figure 1-15, note that in the 2002–2003 timeframe, video over IP services will become significant market factors as well.

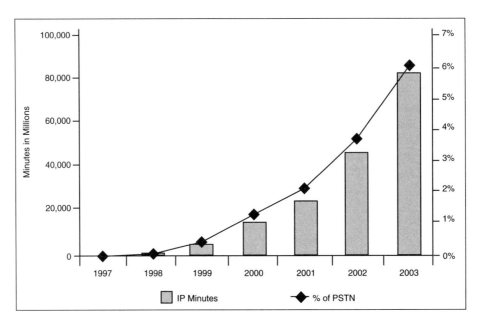

Figure 1-16 Percentage of Long-Distance Minutes Moving to IP Networks
(Courtesy of U.S. Bancorp Piper Jaffray, Inc.)

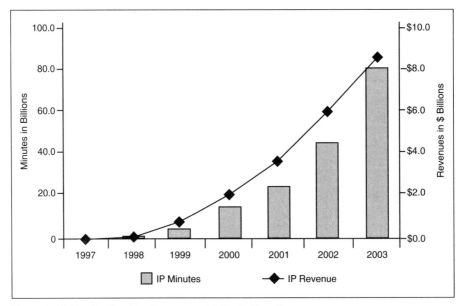

Figure 1-17 Service Provider Revenue and Minute Growth
(Courtesy of U.S. Bancorp Piper Jaffray, Inc.)

1.5 Benefits of the IP-Centric Network

Let us summarize the major hypotheses that have been presented thus far:

◆ The idea of converging voice and data traffic into a single network is not new.

◆ The Internet Protocol, and IP-related technologies, are well understood and widely implemented (near-ubiquity) within the telecommunications industry.

◆ For many reasons, data networks, which incorporate packet switching technologies, are generally more efficient than voice networks, which use circuit switching technologies.

◆ The growth of traffic from voice networks is relatively flat, in sharp contrast to the growth of traffic from data networks, which is very steep.

◆ Given the large number of voice communication, data communication, and Internet communication users, plus the large volumes of revenues from these industries, the total market potential for the voice, fax, and video over IP technologies is very large.

With these hypotheses in mind, consider the following:

Given the current environment, does it still make sense to enhance the capabilities of the voice network to transport data, or, instead, to enhance the capabilities of an IP-centric data network to carry additional applications (voice, fax, and/or video)?

Assuming that such an IP-centric network is deployed, it is important to define the services that it can support. Nortel Networks' document, "Enhancing IP Network Performance" [1-17], divides IP services into three categories: application services, enabling services, and internetworking services. Figure 1-18, which is modeled after the seven-layer reference model, employs an IP-centric system to tie the networking infrastructure at the lower layers to the applications at the higher layers. The three key application services include mission-critical applications, such as human resources, finance, customer support, and so on; voice and fax over IP; and multimedia over IP, such as video conferences, distance learning, and so on. The enabling services enhance the capabilities of IP-based networks, dealing with issues such as traffic management, security, directory services, policy-based networking, and virtual private networks (VPNs) with remote access and extranet support. Internetworking services provide access to the IP-based network from non-IP-centric networks (such as SNA or X.25 WANs). Note that the core of this technology is the Internet Protocol.

The benefits of such a converged network could include:

◆ A reduction in the overall complexity of the networking infrastructure: fewer protocols, operating systems, and so on.

◆ Synergies between carrier circuits supporting voice and data, and possible elimination of circuit redundancy.

◆ Possible reduction in carrier circuit charges.

◆ Integrated management systems and strategies that can support both the voice and data networks, instead of separate management systems.

◆ More consistent user interfaces, such as integrated fax and email.

◆ Access to enhanced applications, such as integrated messaging, voice-enabled Web sites, desktop video conferencing, and others.

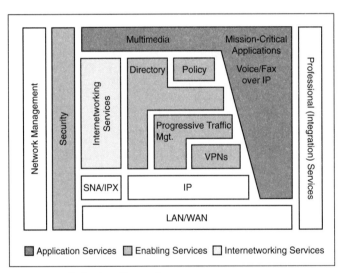

Figure 1-18 IP Services Categories
(Courtesy of Nortel Networks)

The next section will consider how the converged network can be deployed.

1.6 Provisioning the Converged Network

Thus, the IP telephony network would include a number of elements – some from traditional voice networks, such as telephones, fax machines, and PBXs; some from traditional data networks, such as terminals, hosts, and servers; and some from new systems, such as gateways and gatekeepers, that are designed as the glue to hold all of these disparate systems together. Figure 1-19 illustrates some of these various elements, which could incorporate many different subsystems, including the PSTN, dedicated WAN connections, IP routers, wiring hubs and end stations, and many others.

A call over an IP network could start with a local PSTN connection, and the conversion of the analog voice signal to a digital pulse stream at the client end station, PBX, or gateway. That pulse stream will likely undergo some signal processing, including silence suppression and echo cancellation. The gateway may consult with a gatekeeper and/or Domain Name Service (DNS) server to obtain information about the desired destination, such as its transmission capabilities and IP address. The voice signal is then converted into packets, transmitted over the IP-based network to a destination gateway, and the digital pulse stream is reconstructed. As a final step, the digital pulse stream is then converted into an analog signal and delivered to the desired destination.

1.7 Challenges of the Converged Network

Like most good ideas, the path from theory and concept to implementation and reality can have a few obstacles and detours along the way. In the case of voice, fax, and video over IP systems, the challenges come in several areas: the existing mindsets of the networking constituents, the large number of players in the marketplace, and the technical challenges afforded by the marriage of voice and data systems.

1.7.1 Voice and Data Networking Mindsets

As was discussed above, voice and data networks have been designed to address different challenges and, as a result, those who design, configure, and manage these two types of networks approach their respective challenges from different viewpoints. For example, in many organizations, voice telephone service is treated as a utility, much like the electric or water utilities (and possibly taken for granted). As such, it is not always afforded the high technology moniker that is given to the computing side of the house.

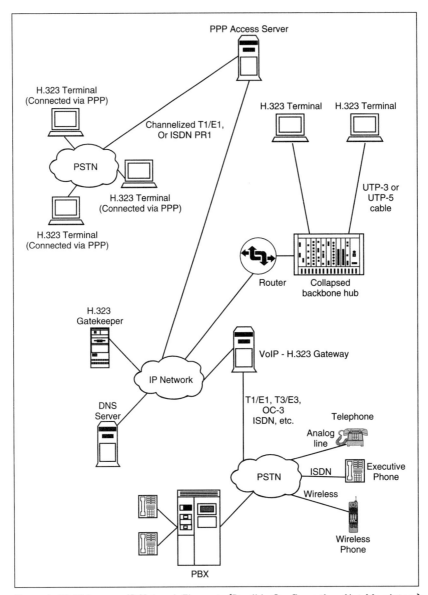

Figure 1-19 Voice over IP Network Elements (Possible Configuration, Not Mandatory)
(Source: IMTC Conferencing over IP (CoIP) activity group)

Data networking requirements are often driven by the applications they support, such as a customer database. Thus, the data network is more likely to be associated with the success (or lack of success) of the entire enterprise. (If you doubt this, pick up a networking journal and look at a typical testimonial advertisement. The typical message is: "we installed XYZ networking products, our downtime decreased, our throughput increased, and we all lived happily ever after. If you buy XYZ products, you will become successful as well.")

Thus, when one considers implementing an integrated network, which will comprise elements from both the voice and data networks, some key issues, such as who will fund, who will manage, and who will be ultimately responsible for the converged network will need to be resolved.

1.7.2 VoIP Market Players

Reviewing Figure 1-13, we noted that there are five categories of segments to the IP telephony marketplace: enabling technology platforms, enterprise solutions, carrier-class solutions, Internet Telephony Service Providers, and end-to-end systems integrators.

Noting the wide diversity in these five categories, and considering the extensive growth factors that were discussed in Section 1.4, it is not hard to realize that a number of different organizations have entered, or will soon enter, this marketplace. Examples include:

- ◆ Traditional carriers: both Inter-Exchange Carriers (IXCs) and Local Exchange Carriers (LECs)

- ◆ Internet Service Providers (ISPs)

- ◆ Internet Telephony Service Providers (ITSPs)

- ◆ Fax service bureaus

- ◆ PBX equipment manufacturers

- ◆ Networking equipment manufacturers

- ◆ Application developers

For completeness, we would need to add the standards organizations, such as the Internet Engineering Task Force (IETF), the International Telecommunications Union (ITU), and the Institute of Electrical and Electronics Engineers (IEEE); plus special interest groups, such as the IMTC Conferencing over IP (CoIP) activity group and the International Multimedia Teleconferencing Consortium (IMTC), which produce work that crosses many of the above technology segments.

1.7.3 VoIP Implementation Challenges

As we have discussed in this chapter, integrating the significant differences between voice and data networks into a single, cohesive system, and then integrating those systems, can be challenging. To identify some of the topics that will be considered in subsequent chapters, as well as to provide some food for thought, consider the following (Figure 1-20):

♦ Numerous standards exist in support of voice and data networks. How will these standards be applied to a converged network?

♦ Voice networks are ultra-reliable. How will this reliability be translated into the converged network?

♦ The convergence industry is at its early stages. Will the products and services that you select from different vendors be interoperable?

♦ Network transmission characteristics, such as latency or delay, are more predictable with voice networks than data networks. How might these differences affect the end user applications?

♦ How will the converged network integrate with any existing systems, such as a PBX or voice mail network?

♦ Does your network infrastructure have enough excess bandwidth to support voice, fax, and/or video applications?

♦ How will the converged network be managed – from the perspective of voice transmission, from the perspective of data transmission, or as an integrated system?

♦ Will regulatory bodies, such as the FCC, impact voice transmission over IP-centric networks, such as the global Internet?

♦ How will the existing levels of Quality of Service (QoS) be maintained?

♦ How should the user interface into the converged network be considered?

♦ How much will the converged network cost, and which department will foot the bill?

1.8 Looking Ahead

In this chapter, we have considered the principles of network convergence, the differences between voice and data networking infrastructures, the projections for growth in these respective areas, and the various players in this marketplace. Independent of these growth factors and which market research you choose to embrace, a general direction in today's networking environments is pointing towards a convergence of the voice and data worlds – a trend that would be difficult to ignore.

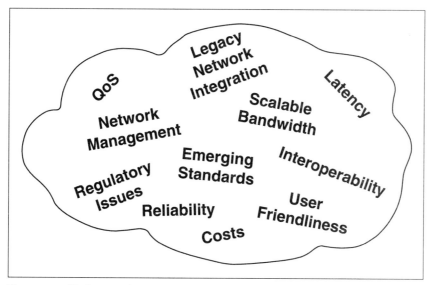

Figure 1-20 Challenges of the Converged Network

In the next and subsequent chapters, we will drill down into these issues in greater detail, beginning in Chapter 2 with a discussion of the applications that require a converged network infrastructure.

1.9 References

[1-1]   The North American ISDN Users' Forum may be contacted at: http://www.niuf.nist.gov.

[1-2]   International Organization for Standardization. *Information Processing Systems – Open Systems Interconnection – Basic Reference Model*, ISO 7498-1984.

[1-3]   Miller, Mark A. *Troubleshooting TCP/IP, 3rd Edition*. Foster City, CA: IDG Books Worldwide, Inc., 1999.

[1-4]   Dix, John. "Convergence: Why I'm buying it this time around." *Network World* (June 14, 1999): 46.

[1-5]   Breidenbach, Susan, et al. "There's no stopping IP." *Network World* (August 10, 1998): 35–50.

[1-6]   Tracey, Lenore V. "Voice over IP – Turning up the volume." *Telecommunications* (March 1998): 28–32.

[1-7]   Thyfault, Mary E. "Resurgence of Convergence." *Information Week* (April 13, 1998): 50–68.

[1-8]   Voice 2000: BCR's Guide to Emerging Voice Technologies. *Business Communications Review Supplement*, October 1998.

[1-9]   Barreca, Tony. "Looking at Real-World Convergence." *3Com Net Age* (Q1 1999): 4–10.

[1-10]   Nicoll, Chris. "Multiservice Integration – Networks Converge on the Data Infrastructure." *Business Communications Review Supplement* (February 1999):1–4.

[1-11]   Miller, Mark A. "Voice, Video, and Fax over Internet Protocol: Possibilities for Converged Networks." *Decision Resources Spectrum Report*, April 15, 1999.

[1-12]   Nokia. "Nokia IP Telephony – Voice and Data Integration White Paper." Available from `http://ww.viennasys.com/public/voicedata_wp.html`, 1999.

[1-13]   Mine, Hillary. "The Evolution of Internet Telephony." Probe Research, Inc., September 1998. For details, contact `http://www.proberesearch.com`.

[1-14]   The number of Hosts and Servers on the Internet at any given time is calculated by Telcordia Technologies (formerly Bellcore) at `http://www.netsizer.com/daily.html`.

[1-15]   Ayvazian, Berge. "One Network – Leveraging Voice/Data Network Convergence." The Yankee Group, Seventh Annual Global Network Strategies Conference, December 1998.

[1-16]   Jackson, Edward R., and Andrew M. Schroepfer. *IP Telephony: Driving the Open Communications Revolution.* Piper Jaffray Equity Research Report, February 1999.

[1-17]   Anderson, Rod. "Enhancing IP Network Performance: A Sensible Solution for Mission-Critical Applications." Nortel Networks Whitepaper WP503-2953EC-A, January 1998.

Chapter 2

Applications for the Converged Network

In the previous chapter, we considered the principles of converged voice and data networks, as well as the challenges that occur when one considers the integration of those different systems. In this chapter, we will take those principles and bring them closer to reality by examining some case studies of real networks that implement these concepts. In doing so, we will look at a number of applications, taken from real networks, that consider voice, fax, video, and various multimedia signals that can be transported over IP-based infrastructures.

This chapter presents a number of case studies that illustrate the breadth of applications that converged networks can support, including voice, fax, video, and web-based implementations. Some of these applications, however, may meet your networking goals more appropriately than others. Therefore, you might want to quickly scan the chapter, and pick out the case studies that are most applicable to your networking objectives and environment. At a later time, you can return to the other case studies as time constraints and applications dictate.

In each example, we will consider the technical challenges and the enabling technologies that were deployed to solve those challenges. In addition, we will introduce some of the functional components, such as gateways and gatekeepers, that are the building blocks of a converged network. Further discussion regarding the operational characteristics of these building blocks will be deferred until Chapter 6.

2.1 Telephone-to-PC Communication via the Internet

Many Internet users have one telephone line into their residence or small business. Therefore, when that user connects to the Internet using a modem and a single telephone line, the telephone line is busy and other telephone calls cannot be received.

There are several solutions to this "busy signal" problem: a second telephone line, a cable or satellite hook-up, ISDN service, and so on. However, all of these solutions require additional installation and monthly costs for the Internet user. In some locations, the time required to order and install that additional service may exceed the patience of the end user as well.

A software-based solution to this problem has been developed by eRing Solutions, Inc. (Montreal, Quebec, Canada). The eRing product allows an Internet user to receive telephone calls directly at their computer connected to the Internet without having to interrupt the Internet session. With eRing, anyone using an ordinary telephone can now talk to an Internet user.

The eRing service consists of three elements: client software, gateways, and a gatekeeper. The client software is installed on the computer of the Internet user. (This software can be downloaded without charge from eRing's Web site, www.ering.net.) The eRing client software runs on Microsoft Windows 95, 98, and NT 4.0, and requires a sound card with microphone and speakers attached. The eRing Gateway is an Internet telephony server that links the Public Switched Telephone Network (PSTN) with IP networks. This gateway enables an Internet user to receive telephone calls directly at the PC from anyone using an ordinary telephone. The eRing GateKeeper is a server connected to the Internet. It manages access to the eRing service for all eRing Gateways and eRing Client Software (end users) around the world.

To use eRing, someone trying to reach the Internet user calls one of the eRing Gateways, where they are asked to enter the telephone number of the Internet user (Figure 2-1a). The eRing Client Software will pop-up on the screen of the Internet user (Figure 2-1b) and enable an exchange of voice messages between the person who is calling (with an ordinary telephone) and the Internet user at the PC (through the microphone and speakers). Note that the eRing service doesn't try to emulate a second phone line and support a real-time full-duplex voice conversation over the Internet connection. Instead, eRing allows an Internet user to be reachable at all times, with no additional costs for a second telephone line. The person calling and the Internet user will exchange a few voice messages in half-duplex mode. If the conversation gets too long to be held through eRing, the Internet user can logoff the Internet modem connection and call back using the telephone.

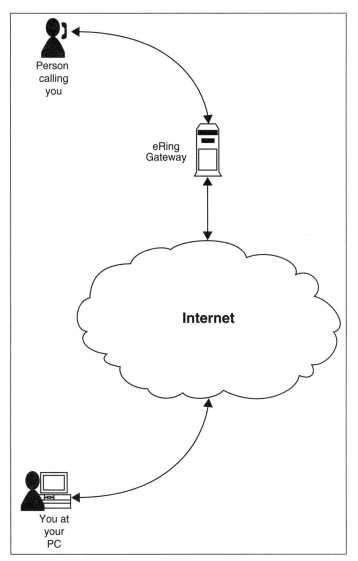

Person
calling
you

eRing
Gateway

Internet

You at
your
PC

Figure 2–1a eRing Client Operation
(Courtesy of eRing Solutions, Inc.)

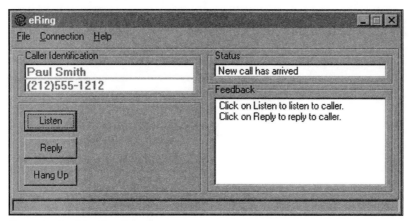

Figure 2-1b eRing User Interface
(Courtesy of eRing Solutions, Inc.

Two primary services are supported by eRing: Phone-to-PC communication and Voice Mail. With the Phone-to-PC service, the caller dials the eRing Gateway and enters the destination phone number. The eRing Gateway sends a request to the eRing Gatekeeper, which replies with the IP address of the Internet user (Figure 2-1c). The eRing Gateway then enables an exchange of unidirectional voice messages between the person who is calling from an ordinary telephone and the Internet user at the PC. If the Internet user is not reachable when the call is placed, the eRing Gateway offers the caller the option of leaving a voice message, which will be delivered to the Internet user the next time he or she connects to the Internet.

Client-to-gatekeeper and gatekeeper-to-gateway communications use the User Datagram Protocol (UDP). Client-to-gateway communications, which carry the actual conversation, use the Transmission Control Protocol (TCP) for greater reliability and communication efficiency. (UDP and TCP operation will be explored in detail in Chapter 4.)

The eRing service offers many additional features, some of which are available only to users of the eRing Plus version, which requires the user to pay a yearly fee or a usage fee. These enhanced features include:

- ◆ A log of the calls received.

- ◆ A message center, which can take a message from the caller if the Internet user is not on line or has declined to accept the call.

- ◆ The ability to receive calls from abroad (for example: someone calls the eRing Gateway in Manila to reach an Internet user in the United States).

- ◆ The ability to receive calls from a user via a toll-free number of the eRing service (for callers who don't have a local eRing Gateway in their calling area).

Further information on the eRing service is available in Reference [2-1].

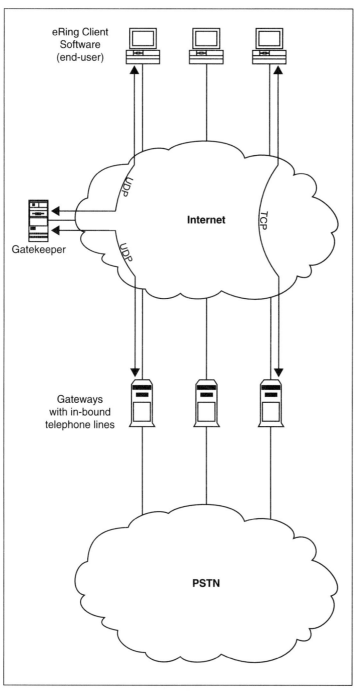

Figure 2–1c eRing Network Components
(Courtesy of eRing Solutions, Inc.)

2.2 International VoIP Network Consortium

One of the key business incentives for moving toward a VoIP network topology is the potential savings in long distance (toll) charges between various company locations. And when the toll charges under consideration are international, not domestic, the savings can be considerable. (More information on the business issues surrounding VoIP technologies is provided in Chapter 3.) This case study will look at the topology and operation of an international network service that has been designed to meet the needs of multinational business customers.

OzEmail Interline Pty Limited, an Australian company, has distinguished itself as the world's very first IP telephony service provider (ITSP) that also owns all of its service technology. Interline was formed with the principal purpose of developing a world class Internet telephony service, beginning operations in mid-1996 and delivering its first commercial voice gateway equipment by the end of that year. OzEmail Interline's commercial Internet telephony service was subsequently launched in January 1997.

Interline's principal business is that of a service provider to the VoIP service industry, with a special emphasis on passing international traffic. As such, it has formed a consortium of ITSPs around the world, creating an international VoIP network that provides high quality, low cost, international voice services. These services can be accessed through standard tone phones for the "Phone-to-Phone" service. The consortium has deployed a number of IP-PSTN gateways, called Voice Interface Nodes, or VINs, which provide high quality voice services to all regions of the world (Figure 2-2a).

The Interline service model includes two key elements: IP/PSTN Gateways, located in strategic areas of the world, and a Call Management System (Figure 2-2b). The Gateways, which are presently designed and manufactured by Interline, are positioned at each access location. The Gateways can be provided with a number of alternative PSTN interfaces. For example, the E1 Primary Rate Interface (PRI) version can handle up to 30 simultaneous calls. Multiple Gateways can be colocated and cascaded to form a non-call-blocking architecture for any number of ports. The Gateways are under the control of the Back End Server, which manages the call process. The Back End Server also provides the call billing services, such as tracking call origin, destination, duration, and other information.

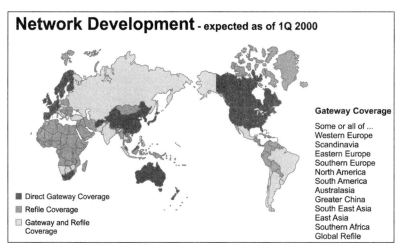

Figure 2-2a Interline Network Development
(Courtesy of OzEmail Interline Pty Limited)

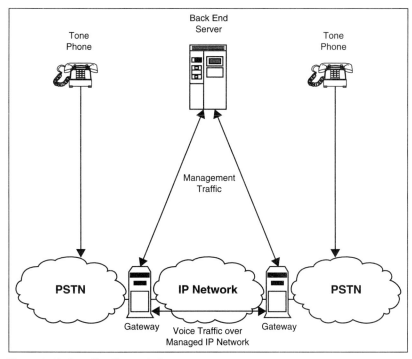

Figure 2-2b Interline Network Components
(Courtesy of OzEmail Interline Pty Limited)

For example, a consortium member in Japan is Dream Train Internet (DTI), a subsidiary of Mitsubishi. A consortium member such as DTI might offer the service to businesses and install a Gateway in the customer's premises. To establish an international call via Interline, the customer would establish or use an existing dedicated IP connection between their premises and DTI's IP network. The customer's premises switch (PBX) would be programmed to direct international traffic from PBX handsets to the on-premises Gateway, instead of to the international PSTN. Once a call is redirected to the Gateway, it is converted into an IP datagram, sent through DTI's IP backbone, and then sent to a consortium partner's backbone network via the Internet. A second Interline Gateway is connected to the partner's network, and from there to the foreign PSTN. At that distant Gateway, the IP datagrams that comprise the telephone call are converted back into a switched circuit format, and from there are delivered via the local PSTN to the destination telephone. Support systems, which include the Interline Back End Server, handle the overall management of the calls (authentication, authorization, routing, number to dial translation and rating) and the network (Gateway, IP bandwidth and PSTN quality of service, or QoS monitoring) and all billing functions. The consortium member is responsible for customer inquiries.

The consortium member might also offer services to businesses or to the general public in different ways. A wide range of services is currently offered by members of the Interline Consortium. These include: prepaid calling cards (where the customer simply dials a publicly advertised access number), Signaling System 7 (SS7)–based interconnect to traditional and mobile telecommunications carriers, large scale enterprise PBX installations (of the type described above), credit based accounts, transit systems for telecommunications carriers, and many other models.

Further information on the Interline Consortium is available in Reference [2-2].

2.3 Replacing International Leased Lines

OpenTel Communication, Inc., is an international long distance carrier based in San Francisco, California, which focuses on traffic between the United States and Asia. The voice traffic passes through an OpenTel Central Office switch and then is routed to voice gateways provided by Nuera Communications, Inc., of San Diego, California, for compression and transmission to the destination city. The voice gateways compress the traffic to between 4.8 Kbps and 9.6 Kbps depending on the route. To ensure voice quality, OpenTel uses leased lines operating between 256 and 1,544 Kbps to interconnect their points of presence (POPs) between the United States and Asia (Figure 2-3).

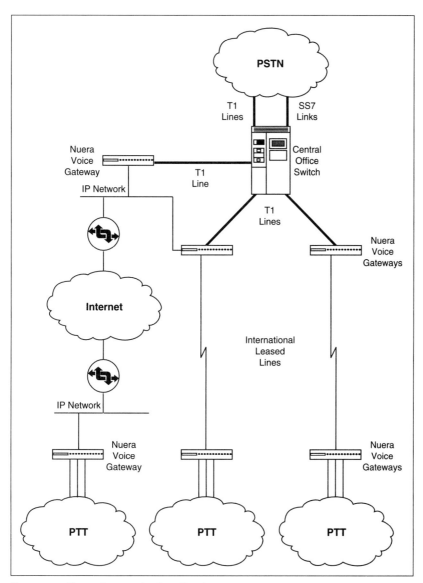

Figure 2–3 Nuera Communications Topology
(Courtesy of Nuera Communications, Inc.)

Due to increased competition in the marketplace, OpenTel was under pressure to reduce the rates it charged to serve the Pacific Rim region. This required OpenTel to investigate new methods to reduce its own monthly costs for providing these services, much of which revolved around the leased line costs between the United States and Asia. For example, typical costs for these leased lines were around $5,000.00 per month per 128 Kbps of bandwidth, with some route costs as high as $10,000.00 per month per 128 Kbps of bandwidth.

Two options were available: reduce the bandwidth required per call or reduce the cost of that bandwidth. The first option was rejected because the calls were already being compressed to 4.8 Kbps, and it was determined that further compression could reduce the voice quality and potentially lead to customer dissatisfaction.

In attempting to reduce the cost of that bandwidth, OpenTel considered both frame relay and IP transport alternatives to the existing leased lines. Frame relay connections promised to lower the costs by about 25%, but had the downside of a potential reduction in voice quality if congestion occurred. In addition, frame relay connections were not always available in Asia, which would mandate long and expensive leased line tail circuits to reach the service provider POPs.

An IP-based transport solution proved to be much more economical and readily available. The service sites for the Internet were more numerous, which cut down the "last mile" tail circuit costs. Furthermore, the circuit cost was not based on the international bandwidth used, but only on the port speed provided, and was typically in the range of $2,000.00–$3,000.00 per month for T1 speeds. On the Asian sides the connection was more expensive, but was still lower than the alternative frame relay connections, with an average cost of $2,000.00 per 128 Kbps of bandwidth. Therefore, OpenTel concluded that an IP solution was both faster and less expensive to provision than the leased lines or the frame relay network alternatives.

OpenTel started slowly by providing Internet access to the major POPs with known good IP performance. They were able to use the same Nuera gateways they had been using for the frame relay connections by simply reconfiguring these gateways to have IP as their primary route between systems. After about a month of testing, the first T1 circuit was cut over to use IP as the primary route. After a month of testing under live traffic conditions, additional routes were converted to the IP-based infrastructure and several leased lines were removed. An additional benefit of this topology is its redundancy – where existing leased lines are still in place, the Internet can be used as an alternate route in the event that those leased lines experience outages.

Further information on OpenTel Communications services is available in Reference [2-3].

2.4 Voice-Enabled Electronic Commerce

Many potential customers come to a vendor's Web site browsing for information. Sometimes they find what they are looking for, and sometimes they don't. But *browsers* are not necessarily *buyers*, as they may encounter several roadblocks along the way. For example, they may not be able to find the information they are seeking, they may have found some information but still have some questions, or perhaps they are ready to make a purchase but are reluctant to enter their credit card information for security reasons.

WebLine Communications Corp.'s products respond to these electronic commerce challenges by integrating voice or chat and visual communication in several ways. The Web/call center integrates the capabilities of the Internet, the vendor's PBX, and Automatic Call Director (ACD), the vendor's customer call center, into a single system to enhance customer support. Cyber seminars provide one-to-many online conferences over the Internet. "Meet me "collaboration demonstrations allow customers to meet a sales representative at a selected time and URL for product details and demonstrations.

The Web-enabled call center provides the customer with a simple, one-click button to connect them with a live customer service agent for further assistance. And this further assistance can take a form that best meets the needs of that customer: a telephone call from a customer support representative, an email response, a chat room facility, or a voice over IP connection (see Figure 2-4a).

The blended collaboration application allows a vendor to implement a customer integration strategy that addresses that customer's specific needs and communication capabilities. The call is initiated by a potential customer who accesses the vendor's Web site, realizes the need for further information, and clicks a button on the browser's screen for more information (step 1 in Figure 2-4a). That request is transmitted via the Internet to a WebLine Collaboration Server, and from there to the WebLine Media Blender, which enables the blending of multiple communication channels, such as Web, telephone, VoIP, text chat, email, and fax (step 2). If VoIP is selected, and the customer has the appropriate workstation configuration, including an H.323 client (H.323 is an ITU-T standard for the transport of multimedia signals over nonguaranteed quality of service LANs), and an Internet telephony gateway (step 3), the customer may then participate in a VoIP call (step 4). The Internet telephony gateway also interacts with the vendor's PBX, which selects the next available agent to handle the customer's call (step 5). The ACD (step 6) and the agent (step 7) maintain a connection with the WebLine Collaboration Server, which controls the information content relayed from the agent back to the customer.

Examples of the screens that are seen by both the customer and the call center agent are shown in the following figures.

The customer accesses the vendor's Web page (Figure 2-4b), gathers some information on their products and services, and realizes that more information is required. The customer locates a button on the Web page that says "click to speak with a representative," and a second window is activated (Figure 2-4c).

The customer then completes a short form with his contact information, products of interest, and so on, and sends this form to the call center (Figure 2-4c).

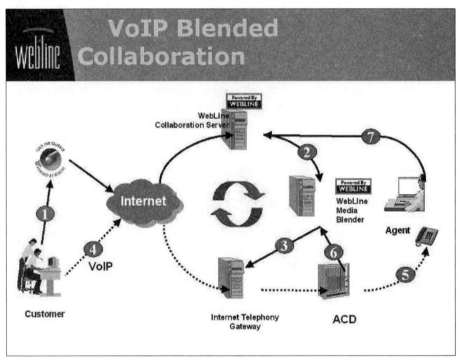

Figure 2–4a Web-enabled Call Center Information Flow
(Courtesy of WebLine Communications Corp.)

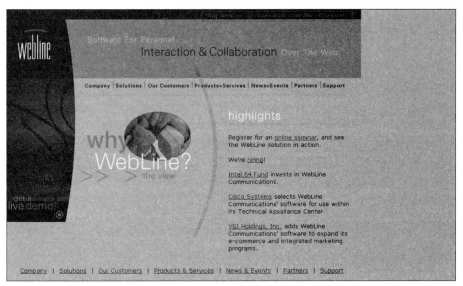

Figure 2-4b WebLine Homepage
(Courtesy of WebLine Communications Corp.)

Figure 2-4c WebLine Caller Information Form
(Courtesy of WebLine Communications Corp.)

At the call center, an agent is waiting for the next call, and his terminal indicates that he does not currently have a call in session. (Figure 2-4d)

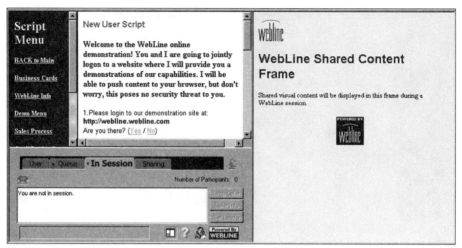

Figure 2-4d Call Agent Terminal Prior to Call Connection
(Courtesy of WebLine Communications Corp.)

After receipt of the completed caller information form from the customer, the call center agent connects to that customer (Figure 2-4e).

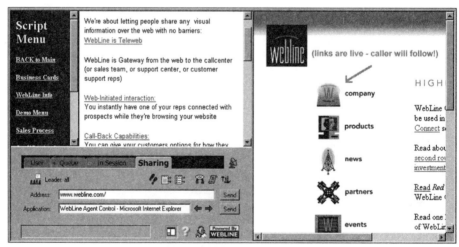

Figure 2-4e Call Agent Screen with Live Links
(Courtesy of WebLine Communications Corp.)

At the call center, information about the next caller in queue is displayed at the agent's workstation. The call agent also has contact information about that caller, which product that caller is interested in, and whether or not the caller is in the vendor's contact database (Figure 2-4f).

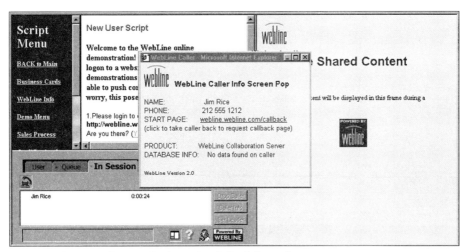

Figure 2-4f Agent's Screen with Incoming Caller Information
(Courtesy of WebLine Communications Corp.)

The agent screen splits into two parts: a sales script on the left, and content pages that will be sent to the caller on the right. Another window indicates that current session (Figure 2-4g).

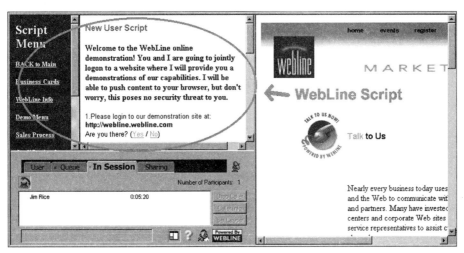

Figure 2-4g Agent Screen with Script and Sample Pages
(Courtesy of WebLine Communications Corp.)

The call agent has two elements of information at his disposal: one part which is a script to be read to the caller over the telephone, and one part which pushes pages to the caller (Figure 2-4h).

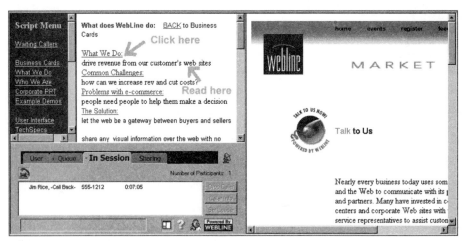

Figure 2-4h Agent Screen in Operation
(Courtesy of WebLine Communications Corp.)

Through the split screen, the agent can also see the content that is being pushed to the caller (Figure2-4i).

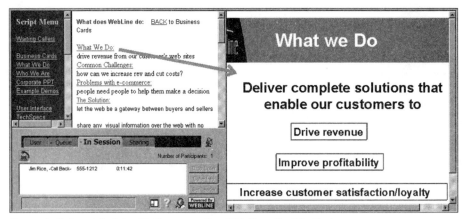

Figure 2-4i Agent Script with Corresponding Web Page Sent to Customer
(Courtesy of WebLine Communications Corp.)

The call can be transferred to a manager or another agent for consultation (Figure 2-4j).

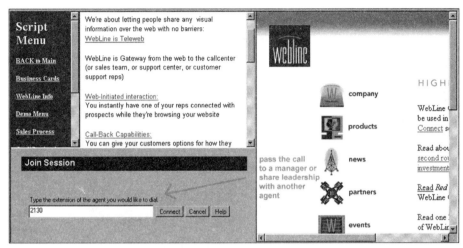

Figure 2-4j Agent Screen with Agent Consultation Option
(Courtesy of WebLine Communications Corp.)

Other agents, perhaps those with special expertise, may then join the conference session in progress as consultants (Figure 2-4k).

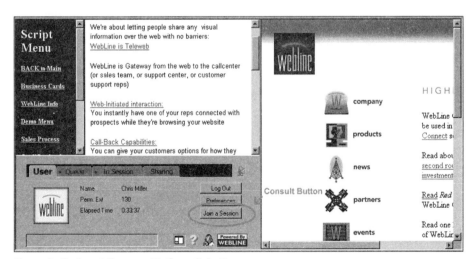

Figure 2-4k Agent Screen with Consult Button
(Courtesy of WebLine Communications Corp.)

When the caller's questions have all been answered, the call center agent displays his business card and any personal information, such as a photograph (Figure 2-4l).

Figure 2-4l Call Agent's Business Card
(Courtesy of WebLine Communications Corp.)

When the call is complete, the call center agent disconnects the call, and prepares for the next customer(Figure 2-4m).

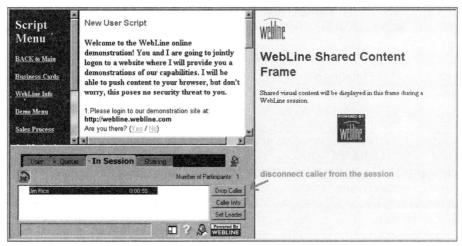

Figure 2-4m Agent Screen with Drop Caller Button
(Courtesy of WebLine Communications Corp.)

In summary, a Web-based call center provides many benefits for both the customer and the vendor. For the customer, questions can be answered immediately, using audio, video, and textual media. For the vendor, the leads that access and then request live information are more qualified as a customer with a sincere interest in the vendor's products or services. When the interactive session is provided, complete information is presented to the prospects, improving the chances of closing a sale. Examples of firms that used WebLine's products for their Web sites include AutoNation, Cisco Systems, Hewlett-Packard Company, MCI Worldcom, TeleSales, Inc., and others.

Further information on WebLine's applications is found in Reference [2-4].

2.5 Fax over IP Networks

Much of the interest regarding convergence technologies has focused on the realm of voice communication; however, facsimile, or fax transmission, is a key communication facility within the business world. By most estimates, annual fax transmission volumes continue to increase and can represent a substantial portion of an organization's overall telecommunications expenses. Fax is preferred over many forms of communication, such as postal mail or courier services, because of its speed and immediate delivery of information. It also provides some elements of security that may be lacking with email attachments, as the letterhead, signature, and so on of the sending party can be easily identified by the recipient, without the need for more extensive authentication schemes.

Fax transmissions can originate from one of three sources: stand-alone fax machines, desktop computers with installed fax/modem boards, or large faxing systems, such as those that serve fax-on-demand or broadcast fax systems. The document to be transmitted is first converted into a fax format by either scanning the document or converting the electronic file into a fax-compatible format. At that point, the information to be transmitted is in a binary format. The next question then becomes one of transmission – should the fax be sent using a modem via the analog PSTN, or converted into an IP datagram and sent via the Internet or via an IP-based corporate intranet. When an IP-based transmission facility is selected, the overall nature of the fax transmission looks very similar to a VoIP call, complete with technical requirements for call setup, data transmission, call disconnect, billing functions, and so on.

One advantage of IP-based faxing, much like VoIP services, is the savings in toll charges, especially for international connections. With IP-based fax, however, another advantage is an increase in productivity. For example, end users can fax documents directly from their workstations, without getting up and walking to the fax machine. Received faxes can be treated much like email and stored in end users' mailboxes for later retrieval or accessed like email when traveling. With a location-wide fax server, economies of scale are likely to result: many, if not all, of the individual fax machines and their attached telephone lines can be eliminated, thus saving on monthly operating expenses.

A number of specialized carrier services, including GTE Internetworking, Singapore Telecom, PSInet, and .comfax, use an Internet faxing system developed by NetCentric Corporation, Bedford, Massachusetts, for their customers. The operation is much like accessing the Internet for sending email or accessing Web pages. A fax account is first established with a fax service bureau, which provides the end users with client software that is loaded onto a Windows 95 or NT 4.0 workstation. The client software provides the user interface where the destination fax number, broadcast fax lists, and other user-specified criteria are entered (Figure 2-5a).

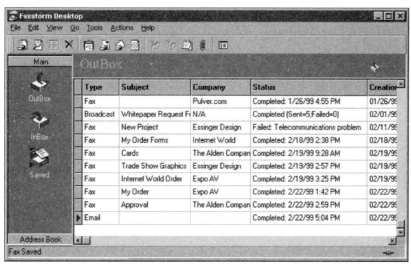

Figure 2-5a Faxstorm Client Desktop
(Courtesy of NetCentric Corporation)

Once the end user has specified the documents to be sent, they are encrypted and then sent to a NetCentric FaxStorm server that is connected to the Internet. At the destination, another FaxStorm server delivers the fax to the desired destination fax machine via local telephone lines, or to another computer as an email attachment if desired. The network provider has the option to establish individual fax mailboxes that electronically capture a user's incoming faxes, and then save them for later retrieval by a PC or forwarding to another fax machine.

The key components of an Internet-based fax network are illustrated in Figure 2-5b. These include: the originating fax devices such as PCs, fax machines, and fax servers; the existing Internet connection that provides access to the fax service bureau's point of presence; a network operations center, which includes the fax server; and the destination devices, such as email systems and desktop applications at the other end of the connection.

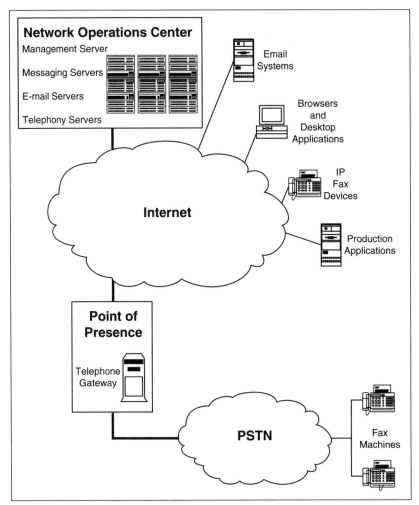

Figure 2–5b Fax over IP Network Components
(Courtesy of NetCentric Corporation)

Note that the majority of the investment in Internet fax equipment is within the network service provider's (NSP's) network, as shown in Figure 2-5c. This equipment includes a Telephony Server and PSTN Gateway, a Messaging Server, and a Management Server.

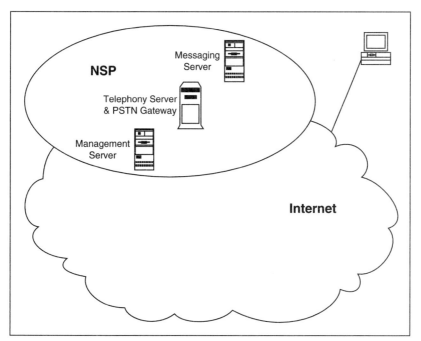

Figure 2-5c Network Service Provider Components
(Courtesy of NetCentric Corporation)

Three different applications are possible with this network topology. In the long distance scenario (Figure 2-5d), a user in Region A accesses the FaxStorm Telephony Server to broadcast a fax to destinations in Regions B and C.

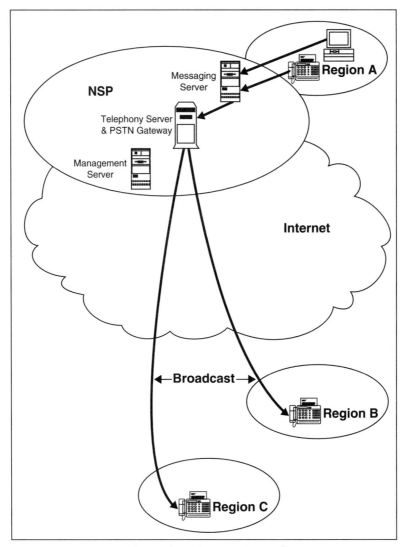

Figure 2-5d Desktop Fax Service (Long Distance Scenario)
(Courtesy of NetCentric Corporation)

The second possible scenario is called the Last Mile Scenario, where the Messaging Server communicates with a local Telephony Gateway to make the local connection for fax machines that are not Internet connected (Figure 2-5e).

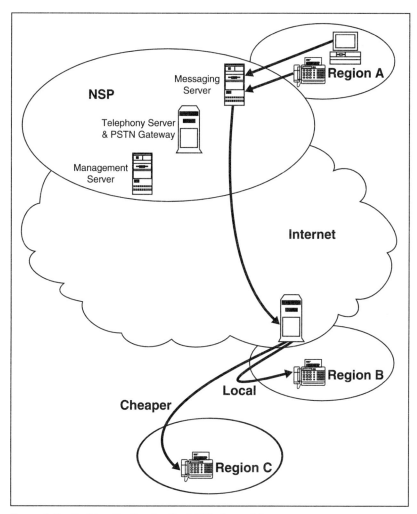

Figure 2-5e Desktop Fax Service (Last Mile Scenario)
(Courtesy of NetCentric Corporation)

The third communication scenario is the Inbox Service (Figure 2-5f), where an originated fax can be forwarded by the Messaging Server to an email address or a destination fax machine.

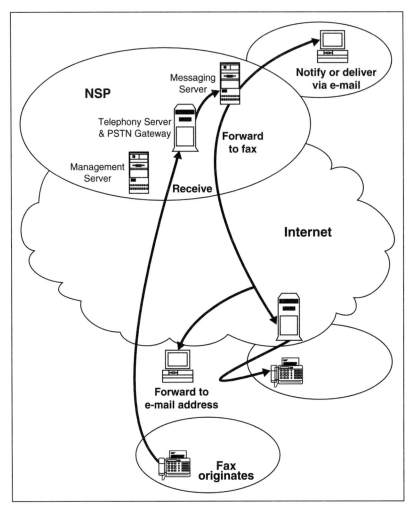

Figure 2-5f Inbox Service
(Courtesy of NetCentric Corporation)

To summarize, the use of Internet fax services provides one more opportunity to leverage an existing IP-based infrastructure to enhance communications and end-user productivity. Further information on NetCentric's products and network partners is found in Reference [2-5].

2.6 Video over IP: The Adirondack Area Network

Several years ago, a project was initiated to link the local area networks of institutions in the northern part of New York State to provide the local communities in the rural Adirondack Mountains region with continuing medical education, distance learning, video conferencing, telemedicine, and remote legal advice. The teleconferencing solution needed to be inexpensive, yet provide all of the traditional line services and video conferencing capabilities.

The Adirondack Region posed a variety of challenges to those creating this network. Technology infrastructure and high bandwidth lines were lacking in many areas that would be required for the planned applications. Of these applications, one of the most desirable was telemedicine, as there was a limited number of health care facilities in the Adirondacks, and therefore limited access to medical specialists. Network applications in support of the medical field included high-resolution data transfers of diagnostic procedures, such as X-ray, magnetic resonance imaging (MRI), and other tests, facilitating access to medical specialists, and expedited patient diagnosis. When consultations were required, physicians at one hospital wanted to easily connect with their colleagues at other network-connected institutions in the area. Another networking challenge was financial, as the ultimate network design and its telecommunications services had to be delivered as cost-effectively as possible.

Today, that project, known as the Adirondack Area Network, or AAnet (www.aanet.org), serves more than 150 institutions, including colleges, school districts, health care centers, legal organizations, hospitals, and the St. Regis Mohawk Tribe. In addition to connections averaging four per week within New York State, institutions from the neighboring states and the Canadian province of Quebec want to join the network. In fact, the Adirondack Area Network is confident that it will have 150 additional members on line by the year 2000. The network started as a collaborative effort among The Sage Colleges, Albany Medical Center, Franklin-Essex-Hamilton Board of Cooperative Educational Services in Malone, New York, Champlain Valley Educational Services in Plattsburgh, Bell Atlantic, RADVision Inc., Tandberg, Cisco Systems, the New York State Education and Research Network (NYSERNet), New York State, and other organizations.

During the design phase of the network, a number of infrastructure alternatives were considered. The LANs had various technologies, including FDDI, switched segments, and 10BASE-T, which also added to the design challenges. On the WAN side, ATM technology was available in the region but was eliminated because of cost. ISDN was considered, but its low bandwidth and lack of universal service in the region were concerns. Satellite up- and down-links were considered for distance learning, but they were considered too expensive for two-way interactive video conferencing. Fractional T1 lines were also ruled out because of cost. As a result, frame relay was identified as the only economical, comprehensive WAN solution.

Thus, a hybrid cloud infrastructure, using frame relay and TCP/IP at the core and other technologies for access, offered an innovative solution to the region's networking needs. Some of these other technologies included VoIP, ISDN, T1, T3, ATM, plus the various LANs and end-user applications (Figure 2-6).

Member institutions access AAnet through a virtual connection (PVC) into the frame relay network. Frame relay is a flat rate service so there are no long distance charges within the cloud. Fractional bandwidths are possible and high bandwidth pipes, with transmission rates from 1.5 Mbps (T1) to 45 Mbps (T3) are available. A frame relay network is a shared resource, and therefore the cost is substantially less than for traditional dedicated network models such as ISDN. By creating logical circuits in the frame relay cloud dedicated to video applications and other circuits dedicated to data, the AAnet guarantees the necessary bandwidth for high quality video. Instead of costly point-to-point connections, sites need only to connect to the nearest access point for the cloud. Sites receive Internet connectivity and high quality video connections for about the price of Internet connectivity by other means. The audio/video signal is of television/compact disc quality, even at 384 Kbps bandwidth. The video signals can adhere to a number of standards, including ITU-T H.323e, IP encapsulated H.320, or H.323. Multipoint video calls are also supported in this environment.

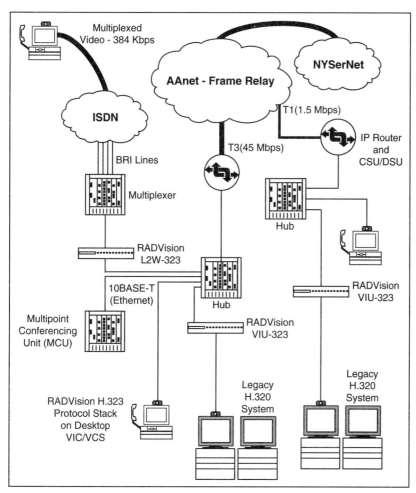

Figure 2-6 The Adirondack Area Network Topology
(Courtesy of RADVision, Inc.)

Much of the network infrastructure hardware was supplied by RADvision, Inc., of Mahwah, New Jersey. Two RADVision products were instrumental in the creation of this ground breaking video conferencing solution: OnLAN VIU-323 (Video Interface Unit) and OnLAN L2W-323 Gateway. By using the Video Interface Unit and connecting it to the room video conferencing hardware, developers found a way to enable the network to assess the video data as just another piece of information content that needed to be routed. The Video Interface Unit accomplishes this by taking the video data, a stream of data compliant with the ITU-T H.320 standard, and converting it into an IP-encapsulated H.323 stream or a pure H.323 stream.

The gateway functions as a video PBX that allows H.320 systems from the PSTN (ISDN) into the frame relay IP cloud. The Video Interface Unit (VIU) contacts the RADVision L2W Gateway, requesting the network address of the ISDN lines. Thus, the gateway enables the VIU to establish its network connection. In addition, the gateway, through its WAN ports, also enables video conferencing users to make multipoint calls. In other words, the gateway makes possible video conference calls that involve more than two participants through legacy multipoint control units (MCUs). The gateway also translates telephone numbers to IP addresses, in effect serving as a video conferencing PBX, with support for both Basic Rate Interface (BRI) and Primary Rate Interface (PRI) ISDN lines. As noted above, ISDN service is not available at all member locations; however, calls can still be made via the frame relay cloud through the gateways to the ISDN connection. Thus, institutions that are remote from ISDN services may still use full ISDN capabilities. In addition, the flexibility of being able to move video conferencing equipment from room to room without ever having to move lines is also provided.

Each institution on the Adirondack Area Network has its own programming and video conferencing-based content distribution as well. Producers have the option of posting their sessions to a public calendar with programs that are open to outside viewers. Those interested in a particular program ask for a port on the multipoint control unit (MCU) and can participate actively or just watch a session.

One example of such programming is offered by the Albany Medical Center, Albany, New York. In January 1999, the hospitals connected to the AANet participated in the first live minimally invasive surgery, a technique that allows the surgeon to perform the operation from outside the patient's body. Scopes, lasers, and other surgical devices are placed through portholes within the patient's body. During the surgery, the surgeon's scopes and workspace video are encoded and digitally mixed in real time. The patient's surgery and the instruments are visible in a split screen, while the surgeon is viewed in the other portion of the screen. To make this procedure visible to all call participants, the operation was broadcast to two rooms on the host campus, plus five other sites that joined via the frame relay network. The multipoint call is completely interactive; the surgeon can be seen and heard by participants, and those participants may pose questions to the operating room during the procedure.

A second example of the network's utility is in its support of natural disaster recovery efforts. When a savage ice storm ravaged this North County region during January 1998, New York State's Department of State deployed the Adirondack Area Network to assist and speed up disaster recovery. By using the AAnet, the Department of State was able to maintain direct voice and video contact with its lead people who were working around the clock to rebuild the shattered electric power and telephone systems in the stricken region. The network, which doesn't rely on standard telephone lines, was especially useful in areas that were without regular phone service for several weeks. Shortly after this devastating ice storm, floods hit many of the same areas. Again the design held up as a valid disaster recovery plan. Since that period many AAN institutions have implemented these processes into their individual disaster recovery plans.

By using frame relay and this network model, the average connection costs less than $1,000.00 per month. Other teleconference systems might cost as much as $100.00 per hour for video conferencing alone. A school or health care organization could purchase everything necessary for joining the network for about $70,000.00. Development of the network was supported in part by a $1.4 million grant from the Bell Atlantic Foundation, which thus reduced total project costs.

Further information on RADVision's products is found in Reference [2-6].

2.7 Looking Ahead

In this chapter, we have considered the wide breadth of applications that can be run over converged networks, supporting voice, fax, data, and video transmission. But the technical viability of these applications is only part of the story – they must be financially viable as well. In the next chapter we will discuss this second part and consider the business case for converged networks.

2.8 References

[2-1]   Additional information regarding the eRing service is available at www.ering.net.

[2-2]   Additional information regarding Interline's international VoIP services is available at www.interline.aust.com.

[2-3]   Additional information regarding OpenTel Communication Inc.'s services is available at www.opentel.com.

[2-4]   Additional information regarding WebLine Communication Corp.'s products is available at www.webline.com.

[2-5]   Additional information regarding NetCentric Corp.'s products and business partners is available at www.faxstorm.com.

[2-6]   Additional information regarding RADvision, Inc.'s products is available at www.radvision.com.

Chapter 3

The Business Case for Converged Networks

As a quick review, recall that we looked at the principles of converged networks in Chapter 1 and considered applications and case studies for those converged networks in Chapter 2. At some point along the way, however, someone will likely ask for some cost justification before a converged network design can move beyond the testing phase and into the enterprise-wide implementation phase.

This fundamental cost question may require additional analysis before a clear answer emerges. For example, there may be an assumption that combining voice and data networks into a converged system will lower the overall telecommunication expenses for the enterprise, but one may not know the extent of these savings until the converged network is actually implemented. The amount of network traffic to be re-routed to the converged network will be a factor, but so will the mix of domestic and international calls. Since carrier charges may be dependent upon the destination, do you have billing records available that can provide these necessary details? If integrated applications are successfully implemented over that converged system, benefits should also be derived – such as more effective use of staff resources, or higher customer satisfaction – both of which could have a positive impact on the organization's financial picture. But again, quantifying these expected benefits prior to implementation may be challenging.

It is the goal of this chapter to provide some guidelines that will assist in answering financial questions such as these. A case study, taken from one firm's actual experiences, will be presented at the end of this chapter to summarize some of the key points from the chapter.

But before we get into this analysis, a few caveats are in order. First, internetworks, by their very nature, are enterprise-specific entities. Put another way, your network is unique from any other, and, likewise, the costs associated with your network, and the way in which you justify those costs, are also unique from any other. An expense that I feel is quite appropriate might be considered unreasonable in your circumstances, or for your application. Therefore, some of the assumptions that are presented in this chapter may require modification in order for them to be applicable to your circumstances.

Second, there are a number of factors in any analysis of this type that are difficult to quantify. What about intangible or "blue sky" factors, such as the value of your customer service reputation? If you significantly change your network infrastructure, are any elements of your current operation at risk? These factors should be considered, as they may impact your financial assumptions.

Before proceeding, let's consider two basic assumptions.

3.1 Fundamental Financial Assumptions

With the caveats from the above discussion in mind, the first fundamental assumption for this chapter could be stated as follows:

> *Assumption 1: Assuming a given level of network performance, operating one network is less expensive than operating two networks.*

We will take it as a given that the readers of this book have at least two networks in place: one that serves data networking requirements, and one that serves voice networking requirements (Figure 3-1). If you wanted to extend this discussion further, you could probably subdivide these two categories. For example, the data network may include elements for Internet access, client/server computing, mainframe database access, and others. The voice network would include dial-up access to the PSTN, but may also include leased line connections supporting a private voice network, such as T1 lines operating at 1.544 Mbps or other tie trunks that connect the PBXs at the various locations.

Next, we will assume that the topology of an integrated network (Figure 3-2) would include some new elements that must be purchased, leased, or otherwise acquired. This would likely involve some hardware elements, such as VoIP gateways, but may also include upgrades to existing systems, such as routers and PBXs. Client applications, such as desktop video conferencing equipment, cameras, and so on, may also be involved. Thus, the total cost for the converged network may include several components: acquisition (or first) cost for new equipment, plus the ongoing operating cost for that new equipment, which could include employee training, maintenance contracts, and so on.

Before we embark on this financial study, a second key assumption needs to be stated:

> *Assumption 2: Support for new end-user applications will also be a financially motivating factor, but one that is much harder to quantify.*

For example, let us suppose that your proposed application is a Web-enabled call center. You know that your competition recently implemented a similar service, and have read industry reports that their sales have substantially increased. (During the same period, you have also noted that your sales have *decreased*, and have possibly wondered if these two facts are somehow related.)

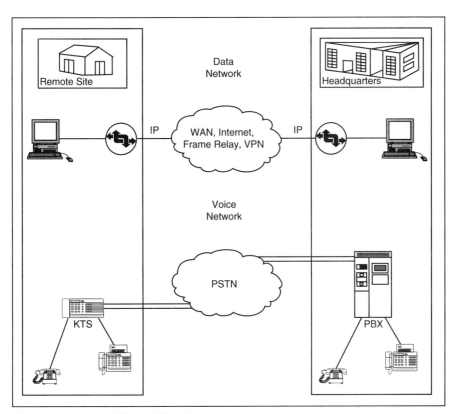

Figure 3-1 Separate Voice and Data Networks
(Courtesy of Netrix Corporation)

In any event, you have a second objective when network convergence is considered – protection of your installed base of customers through the implementation of a new customer application. For most people, this is the most difficult part of the analysis – quantifying the "blue sky" elements of that financial decision. Or, stated another way, how do you quantify the impact of *not* implementing the converged network and/or applications? As with most rhetorical questions, formulating an answer is left to the reader.

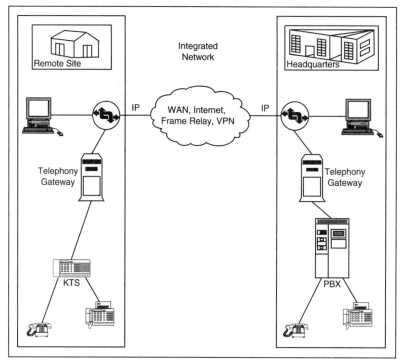

Figure 3-2 Integrated Voice and Data Networks
(Courtesy of Netrix Corporation)

3.2 Network Traffic Assumptions

Before developing a business case for a converged network, the technical characteristics of the existing network must be known. An important element of this business case will be the underlying assumptions regarding both current and future network traffic that will impact much of the financial work. For example, if you consider adding voice traffic onto your existing data network, do you know if your data network has the excess capacity to handle that additional traffic? For that matter, do you have baseline or historical information that allows you to predict network growth trends?

Another important factor to consider is whether or not any historical information that you might have available would even be relevant to the new application. In other words, a new application, such as a Web-enabled call center, may be so different in its traffic handling and loading characteristics that any current network statistics do not provide a good indication of how the network might respond to this new application. If that is the case, the network manager will have to make some initial estimates, and then refine those estimates as more complete information, perhaps from a lab-based test network, becomes available.

Most vendors of VoIP equipment have software tools available to assist their customers with the design and provisioning of a converged network. However, in order to expedite this process, the network manager should have the following information available before contacting prospective vendors:

◆ Network topology information and drawing showing up-to-date network configurations.

◆ Network connectivity information showing the types and capacities of the communication lines between various network locations.

◆ Network utilization information, including historical data that shows the growth in network traffic on those communication lines over the last 12–24 months.

◆ Growth projections, indicating areas in which network traffic is likely to be impacted. For example, the construction of a new manufacturing facility, the acquisition of a smaller, related firm, a joint venture with a business partner, or significant increases or decreases in the number of personnel would all impact network traffic.

◆ Impacts on network operation that come from end-user applications or the deployment of new applications. For example, the addition of a new distributed database, a customer support center, a fax-back service, or other communication-intensive application may impact the network traffic and its operation.

◆ Impacts on network operations that are seasonal or cyclical in nature. For example, one would assume that network traffic would increase at the end of the month (payroll processing) and at the end of the quarter (tax return and deposit processing). But if you are in the retail business, you likely have an increase in traffic during December and January as well, as a result of holiday purchases. Have you been able to quantify these cyclical trends?

◆ The sources of traffic on your network, divided by media type such as voice, fax, data, and video. Do you know what percentage of your traffic is a result of fax transmissions? If you do not, then the deployment of a network of fax gateways may be more difficult to justify.

If the preceding questions prompted any concerns or unresolved issues, then it would behoove you to do this research before significantly proceeding with any further design or financial commitments. It is difficult to design a network application if you don't know the characteristics of your existing network. Fortunately, a number of tools are available to assist with network monitoring, analysis, and traffic management functions. Further discussion on this subject is beyond the scope of this text; however, a few hours searching industry journals or the World Wide Web for products that would meet your requirements would be a worthwhile investment.

Once these baseline questions can be answered, both the network manager and the prospective vendors are in a better position to proceed. As part of their sales proposal, the vendors are likely to consider some additional factors:

◆ The type of WAN circuits to be used, such as Internet, ISDN, frame relay, or ATM.

◆ The maximum number of simultaneous calls possible at each location.

◆ The traffic matrix, or where most of the calls originate and terminate.

◆ The typical length or duration of the calls.

◆ The voice compression protocol options available or desirable.

◆ Interoperability with existing systems, such as the PBX or voice mail adjunct processor, that may be impacted by this conversion.

The sections that follow will include examples of various financial scenarios for consideration. As noted above, these examples are intended to serve as a guide, not necessarily the last word. Any network implementation should pass through the reality check of your own network's objectives and current operation before proceeding.

3.3 Quantifying the Business Case

To summarize our discussion thus far, your interest in moving toward a converged network topology may be rooted in several factors: improving network performance, increasing network redundancy, adding a new application, and/or decreasing communications costs. Putting a value on the first three factors is difficult — how do you quantify the potential payback from a more satisfied customer or determine if the cost of that redundant communication circuit paid off? On the other hand, if you install some new equipment and observe that your monthly telecommunications charges decrease, then a value-based analysis is more understandable.

Thus, your business case should be principally based on the hard numbers (such as decreases in monthly telecommunications expenses) rather than the soft numbers (such as customer satisfaction). A simple spreadsheet could be used to summarize this information and determine how quickly the investment in new equipment would pay for itself. For example, suppose that a network with four offices was converted from separate voice and data networks to a converged VoIP network. For each office, estimates could be made regarding the monthly expenses such as toll charges, personnel, maintenance, and so on, that would be saved by converting to the converged VoIP network, as seen in Column A of Worksheet 1(Figure 3-3). In a similar manner, the costs to purchase the new equipment at each location to support the converged network could be determined Column B of Worksheet 1. Dividing the Total Cost from Column B by the Monthly Savings from Column A would determine the approximate number of months needed for this new equipment to pay for itself.

For example, suppose that some of these offices are located outside of the United States and a traffic analysis indicates that some of the toll charges between locations could be eliminated if a converged network was installed. A comparison between the expected savings and expected costs of the new equipment would determine the payback period of this investment. To take this example a step further, suppose that an analysis strictly based on these hard cost savings indicates that return on this project is somewhat marginal. A more thorough analysis could then be made, which could take into account the value of the soft factors, such as customer satisfaction, potential increased sales, and so on, that might show the project in a more favorable light.

A similar analysis could be made if the equipment at each location were leased instead of purchased, as seen in Worksheet 2 (Figure 3-4). In this case, the monthly savings in network expenses (Column A) would be compared with the monthly lease payment for the new equipment (Column B), with the net monthly savings determined in Column C. As before, consideration of the easily quantifiable (hard) cost savings should be made before considering any of the more intangible (soft) cost savings.

Column A		Column B	
Office A: monthly savings in network expenses	$	**Office A:** cost for VoIP equipment	$
Office B: monthly savings in network expenses	$	**Office B:** cost for VoIP equipment	$
Office C: monthly savings in network expenses	$	**Office C:** cost for VoIP equipment	$
Office D: monthly savings in network expenses	$	**Office D:** cost for VoIP equipment	$
Subtotal:	$		$
Federal, State, and Local Taxes:	$		$
Total:	$		$

Figure 3-3 Worksheet 1 : Payback Period Calculations for Purchased VoIP Equipment (Courtesy of Netrix Corporation)

Column A		Column B		Column C	
Office A: monthly savings in network expenses	$	**Office A:** monthly lease payment for VoIP equipment	$	**Office A:** net monthly savings	$
Office B: monthly savings in network expenses	$	**Office B:** monthly lease payment for VoIP equipment	$	**Office B:** net monthly savings	$
Office C: monthly savings in network expenses	$	**Office C:** monthly lease payment for VoIP equipment	$	**Office C:** net monthly savings	$
Office D: monthly savings in network expenses	$	**Office D:** monthly lease payment for VoIP equipment	$	**Office D:** net monthly savings	$
Subtotal:	$		$		$
Federal, State, and Local Taxes:	$		$		$
Total:	$		$		$

Figure 3-4 Worksheet 2: Monthly Savings Calculations for Leased VoIP Equipment (Courtesy of Netrix Corporation)

The following examples will consider various network reconfiguration scenarios that could potentially increase the productivity of a network while also reducing the expenses of that network.

3.4 Example Scenarios for Converged Networks

Converging voice and data networks into a single system may solve a number of networking challenges and provide a number of benefits. The examples given in this section, taken from Reference [3-1], illustrate scenarios where cost savings may occur. As noted above, modification of these scenarios to incorporate network-specific factors would be required in most, if not all, of these examples.

3.4.1 Reducing Interoffice Toll Charges

Corporate interoffice long distance is one of the greatest telecommunications expenses that managers of large voice and data networks face. Aside from the company's sales staff, the average manager of any firm is on the phone much of the day conferring with coworkers at other offices of the same corporation. This is especially true in high technology firms where engineers must collaborate with teammates around the world. And, in many cases, these voice and data networks link the same pairs of locations, or in other words are *parallel networks*. If these two parallel networks can be integrated into a single network infrastructure, some economies of scale are likely to be realized.

If the business routes its interoffice long distance voice traffic over its existing corporate data WAN, virtual private network (VPN), the public Internet, or a public frame relay network, these economies are likely to be realized, and the expense for the interoffice toll charges reduced.

To implement such a converged topology will require some additional equipment in the form of a VoIP gateway, adjunct to the existing voice PBX, or other hardware. Worksheet 1 can be used to determine the payback period for this additional hardware. To complete Column A of that worksheet, the network manager must examine the interoffice traffic between that location and all other company locations. An estimate of the savings in monthly toll charges, assuming that the two parallel networks are combined into a single integrated network, is entered in Column A. This estimate should be based on the current network utilization, the amount of excess capacity available on those voice and data links, and the voice compression efficiencies that are anticipated. The cost to purchase the associated VoIP equipment is entered in Column B. By dividing the value in Column A into the value in Column B, a payback period, given in months, may be calculated. For example, suppose that the toll charge savings at Office A is estimated at $800.00 per month, and that the VoIP equipment costs for Office A are $8,000.00. The resulting payback period would be $8,000.00/$800.00, or 10 months.

In some cases, it will be more desirable to lease the VoIP equipment than to make an outright purchase. Worksheet 2 (Figure 3-4) is used for this situation. In this case, the monthly savings in interoffice toll charges (in Column A) would be used to offset the monthly lease expenses (in Column B). The difference between these two numbers represents the net monthly savings (in Column C).

3.4.2 Reducing Non-interoffice Toll Charges

Is much of your long distance traffic destined for the same calling areas such as area codes 303, 408, 212, 612, and so on? By installing a VoIP gateway in each of these local calling areas and activating the off-net dialing function of the gateway, end users can dial in from their location, get dial tone in those local calling areas or overseas, call any number in that local calling area, and therefore incur no long distance charges (Figure 3-5). A firm can further reduce its costs for its VoIP equipment and WAN connections by leasing ports on its gateway, or even by selling connect time minutes to other firms.

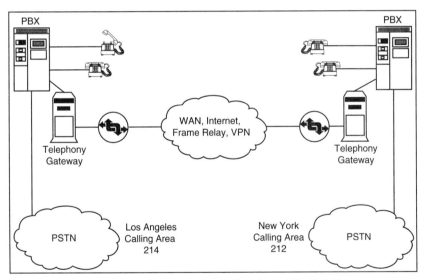

Figure 3-5 Using Off-net Dialing to Eliminate Non-interoffice Toll Charges
(Courtesy of Netrix Corporation)

3.4.3 Reducing In-bound Customer Call Charges

Many organizations provide toll-free (800/888) numbers for their customers' convenience. If VoIP gateways are installed on the premises of these regular customers, then calls from those customers are routed via an IP network to that vendor (Figure 3-6). As a result, those calls do not incur the typical charges associated with the use of the toll-free number. The payback period for this scenario can be calculated by comparing the monthly toll-free savings at each location with the cost of purchasing the VoIP equipment to support that location.

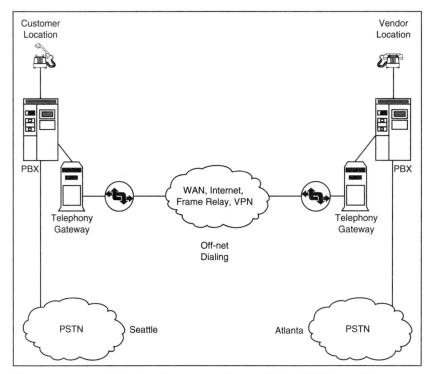

Figure 3-6 Inbound Calls from Customers to Vendors Using VoIP Points of Presence (Courtesy of Netrix Corporation)

3.4.4 Reducing In-bound Call Center Charges

Now, let's extend the in-bound call center scenario by considering that multiple, separate customers are calling about a vendor's products or services. For example, perhaps your organization has recently focused its advertising efforts in four cities: Los Angeles, Denver, Chicago, and New York. As a result, a high percentage of your in-bound customer calls are from area codes 213, 303, 312, and 212. Or perhaps you are in the banking industry, with a number of branch banks scattered around the country. You would like to provide your customers with a local telephone number for customer service, yet have those calls go to a centralized processing center.

Both of these challenges share a common solution: install a VoIP point of presence (POP) in the local calling area, and address that POP with a local telephone number (Figure 3-7). Using that local number, the customers access a VoIP gateway installed in their local calling area. That gateway connects to an IP-based network connection and communicates with a similar gateway at the distant call center location. From the customer's perspective, the call, and the call center, are both local operations. In this case, both the customer and the vendor benefit – the customer does not have to make a toll call to access the call center, and the vendor pays for local telephone circuits instead of toll circuits. The payback period for this scenario can be calculated by comparing the savings in communication line charges (the difference between the 800/888 access lines and the local access lines) with the cost of the VoIP equipment to support each location.

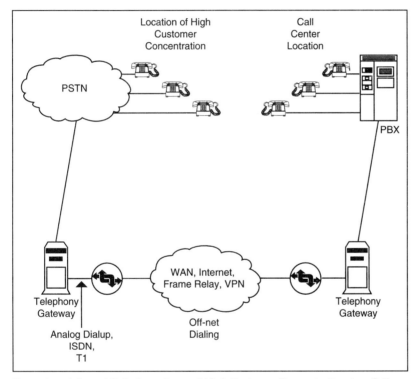

Figure 3-7 Inbound Calls from Areas of High Customer Concentration to a Call Center Using VoIP Points of Presence (Courtesy of Netrix Corporation)

3.4.5 Consolidating Network Operations within One Calling Area

If all corporate offices are in the same local calling area, and thus no toll charges apply, VoIP technologies may still be deployed for potential cost savings. These savings are derived by reducing the number of trunk lines that are required from the local exchange carrier (LEC). By routing the voice traffic over a firm's WAN or even the public Internet, the firm need not lease so many lines from the local exchange carrier. In effect, the data network replaces the local loop (Figure 3-8). The number of lines that could be replaced would be based on the results of the traffic studies, as discussed above in Section 3.2. In addition, good disaster recovery procedures would dictate that some voice lines from the LEC remain in place for contingency purposes.

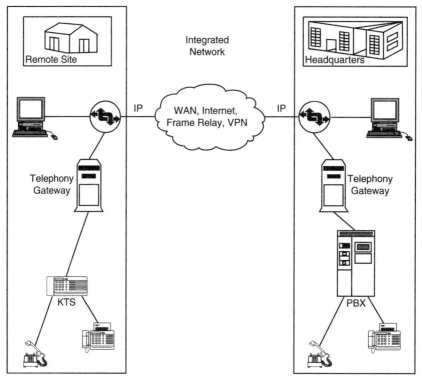

Figure 3-8 Routing Voice Traffic over the Existing Data Network
(Courtesy of Netrix Corporation)

3.5 Case Study: ALARIS Medical Systems

As an example of the business processes that a firm must consider when converging their voice and data networking infrastructures into a single, cohesive system, consider the experiences of ALARIS Medical Systems of San Diego, California (www.alarismed.com). ALARIS Medical's principal line of business is the design, manufacture, and marketing of intravenous infusion therapy products and patient monitoring instruments. In addition to its San Diego world headquarters and manufacturing facility, the company operates manufacturing facilities in Creedmoor, North Carolina, Basingstoke, England, and Tijuana, Mexico. The firm has three strategic business units: North America, which includes the United States and Canada; Instromedix; and International, which includes all other international operations, including Europe, Asia, Australia, and Latin America.

The need for additional bandwidth over their WAN has grown significantly from the recent additions of SAP/R3 applications and a new corporate email system, Microsoft Outlook. The firm quickly found itself lacking bandwidth needed to support these applications. Rather than invest in additional expensive T1 lines, they enlisted a local consulting group to assist in identifying other alternatives.

A conversion to an asynchronous transfer mode (ATM) backbone was considered; however, that would require an entirely new routing structure as well as a significant capital investment. Voice over IP systems were then researched, and appeared to provide a viable solution. However, a VoIP solution needed to be compatible with the existing voice network, which consisted of networked NEC NEAX PBX systems.

The NEC NEAX PBX uses a proprietary signaling protocol called Common Channel Interoffice Signaling, or CCIS. The CCIS protocol is based on the well-known Signaling System 7 (SS7) protocol that provides transparent network voice connectivity between PBXs. For example, CCIS operations facilitate functions such as call forwarding, centralized call accounting, voicemail, and attendant services. This CCIS channel operates within the confines of a T1 circuit in much the same way that an ISDN D-channel operates on an ISDN Primary Rate Interface (PRI) circuit, by providing a specific amount of reserved bandwidth for inter-switch communications. This signaling channel must operate at a full 64 Kbps rate, without compression or echo cancellation functions being applied. In summary, a VoIP solution would have to accommodate the existing investment in NEC PBXs and their proprietary CCIS channel in order for the converged network topology to be viable.

After reviewing a number of vendors' VoIP proposals, ALARIS selected the Network Exchange 2210 gateway, manufactured by Netrix Corporation of Herndon, Virginia. This gateway could fully support the CCIS signaling protocol, thus requiring no change to ALARIS' existing voice infrastructure.

The first VoIP connections were between the headquarters facility in San Diego, California, and a remote office in Creedmoor, North Carolina (Figure 3-9). This installation replaced a T1 private line between facilities, which distributed the voice and data channels using a drop and insert Channel Service Unit/Data Service Unit (CSU/DSU).

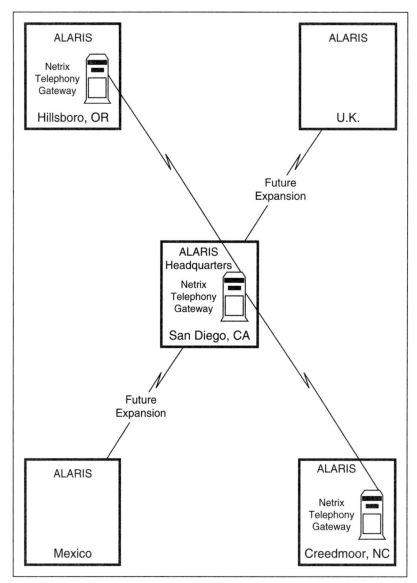

Figure 3-9 ALARIS Medical Systems VoIP Network Topology
(Courtesy of ALARIS Medical Systems

Due to the distance between the two locations, signal echoes can occur. ALARIS used the built-in echo cancellation features of the Netrix gateway to solve this challenge. By using this built-in feature, ALARIS did not have to purchase the echo cancellation capability from their WAN provider, which would have been an additional expense. In addition, they tested various voice compression algorithms that are available for the Netrix gateway, and found one that provided near toll-quality voice without impairing the data transmission characteristics of the circuit. The Netrix gateways also have built-in voice activity detectors than can minimize the bandwidth consumption of voice circuits that are not in use, thus providing additional bandwidth resources for data transmission. (We will study the characteristics of voice transmission, compression algorithms, and quality in detail in Chapter 6.) A second installation connected the San Diego headquarters with a remote facility in Hillsboro, Oregon. Like the previous connection, this circuit provided ample bandwidth for both voice and data connectivity.

As a result of the gateway's voice optimization algorithms, ALARIS had more bandwidth between the locations than was actually required, and was therefore able to eliminate one T1 line from each location, saving over $10,000.00 per month in circuit charges. This resulted in a payback period of about three months for the VoIP equipment. As a result of these positive experiences, ALARIS plans to expand their VoIP network and install Netrix gateways in Mexico and the United Kingdom.

3.6 Other Business Considerations

To summarize our discussion, VoIP technologies give the promise of reduced telephone charges and access to new applications designed to increase the productivity of a firm's staff, customers, or both. But since every network implementation is unique, a thorough analysis of business goals, objectives, and network traffic is required to make an adequate judgement regarding the viability of these technologies for your specific enterprise.

Two additional factors may enter into the decision process. First, firms with a significant percentage of international voice and data traffic will find that the charges for these connections may bias their results. In most cases, rates for domestic United States telephone service can be negotiated for $0.10 per minute or less. In contrast, rates for international calls are considerably higher – often ten to thirty times higher, depending on the desired destination and the time of the call. Thus, a significant amount of international toll traffic on the voice network may dramatically improve the business case for VoIP equipment investments.

Second, some firms negotiate long-term contracts with their carriers to obtain more favorable rates. In some cases, termination charges would be applied if a traditional network connection contract were cancelled in favor of an IP-based solution. Any such termination charges should be factored into the business case calculations accordingly. Reference [3-2] chronicles several such cases of customer-carrier contract issues. References [3-3] through [3-8] discuss some of the business and operational issues that impact VoIP network implementations.

3.7 Looking Ahead

In this chapter, we have considered the business case aspects for planning a Voice over IP network. In the next chapter, we will begin examining the underlying technologies that comprise a VoIP network.

3.8 References

[3-1]   Ohrtman, Frank. "Make All Your Calls Local Calls." Netrix Corporation White Paper, July 1999.

[3-2]   Rohde, David. "Beware Binding Telco Contracts." *Network World* (March 8, 1999): 1.

[3-3]   Misunas, David. "Routing Voice and Fax Over Corporate IP Networks." *CTI* (September 1997): 82.

[3-4]   Bajorek, Chris, Dr. "Big Call Centers for Small Companies." *Computer Telephony* (October 1997): 34–36.

[3-5]   Udall, Jim. "Extending the PSTN: Voice Over IP Gateways." *CTI* (February 1998): 114–118.

[3-6]   Fromm, Laurence J. "The Case for IP Telephony." *Internet Telephony* (Second Quarter 1998): 34–37.

[3-7]   McConnell, Brian. "IP Telephony in The Local Loop." *Computer Telephony* (April 1998): 30–37.

[3-8]   Kim, Gary. "IP Telephony Places New Challenges on Traditional Long Distance." *Sounding Board* (May/June 1998): 46–49.

Chapter 4

Protocols for the Converged Network

Thus far, we have discussed the principles of network convergence, applications that can operate over converged networks, and some of the business decisions that may be required before implementing these technologies. In this chapter, we will consider the infrastructure of an Internet Protocol system, looking at the background that went into the development of the Internet protocol, the architecture and protocols of IP-based internetworks that support data transport, and finally, the additional protocols that are required to support VoIP applications.

Some readers will already be familiar with the architecture and operation of IP-based internetworks. You may feel comfortable with the details of the IPv4 and IPv6 packet headers; IPv4, and IPv6 addressing formats; routing protocols, such as RIP and OSPF; the purpose of the Domain Name Service; and the functional differences between UDP and TCP. If you fall into this category, skip directly to Section 4.8, and read about the additional protocols that are required to support voice and video transport over IP networks. However, if you feel lacking in any of the above topics, proceed with Section 4.1, so that you will more fully understand the more advanced topics that come later in this text.

4.1 The ARPA Network Architecture

Recall from our discussion in Chapter 1 that the Internet protocols were developed, in part, by the U.S. Advanced Research Projects Agency (ARPA). The ARPA internetwork architecture (Figure 4-1) consisted of networks connected by gateways [4-1]. The ARPA model assumed that each network used packet switching technology and could connect to a variety of transmission media (LAN, WAN, radio, and so on). Note that the term "gateway" is somewhat historic and has been replaced with the term "router." Subsequent references in this text will use the term router.

The ARPA Internet architecture consisted of four layers (Figure 4-2). The lowest layer was called the Network Interface Layer (it was also referred to as the Local Network or Network Access Layer) and comprised the physical link (e.g., LAN) between devices. The Network Interface Layer existed in all devices, including hosts and gateways.

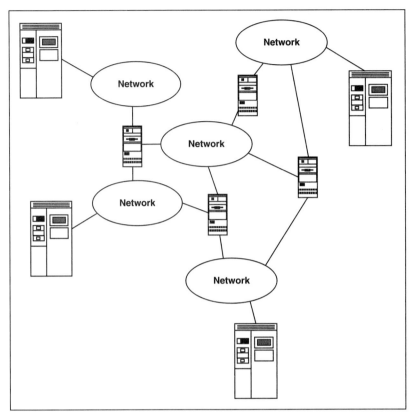

Figure 4-1 Networks Connected with Gateways to Form an Internetwork

The Internet Layer insulated the hosts from network-specific details, such as addressing. The Internet Protocol (IP) was developed to provide end-to-end datagram service for this layer. (Datagram service is analogous to a telegram in which the information is sent as a package.) The Internet Layer (and, therefore, IP) existed only in hosts and gateways.

While the Internet Layer provided end-to-end delivery of datagrams, it did not guarantee their delivery. Therefore, a third layer, known as the Service Layer (now called the Host-to-Host Layer), was provided within the hosts. As its name implies, the Service Layer defined the level of service the host applications required. Two protocols were created for the Service Layer: the Transmission Control Protocol (TCP) for applications needing reliable end-to-end service, and the User Datagram Protocol (UDP) for applications with less stringent reliability requirements. A third protocol, the Internet Control Message Protocol (ICMP), allowed hosts and gateways to exchange monitoring and control information. All three of these protocols – TCP, UDP and ICMP – are employed with VoIP networks. TCP is used to establish the VoIP call, a function that requires high reliability. UDP is used to transport voice samples, a function that requires maximum efficiency with a minimum of overhead. ICMP is used by IP-based VoIP equipment to verify connectivity and resolve communication problems.

The highest ARPA layer, the Process/Application Layer, resided only in hosts and supported user-to-host and host-to-host processing or applications. A variety of standard applications were developed. These included the Telecommunications Network (TELNET) for remote terminal access, the File Transfer Protocol (FTP) for file transfer, and the Simple Mail Transfer Protocol (SMTP) for electronic mail.

Figure 4-2 compares the OSI architecture which is more theoretical, with the ARPA architecture which is more practical, and better describes how IP-based networks, including VoIP systems, are actually implemented. Note that the OSI Physical and Data Link Layers represent the ARPA Network Interface (or Local Network) Layer; the OSI Network Layer corresponds to the Internet Layer; the OSI Transport Layer is functionally equivalent to the Host-to-Host (Service) Layer; and the OSI Session, Presentation, and Application Layers comprise the ARPA Process/Application Layer. Reference [4-2] further describes the development of the ARPANET Reference Model and protocols.

OSI Layer	ARPA Architecture
Application	Process / Application Layer
Presentation	
Session	
Transport	Host-to-Host Layer
Network	Internet Layer
Data Link	Network Interface or Local Network Layer
Physical	

Figure 4-2 Comparing OSI and ARPA Models

To connect to LANs, the Network Interface Layer must exist in all hosts and routers, although its implementation may change across the internetwork (see Figure 4-3). Thus Host A must have a consistent attachment to Router B, but the destination Host Z may be of a different type. In other words, you can start with an Ethernet, traverse a frame relay network, and end with a token ring as long as you maintain pair-wise consistencies.

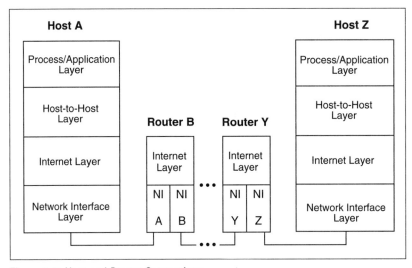

Figure 4-3 Host and Router Connections

The Internet transmission frame that originates at a host, and then subsequently passes through the routers on its way to the destination host, is illustrated in Figure 4-4. This frame would have the format of the local or wide area network in use, such as Ethernet or frame relay. A local network header would begin the frame, which would contain addressing information required to deliver that frame to the appropriate location, such as the router, on a local network. The upper layer headers, IP, UDP/TCP, and Application, would following the local network header. At the end of the frame would be the local network trailer, which would include error control information such as a checksum.

Reviewing Figure 4-3, note that the local network frame formats may change as they pass through various topologies. For example, if the transmission started on an Ethernet LAN, the initial frame format would adhere to the Ethernet specification. If this Ethernet then connected to a frame relay WAN, a conversion in the frame format from Ethernet to frame relay would be made at the first router with a frame relay connection. This frame relay frame would travel to the destination LAN (such as a token ring), where another frame format conversion would be made. Through this process, the *packet* inside that *frame* (the IP header, UDP/TCP header, Application Data, and so on) would be largely undisturbed, unless a packet size conversion (known as fragmentation and reassembly) became necessary.

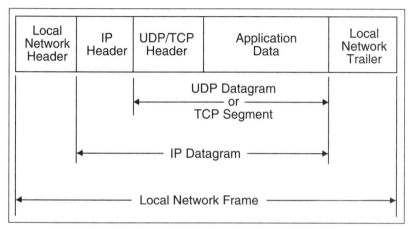

Figure 4–4 The Internet Transmission Frame

4.2 The ARPA Protocols

The ARPA model is the architecture upon which all of the Internet Protocols were based. To better understand the interworkings of a VoIP system, one must first have a good grasp on the underlying protocols, including the architecture surrounding those protocols.

The ARPA model was designed to connect hosts serving the academic, research, government, and military populations, primarily in the United States. In contrast, the Open Systems Interconnection Reference Model (OSI-RM) was broader in scope. It was designed to address a much broader charter, the interconnection of Open Systems, and was not constrained by the type of system to be connected (e.g., academic, military, and so forth). As a result, the OSI-RM added some additional granularity to the definitions of the layer functions and developed a seven-layer model in contrast to ARPA's four-layer model. To summarize, the ARPA world was more specific, the OSI world more general. The result was two architectures that are almost, but not quite, parallel, as shown in Figure 4-5.

ARPA Layer	Protocol Implementation								OSI Layer
	Hypertext Transfer	File Transfer	Electronic Mail	Terminal Emulation	Domain Names	File Transfer	Client / Server	Network Management	
Process / Application	Hypertext Transfer Protocol (HTTP) RFC 2068	File Transfer Protocol (FTP) MIL-STD-1780 RFC 959	Simple Mail Transfer Protocol (SMTP) MIL-STD-1781 RFC 821	TELNET Protocol MIL-STD-1782 RFC 854	Domain Name System (DNS) RFC 1034, 1035	Trivial File Transfer Protocol (TFTP) RFC 783	Sun Microsystems Network File System (NFS) Protocols RFCs 1014, 1057, and 1094	Simple Network Management Protocol (SNMP) v1: RFC 1157, v2: RFC 1901-10, v3: RFC 2271-75	Application
									Presentation
									Session
Host-to-Host	Transmission Control Protocol (TCP) MIL-STD-1778 RFC 793					User Datagram Protocol (UDP) RFC 768			Transport
Internet	Address Resolution ARP RFC 826 RARP RFC 903	Internet Protocol (IP) MIL-STD-1777 RFC 791					Internet Control Message Protocol (ICMP) RFC 792		Network
Network Interface	Network Interface Cards: Ethernet, Token Ring, ARCNET, MAN and WAN RFC 894, RFC 1042, RFC 1201 and others								Data Link
	Transmission Media: Twisted Pair, Coax, Fiber Optics, Wireless Media, etc.								Physical

Figure 4-5 Comparing ARPA Protocols with OSI and ARPA Architectures

We see some of these parallels when considering the protocols that are implemented in support of IP-based internetworks. Reviewing our earlier discussion, recall that the first layer of the ARPA model is the Network Interface Layer, sometimes called the Network Access Layer or Local Network Layer; it connects the local host to the local network hardware. As such, it comprises the functions of the OSI Physical and Data Link Layers: it makes the physical connection to the cable system, it accesses the cable at the appropriate time (e.g., using a Carrier Sense Multiple Access with Collision Detection (CSMA/CD) or token passing algorithm), and it places the data into a frame. The frame is a package that envelops the data with information, such as the hardware address of the local host and a check sequence to ensure data integrity. The frame is defined by the hardware in use, such as an Ethernet LAN or a frame relay interface into a WAN. The ARPA model shows particular strength in this area — it includes a standard for virtually all popular connections to LANs, MANs, and WANs. (Internet standards are defined in Request for Comments documents, or RFCs. Further details on these Internet standards are provided in Appendix G.) These include Ethernet (RFC 894); IEEE 802 LANs (RFC 1042); ARCNET (RFC 1201); Fiber Distributed Data Interface — FDDI (RFC 1103); serial lines using the Serial Line Internet Protocol or SLIP (RFC 1055); PSPDNs (RFC 877); frame relay (RFC 1490); Switched Multimegabit Data Service or SMDS (RFC 1209); and the Asynchronous Transfer Mode (ATM), defined in RFC 1438.

The Internet Layer transfers packets from one host (the computing device that runs application programs) to another host. Note that we said packet instead of frame. The packet differs from the frame in that it contains address information to facilitate its journey from one host to another through the internetwork; the address within the frame header gets the frame from host to host on the same local network. The protocol that operates the Internet Layer is known as the Internet Protocol (the IP in TCP/IP). Several other protocols are also required, however.

The Address Resolution Protocol (ARP) provides a way to translate between IP addresses and local network addresses, such as Ethernet, and is discussed in RFC 826. The Reverse Address Resolution Protocol (RARP), explained in RFC 903, provides the complementary function, translating from the local address (again, such as Ethernet) to IP addresses. (In some architectural drawings, ARP and RARP are shown slightly lower than IP to indicate their close relationship to the Network Interface Layer. In some respects, ARP/RARP overlap the Network Interface and Internet Layers.)

The Internet Control Message Protocol (ICMP) provides a way for the IP software on a host or gateway to communicate with its peers on other machines about any problems it might have in routing IP datagrams. ICMP, which is explained in RFC 792, is a required part of the IP implementation. One of the most frequently used ICMP messages is the Echo Request, commonly called the Ping, which allows one device to test the communication path to another.

As the datagram traverses the Internet, it may pass through multiple routers and their associated local network connections. There's a risk that packets may be lost or that a noisy communication circuit may corrupt data. The Host-to-Host Layer guards against these problems, however remote, and ensures the reliable delivery of a datagram sent from the source host to the destination host.

The Host-to-Host Layer defines two protocols: the User Datagram Protocol (UDP) and the Transmission Control Protocol (TCP). The minimum security UDP, described in RFC 768, provides minimal protocol overhead. UDP restricts its involvement to higher layer port addresses, defining the length and a checksum. TCP, detailed in RFC 793, defines a much more rigorous error control mechanism. TCP (of the TCP/IP nomenclature) provides much of the strength of the Internet protocol suite. TCP provides reliable datastream transport between two host applications by providing a method of sequentially transferring every octet (8-bit quantity of data) passed between the two applications.

End users interact with the host via the Process/Application Layer. Because of the user interface, a number of protocols have been developed for this layer. As its name implies, the File Transfer Protocol (FTP) transfers files between two host systems. FTP is described in RFC 959. To guarantee its reliability, FTP is implemented over TCP. When economy of transmission is desired, you may use a simpler program, the Trivial File Transfer Protocol (TFTP), described in RFC 783. TFTP runs on top of UDP to economize the Host-to-Host Layer as well.

Electronic mail and terminal emulation are two of the more frequently used Internet applications. The Simple Mail Transfer Protocol (SMTP), given in RFC 821, sends mail messages from one host to another. When accessing a remote host via the Internet, one must emulate the type of terminal the host wishes to see. For example, a Digital host may prefer a VT-100 terminal while an IBM host would rather see a 3278 or 3279 display station. The Telecommunications Network (TELNET) protocol provides remote host access and terminal emulation.

As internetworks become more complex, system management requirements increase as well. A large number of vendors, including Hewlett-Packard, IBM, Microsoft, SunSoft, and others, have developed network management systems that supply these needs. Common to all of these platforms is the use of a protocol, the Simple Network Management Protocol (SNMP), that was originally developed to meet the needs of TCP/IP-based internets. As its name implies, SNMP uses minimal overhead to communicate between the Manager (i.e., management console) and the Agent (i.e., the device, such as a router, being managed). There are presently three different versions of SNMP defined: version 1 (RFCs 1155, 1157, and 1213), version 2 (RFCs 1901–1910), and version 3 (RFCs 2271–2275).

Many other protocols are defined for the Internet suite that provide address resolution, control, and routing functions; these are illustrated in Figure 4-6. Note that the address resolution protocols are functionally lower than the ARPA Internet Layer, and that the control and routing functions are functionally higher than the Internet Layer.

Thus, an IP-based internetwork is comprised of a number of distinct protocols, all of which must be used at one time or another to transport information from one point to another. And these protocol functions – such as address resolution and routing information updates – are independent of the information content of the data being sent. In other words, ARP, ICMP, TCP, UDP and the other elements of the ARPA protocol suite must be present independent of whether the information that is being transmitted is a file (using FTP), a network management query (using SNMP) or a short sample of digitized voice (which, as we will see in Section 4.8, needs other protocols as well.) With that background into the Internet protocols, the next section will consider the protocols that facilitate packet transport: IPv4 and IPv6.

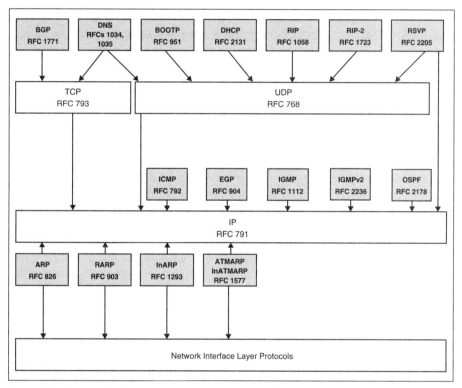

Figure 4-6 Internet Routing, Control, and Address Resolution Protocols

4.3 Packet Transport: IPv4, IPv6, and ICMP

This section will consider the protocols that forward Internet packets: the Internet Protocol, IPv4 and IPv6. In addition, we will discuss a complementary protocol that handles communication within the IP-based network infrastructure, the Internet Control Message Protocol (ICMP). We will consider these protocols individually in the sections that follow and how each relates to Voice over IP.

4.3.1 Internet Protocol version 4

IP, as defined in RFC 791 [4-3], is responsible for the delivery of packets (or *datagrams* as they are known in IPv4 parlance). In other words, the IP destination address facilitates the routing of the datagram to the correct host on the specified network. A port address, found in the UDP or TCP header, then facilitates the routing of the application data within the host to the correct host process.

To deliver datagrams, IP deals with two issues: addressing and fragmentation. The address ensures that the datagram arrives at the correct destination. Datagram transmission is analogous to mailing a letter. When you mail a letter, you write source and destination addresses on the envelope, place the information to be sent inside, and drop the resulting message in a mailbox. With the postal service, the mailbox is a blue (or red, depending on where you live) box. With the Internet, the mailbox service is the node where you enter the network.

Fragmentation is necessary because the sequence of LANs and WANs that any particular datagram may traverse can have differing frame sizes, and the IP datagram must fit within these varying frames (review Figure 4-4). For example, if the endpoint is attached to an IEEE 802.3 LAN with a maximum data field size of 1500 octets (an octet is defined as eight bits of information), IP must fragment the large IP datagram into smaller pieces (fragments) that will fit into the constraining frame. The distant node then reassembles the fragments back into a single IP datagram.

As you can see in Figure 4-7, the IP header contains at least 20 octets of control information, divided into a number of distinct fields. Version (4 bits) defines the current version of IP and should be equal to four. Internet Header Length (IHL, 4 bits) measures the length of the IP header in 32-bit words. (The minimum value would be five 32-bit words, or 20 octets.) The IHL also provides a measurement (or offset) for where the higher layer information, such as the TCP header, begins within the datagram. Type of Service (8 bits) tells the network the quality of service requested for this particular datagram. Values include:

Bits 0–2:	Precedence (or relative importance of this datagram)
	111 - Network Control
	110 - Internetwork Control
	101 - CRITIC/ECP
	100 - Flash Override
	011 - Flash
	010 - Immediate
	001 - Priority
	000 - Routine

Bits 0–2:	Precedence (or relative importance of this datagram)
Bit 3:	Delay, 0 = Normal, 1 = Low
Bit 4:	Throughput, 0 = Normal, 1 = High
Bit 5:	Reliability, 0 = Normal, 1 = High
Bits 6–7	:Reserved for future use (set to 0)

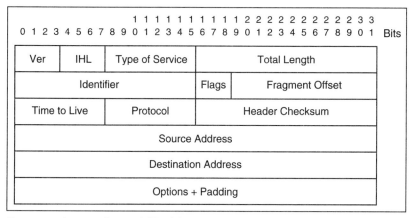

Figure 4-7 Internet Protocol (IPv4) Header Format

The Total Length field (16 bits) measures the length, in octets, of the IP datagram (the IP header plus higher layer information). The 16-bit field allows for a datagram of up to 65,535 octets in length, although at minimum all hosts must be able to handle datagrams of 576 octets in length.

The next 32-bit word contains three fields that deal with datagram fragmentation/reassembly. The sender assigns the Identification field (16 bits) to reassemble the fragments into the datagram. Three flags indicate how the fragmentation process is to be handled:

Bit 0:	Reserved (set to 0)
Bit 1:	(DF) 0 = May fragment, 1 = Don't fragment
Bit 2:	(MF) 0 = Last fragment, 1 = More fragments

The last field within this word is a 13-bit Fragment Offset, which indicates where in the complete message this fragment belongs. This offset is measured in 64-bit units.

The next word in the IP header contains a time-to-live (TTL) measurement, which is the maximum amount of time that the datagram is allowed to live within the internet. When TTL = 0, the datagram is destroyed. This field is a fail-safe measure that prevents misaddressed datagrams from wandering around the internet forever. TTL may be measured in either router hops or seconds, with a maximum of 255 of either measurement. If the measurement is in seconds, the maximum of 255 seconds is equivalent to 4.25 minutes (a long time to be "lost" within today's high-speed internetworks).

The Protocol field (8 bits) identifies the higher layer protocol following the IP header. Examples include:

Decimal	Keyword	Description
1	ICMP	Internet Control Message Protocol
6	TCP	Transmission Control Protocol
17	UDP	User Datagram Protocol

RFC 1700, "Assigned Numbers" [4-4], provides a more detailed listing of the protocols defined. A 16-bit Header Checksum completes the third 32-bit word.

The fourth and fifth words of the IP header contain the Source and Destination Addresses, respectively. Addressing may be implemented at several architectural layers. For example, hardware addresses are used at the ARPA Network Interface layer (or OSI Data Link layer) and are associated with a specific network interface card, usually burned into an address ROM on the card. The addresses within the IP header are the Internet layer (or OSI Network layer) addresses. The Internet address is a logical address that routes the IP datagram through the Internet to the correct host and network (LAN, MAN, or WAN).

4.3.2 Internet Control Message Protocol

If internetworks never experienced errors, datagrams would always be routed to their intended destination without errors. Unfortunately, this is not the case. As discussed previously, IP provides a connectionless service to the attached hosts but requires an additional module, known as the Internet Control Message Protocol (ICMP), to report any errors that may occur in the processing of those datagrams. Examples of errors would be undeliverable datagrams or incorrect routes. The protocol is also used to test the path to a distant host (known as a PING) or to request an address mask for a particular subnet. ICMP is an integral part of IP and must be implemented in IP modules contained in hosts and routers. The standard for ICMP is RFC 792 [4-5].

IP datagrams contain ICMP messages. In other words, ICMP is a user (client) of IP, and the IP header precedes the ICMP message. The datagram would thus be IP header, ICMP header, and finally ICMP data. Protocol = 1 identifies ICMP within the IP header. A Type field within the ICMP header further identifies the purpose and format of the ICMP message. Any data required to complete the ICMP message follows the ICMP header.

Thirteen ICMP message formats have been defined, each with a specific ICMP header format. Two of these formats (Information Request/Reply) are considered obsolete, and several others share a common message structure. The result is six unique message formats, as shown in Figure 4-8.

Network managers need to understand each of these ICMP messages because they contain valuable information about network status. All the headers share the first three fields. The Type field (1 octet) identifies one of the thirteen unique ICMP messages. These include:

Type Code	ICMP Message
0	Echo Reply
3	Destination Unreachable
4	Source Quench
5	Redirect
8	Echo
11	Time Exceeded
12	Parameter Problem
13	Timestamp
14	Timestamp Reply
15	Information Request (obsolete)
16	Information Reply (obsolete)
17	Address Mask Request
18	Address Mask Reply

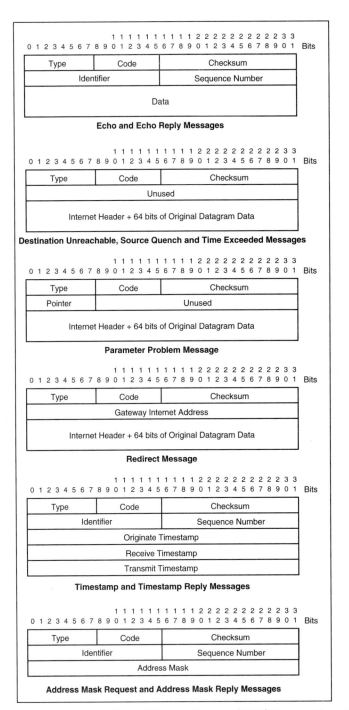

Figure 4-8 Internet Control Message Protocol (ICMP) Message Formats

The second field is labeled Code (1 octet) and elaborates on specific message types. For example, the Code field for the Destination Unreachable message indicates whether the network, host, protocol, or port was the unreachable entity. The third field is a Checksum (2 octets) on the ICMP message. The ICMP message formats diverge after the third field.

The Echo message (ICMP Type = 8) tests the communication path from a sender to a receiver via the Internet. On many hosts, this function is known as PING. The sender transmits an Echo message, which may contain an Identifier (2 octets) and a Sequence Number (2 octets) as well as data. When the intended destination receives the message, it reverses the source and destination addresses, recomputes the checksum, and returns an Echo Reply (ICMP Type = 0). The contents of the Data field (if any) would also return to the sender.

The Destination Unreachable message (ICMP Type = 3) is used when the router or host is unable to deliver the datagram. This message is returned to the source host of the datagram in question, and its Code field includes the specific reason for the delivery problem:

Code	Meaning
0	Net Unreachable
1	Host Unreachable
2	Protocol Unreachable
3	Port Unreachable
4	Fragmentation Needed and DF Set
5	Source Route Failed

Routers use codes 0, 1, 4, or 5. Hosts use codes 2 or 3. For example, when a datagram arrives at a router, it does a table lookup to determine the outgoing path to use. If the router determines that the destination network is unreachable (that is, a distance of infinite hops away), it returns a Net Unreachable message. Similarly, if a host is unable to process a datagram because the requested protocol or port is inactive, it would return a Protocol Unreachable or Port Unreachable message, respectively. Included in the Destination Unreachable message is the IP header plus the first 64 bits (8 octets) of the datagram in question. This returned data helps the host diagnose the failure in the transmission process.

The advantage of the datagram's connectionless nature is its simplicity. The disadvantage is its inability to regulate the amount of traffic into the network. As an analogy, consider the problem that your local post office faces. To handle the maximum possible number of letters, it needs enough boxes to handle the holiday rush. Building many boxes might be wasteful, however, because many of the boxes may not be used fully during the summer. If a router or host becomes congested with datagrams, it may send a Source Quench message (ICMP Type = 4) asking the source of those datagrams to reduce its output. This mechanism is similar to traffic signals that regulate the flow of cars onto a freeway. The Source Quench message does not use the second 32-bit word of the ICMP header, but fills it with zeros. The rest of the message contains the IP header and the first 8 octets of the datagram that triggered the request.

Hosts do not always choose the correct destination address for a particular datagram, and occasionally send one to the wrong router. This scenario can occur when the host is initialized and its routing tables are incomplete. When such a routing mistake occurs, the router receiving the datagram returns a Redirect message to the host specifying a better route. The Code field in the datagram would contain the following information:

Code	Message
0	Redirect datagrams for the network
1	Redirect datagrams for the host
2	Redirect datagrams for the type of service and network
3	Redirect datagrams for the type of service and host

The Redirect message (ICMP Type = 5) contains the router (gateway) address necessary for the datagram to reach the desired destination. In addition, the IP header plus the first 8 octets of the datagram in question return to the source host to aid the diagnostic processes.

Another potential problem of connectionless networks is that datagrams can get lost within the network. Alternatively, congestion could prevent all fragments of a datagram from being reassembled within the host's required time. Either of these situations could trigger an ICMP Time Exceeded message (ICMP Type = 11). This message contains two codes: time-to-live exceeded in transmit (code = 0), and fragment reassembly time exceeded (code = 1). The rest of the message has the same format as the Source Quench message: the second word contains all zeros and the rest of the message contains the IP header and the first 8 octets of the offending datagram.

If a datagram cannot be processed because of errors, higher layer processes recognize the errors and discard the datagram. Parameter problems within an IP datagram header (such as incorrect Type of Service field) would trigger the sending of an ICMP Parameter Problem message (ICMP Type = 12) to the source of that datagram, identifying the location of the problem. The message contains a pointer that identifies the octet with the error. The rest of the message contains the IP datagram header plus the first 8 octets of data, as before.

The Timestamp message (ICMP Type = 13) and Timestamp Reply message (ICMP Type = 14) either measure the round-trip transit time between two machines or synchronize the clocks of two different machines. The first two words of the Timestamp and Timestamp Reply messages are similar to the Echo and Echo Reply messages. The next five fields contain timestamps, measured in milliseconds since midnight, Universal Time (UT). The Timestamp requester fills in the Originate field when it transmits the request; the recipient fills in the Receive Timestamp upon its receipt. The recipient also fills in the Transmit Timestamp when it transmits the Timestamp Reply message. With this information, the requester can estimate the remote processing and round-trip transit times. (Note that these are only estimates, since network delay is a highly variable measurement.) The remote processing time is the Received Timestamp minus Transmit Timestamp. The round-trip transit time is the Timestamp Reply message arrival time minus the Originate Timestamp. With these two calculations, the two clocks can be synchronized.

The subnetting requirements (RFC 950) added the Address Mask Request (ICMP Type = 17) and Address Mask Reply (ICMP Type = 18) to the ICMP message set. It is assumed that the requesting host knows its own Internet address. (If not, it uses RARP to discover its Internet address.) The host broadcasts the Address Mask Request message to destination address 256.256.256.255 and fills the Address Mask field of the ICMP message with zeros, and the IP router that knows the correct address mask responds. For example, the response for a Class B network (when subnet addresses are not used) would be 256.256.0.0. A Class B network using an 8-bit subnet field would be 256.256.256.0.

4.3.3 Internet Protocol version 6

As the applications for the Internet expanded in the early 1990s, and more organizations began using this worldwide communications resource, some of the shortcomings of the Internet Protocol became evident. The most noticeable of these shortcomings was the 32-bit IPv4 address space; there were concerns that this address space would soon be exhausted, thus limiting growth of the Internet. As a result, the Internet Engineering Task Force chartered the Internet Protocol Next Generation (IPng) working group. This working group was tasked with defining the requirements and specifications for the protocols that would take the Internet to the next level of growth.

In December 1993, RFC 1550 was distributed, titled "IP: Next Generation (IPng) White Paper Solicitation." This RFC invited any interested party to submit their comments regarding any specific requirements for the IPng or any key factors that should be considered during the IPng selection process. Twenty-one responses were submitted that addressed a variety of topics, including: security (RFC 1675), a large corporate user's view (RFC 1687), a cellular industry view (RFC 1674), and a cable television industry view (RFC 1686).

The IPng Area commissioned RFC 1726, "Technical Criteria for Choosing IP The Next Generation (IPng)," to define a set of criteria that would be used in the IPng evaluation process. Seventeen criteria were noted:

◆ Scale – The IPng Protocol must scale to allow the identification and addressing of at least 1012 end systems and 109 individual networks.

◆ Topological Flexibility – The routing architecture and protocols of IPng must allow for many different network topologies.

◆ Performance – A state-of-the-art, commercial-grade router must be able to process and forward IPng traffic at speeds capable of fully utilizing common, commercially available, high-speed media at the time.

◆ Robust Service – The network service and its associated routing and control protocols must be robust.

◆ Transition – The protocol must have a straightforward transition plan from the current IPv4.

◆ Media Independence – The protocol must work across an internetwork of many different LAN, MAN, and WAN media, with individual link speeds ranging from a ones-of-bits per second to hundreds of gigabits per second.

◆ Unreliable Datagram Service – The protocol must support an unreliable datagram delivery service.

◆ Configuration, Administration, and Operation – The protocol must permit easy and largely distributed configuration and operation. The automatic configuration of hosts and routers is required.

◆ Secure Operation – IPng must provide a secure network layer.

◆ Unique Naming – IPng must assign all IP-Layer objects global, ubiquitous, Internet unique names.

◆ Access and Documentation – The protocols that define IPng, its associated protocols, and the routing protocols, must be published in the standards track RFCs, be freely available, and be without licensing fees for implementation.

◆ Multicast – The protocol must support both unicast and multicast packet transmission.

◆ Extensibility – The protocol must be extensible; it must be able to evolve to meet the future service needs of the Internet.

◆ Network Service – The protocol must allow the network to associate packets with particular service classes, and must provide them with the services specified by those classes.

◆ Mobility – The protocol must support mobile hosts, networks, and internetworks.

◆ Control Protocol – The protocol must include elementary support for testing and debugging networks.

◆ Private Networks – IPng must allow users to build private internetworks on top of the basic Internet infrastructure.

Of the criteria noted above, the ones most relevant to our discussion of VoIP applications are the multicast and network service requirements. Multicasting allows the same packet to be distributed to more than one destination, such as an audio or video conference call. The network service criteria notes that a particular flow of packets, such as those from that real-time conference call, could be identified for special processing to provide more timely packet delivery. In addition, the overall architecture of IPv6 is designed around 64-bit processors, which run real-time operations more effectively than those processors with a smaller word size (such as 16- or 32-bit machines).

These criteria were used to develop IP version 6, which is currently specified in RFC 2460 [4-6]. These functions are included within the IPv6 base header and extension headers.

4.3.3.1 THE IPV6 HEADER
The IPv6 header is 40 octets in length, with eight fields (Figure 4-9).

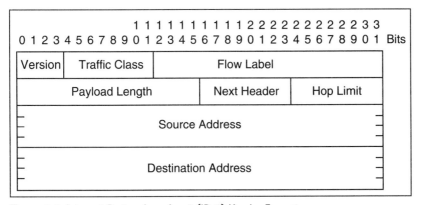

Figure 4-9 Internet Protocol version 6 (IPv6) Header Format

◆ The Version field is four bits in length and identifies the version of the protocol. For IPv6, Version = 6.

◆ The Traffic Class field is eight bits in length and enables a source to identify the desired delivery criteria for its packets.

The Flow Label field is 20 bits in length and may be used by a host to request special handling for certain packets, such as those with a nondefault quality of service.

The Payload Length field is a 16-bit unsigned integer that measures the length, given in octets, of the payload (i.e., the balance of the IPv6 packet). Payloads greater than 65,535 are allowed, and are called jumbo payloads.

The Next Header field is eight bits in length and identifies the header immediately following the IPv6 header. This field uses the same values as the IPv4 Protocol field. Examples are:

Value	Header
0	Hop-by-Hop Options
1	ICMPv4
4	IP in IP (encapsulation)
6	TCP
17	UDP
43	Routing
44	Fragment
50	Encapsulating Security Payload
51	Authentication
58	ICMPv6
59	None (no next header)
60	Destination Options

The Hop Limit field is eight bits in length and is decremented by one by each node that forwards the packet. When the Hop Limit equals zero, the packet is discarded and an error message is returned.

The Source Address is a 128-bit field that identifies the originator of the packet. (Note that this represents a substantial increase in address field size over and above that which was provided with IPv4.)

The Destination Address field is a 128-bit field that identifies the intended recipient of the packet, although possibly not the ultimate recipient of the packet, if a Routing header is present.

4.3.3.2 EXTENSION HEADERS

The IPv6 design simplified the existing IPv4 header by placing many of the existing fields in optional headers. In this way, the processing of ordinary packets is not complicated by undue overhead, while the more complex conditions are still provided for. An IPv6 packet, which consists of an IPv6 packet plus its payload, may consist of zero, one, or more extension headers, as shown in Figure 4-10.

The Hop-by-Hop Options header carries information that must be examined and processed by every node along a packet's delivery path, including the destination node. As a result, the Hop-by-Hop Options header, when present, must immediately follow the IPv6 header. The other extension headers are not examined or processed by any node along a packet's delivery path until the packet reaches its intended destination(s). When processed, the operation is performed in the order in which the headers appear in the packet.

The IPv6 specification recommends that the extension headers be placed in the IPv6 packet in a particular order:

- ◆ IPv6 header

- ◆ Hop-by-Hop Options header

- ◆ Destination Options header (for options to be processed by the first destination that appears in the IPv6 Destination Address field, plus any subsequent destinations listed in the Routing header)

- ◆ Routing header

- ◆ Fragment header

- ◆ Authentication header

- ◆ Encapsulating Security Payload header

- ◆ Destination Options header (for options to be processed by the final destination only)

- ◆ Upper Layer Protocol header (TCP and so on)

Figure 4-10 illustrates the IPv6 and optional headers, with their suggested order.
Further details on IPv6 standards and implementations are available from the IPv6 Industry Page [4-7].

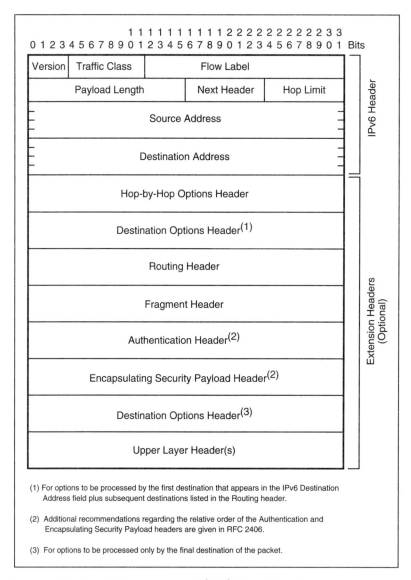

Figure 4–10 Internet Protocol version 6 (IPv6) Packet Format

4.4 Packet Addressing

Following the format of the previous discussion, this section will discuss packet addressing for IPv4 and IPv6, respectively.

4.4.1 IPv4 Addressing

Each 32-bit IPv4 address is divided into Host ID and Network ID sections and may take one of five formats ranging from Class A to Class E, as shown in Figure 4-11. The formats differ in the number of bits they allocate to the Host IDs and Network IDs and are identified by the first four bits.

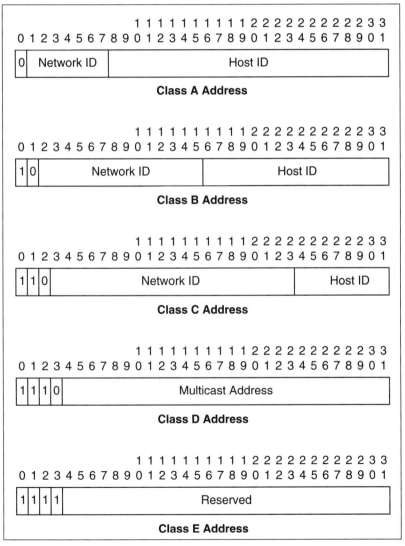

Figure 4-11 Internet Protocol version 4 (IPv4) Address Formats

Class A addresses are designed for very large networks with many hosts. They are identified by Bit 0 = 0. Bits 1 through 7 identify the network, and Bits 8 through 31 identify the host. With a 7-bit Network ID, only 128 Class A network addresses are available. Of these, addresses 0 and 127 are reserved.

The majority of organizations that have distributed processing systems including LANs and hosts use Class B addresses. Class B addresses are identified with the first 2 bits having a value of 10 (binary). The next 14 bits identify the network. The remaining 16 bits identify the host. A total of 16,384 Class B network addresses are possible; however, addresses 0 and 16,383 are reserved.

Class C addresses are generally used for smaller networks, such as LANs. They begin with a binary 110. The next 21 bits identify the network. The remaining 8 bits identify the host. A total of 2,097,152 Class C network addresses are possible, with addresses 0 and 2,097,151 reserved.

Class D addresses begin with a binary 1110 and are intended for multicasting. Class E addresses begin with a binary 1111 and are reserved for future use.

All IP addresses are written in dotted decimal notation, in which each octet is assigned a decimal number from 0 to 255. For example, network [10.55.31.84] is represented in binary as 00001010 00110111 00011111 1010100. The first bit (0) indicates a Class A address, the next 7 bits (0001010) represent the Network ID (decimal 10), and the last 24 bits (00110111 00011111 1010100) represent the Host ID.

Class A addresses begin with 1–127, Class B with 128–191, Class C with 192–223, and Class D with 224–239. Thus, an address of [150.100.200.5] is easily identified as a Class B address.

4.4.2 IPv6 Addressing

As we discussed previously, one of the incentives behind the IPng effort that resulted in IPv6 was the limitations of the 32-bit IPv4 address structure. These new address formats are defined in RFC 2373, "IP Version 6 Addressing Architecture" [4-8].

4.4.2.1 IPv6 ADDRESS TYPES
RFC 2373 defines three different types of IPv6 addresses:

◆ Unicast – an identifier to a single interface. A packet sent to a unicast address is delivered to the interface identified by that address.

◆ Anycast – an identifier for a set of interfaces (typically belonging to different nodes). A packet sent to an anycast address is delivered to one of the interfaces identified by that address (the "nearest" one, according to the routing protocol's measure of distance).

◆ Multicast – an identifier for a set of interfaces (typically belonging to different nodes). A packet sent to a multicast address is delivered to all interfaces identified by that address. The multicast replaces the broadcast function, but with added capabilities to discriminate between packet destinations.

4.4.2.2 IPV6 ADDRESS REPRESENTATION

IPv4 addresses are typically represented in dotted decimal notation. As such, a 32-bit address is divided into four 8-bit sections, and then each section is represented by a decimal number between 0 and 255, for example [129.144.52.38].

Since IPv6 addresses are 128 bits long, a different method of representation is required. As specified in the Addressing Architecture document, RFC 2373, the preferred representation is:

```
X:X:X:X:X:X:X:X
```

where each "x" represents 16 bits, and each of those 16-bit sections is defined in hexadecimal. For example, an IPv6 address could be of the form:

```
FEDC:BA98:7654:3210:FEDC:BA98:7654:3210
```

Note that each of the 16-bit sections is separated by colons, and that four hexadecimal numbers are used to represent each 16-bit section. Should any one of the 16-bit sections contain leading zeros, those zeros are not required. For example:

```
1080:0000:0000:0000:0008:0800:200C:417A
```

may be simplified to:

```
1080:0:0:0:8:800:200C:417A
```

If long strings of zeros appear in an address, a double colon "::" may be used to indicate multiple groups of 16-bits of zeros, which further simplifies the example shown above:

```
1080::8:800:200C:417A
```

The use of the double colon is restricted to appearing only once in an address, although it may be used to compress either the leading or trailing zeros in an address. For example, a loopback address of:

```
0:0:0:0:0:0:0:1
```

could be simplified as:

```
::1
```

For additional details, see RFC 2373.

4.4.2.3 IPv6 ADDRESS ARCHITECTURE

The 128-bit IPv6 address may be divided into a number of subfields to provide maximum flexibility for both current and future address representations. The leading bits, called the *format prefix*, define the specific type of IPv6 address. RFC 2373 defines a number of these prefixes, as shown in Figure 4-12. Note that address space has been allocated for NSAP, IPX, aggregatable global, site local, and other addresses. Also note that multicast addresses begin with the binary value 11111111; any other prefix identifies a unicast address. Anycast addresses are part of the allocation for unicast addresses, and are not given a unique identifier.

A number of forms for unicast addresses have been defined for IPv6, some with more complex structures that provide for hierarchical address assignments. The simplest form would be a unicast address with no internal structure – in other words, with no address-defined hierarchy. The next possibility would be to specify a subnet prefix within the 128-bit address, thus dividing the address into a subnet prefix (with n bits) and an interface ID (with 128 - n bits). For applications where more hierarchy is required, a specific type of address, called the Aggregatable Global Unicast Address, is defined. This address type allows multiple levels of hierarchy, starting with network providers of IPv6 service and graduating down to the networks, subnetworks, and then finally to the end-user devices. In summary, with a 128-bit address space available, a number of addressing structures are possible. RFC 2373 illustrates many of these.

Two addresses have special meanings. The address 0:0:0:0:0:0:0:0 (also represented as 0::0) is defined as the *unspecified address* and indicates the absence of an address. This address might be used upon startup when a node has not yet had an address assigned. The unspecified address can never be assigned to any node.

The address 0:0:0:0:0:0:0:1 (also represented as 0::1) is defined as the *loopback address*. This address is used by a node to send a packet to itself.

Two special addresses have been defined for IPv4/IPv6 transition networks. The first such address is called an IPv4-Compatible IPv6 address. It is used when two IPv6 devices (such as hosts or routers) need to communicate via an IPv4 routing infrastructure. The devices at the edge of the IPv4 would use this special unicast address that carries an IPv4 address in the low order 32 bits. This address has a prefix of 96 bits of zeros. The second type of transition address is called an IPv4-Mapped IPv6 address. This address is used by IPv4-only nodes that do not support IPv6. For example, an IPv6 host would use an IPv4-Mapped IPv6 address to communicate with another host that only supported IPv4. This prefix is 80 bits of zeros, followed by 16 bits of ones.

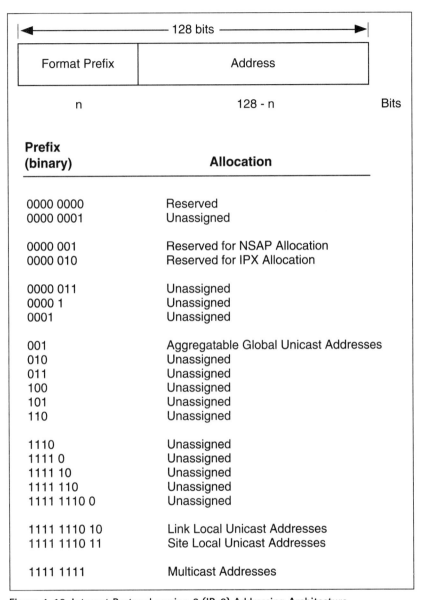

Prefix (binary)	Allocation
0000 0000	Reserved
0000 0001	Unassigned
0000 001	Reserved for NSAP Allocation
0000 010	Reserved for IPX Allocation
0000 011	Unassigned
0000 1	Unassigned
0001	Unassigned
001	Aggregatable Global Unicast Addresses
010	Unassigned
011	Unassigned
100	Unassigned
101	Unassigned
110	Unassigned
1110	Unassigned
1111 0	Unassigned
1111 10	Unassigned
1111 110	Unassigned
1111 1110 0	Unassigned
1111 1110 10	Link Local Unicast Addresses
1111 1110 11	Site Local Unicast Addresses
1111 1111	Multicast Addresses

Figure 4-12 Internet Protocol version 6 (IPv6) Addressing Architecture

4.5 Packet Routing: RIP, OSPF, EGP, and BGP

So far, we've learned that hosts transmit datagrams and use a 32-bit address to identify the source and destination of the datagram. The host drops the datagram into the internetwork, and the datagram somehow finds its way to its destination. That "somehow" is the work of routers, which examine the Destination address, compare that address with their internal routing tables, and send the datagram on the correct outgoing communication circuit (Figure 4-13).

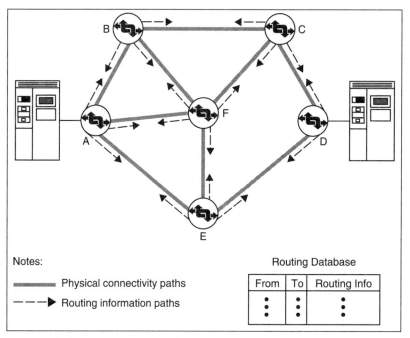

Figure 4–13 Routing Table Information Exchange

Router operation involves several processes. First, the router creates a routing table to gather information from other routers about the optimum path for each packet. This table may be *static* (i.e., manually built) and fixed for all network conditions, or *dynamic* (i.e., constructed by the router according to the current topology and conditions). Dynamic routing is considered the better technique because it adapts to changing network conditions. The router uses a *metric*, or measurement, of the shortest distance between two endpoints to help determine the optimum path. It determines the metric using a number of factors, including the shortest distance, or least cost path, to the destination. The router plugs the metric into one of two algorithms to make a final decision on the correct path. A Distance Vector algorithm makes its choice based on the distance to a remote node. A Link State algorithm also includes information about the status of the various links connecting the nodes and the topology of the network.

The various routers within the network use the Distance Vector or Link State algorithms to inform each other of their current status. Because routers use them for intra-network communication, the protocols that make use of these algorithms are referred to as Interior Gateway Protocols (IGPs). The Routing Information Protocol (RIP) is an IGP based on a Distance Vector algorithm. The Open Shortest Path First (OSPF) protocol is an IGP based on a Link State algorithm. We'll look at these two algorithms separately in the following sections. If one network wishes to communicate routing to another network, it uses an Exterior Gateway Protocol (EGP). An example of an EGP is the Border Gateway Protocol (BGP).

In this section, we will focus on routing within IPv4-based networks. Updates to the various routing protocols in support of IPv6 are under development and implementation. Current information regarding these updates can be found on the IPv6 Industry Home Page [4-7].

4.5.1 Routing Information Protocol

The Routing Information Protocol, described in RFC 1058 [4-9], is used for inter-router (or inter-gateway) communications. RIP is based on a Distance Vector algorithm, in which the routers periodically exchange information from their routing tables. The routing decision is based on the best path between two devices, which is often the path with the fewest hops or router transversals.

RFC 1058 acknowledges several limitations to RIP. RIP allows a path length of 15 hops, which may be insufficient for large internetworks. Routing loops are not possible for internetworks containing hundreds of networks because of the time required to transmit updated routing table information. Finally, the metrics used to choose the routing path are fixed and do not allow for dynamic conditions, such as a measured delay or a variable traffic load.

RIP assumes that all devices (hosts and routers) contain a routing table. This table includes several entries: the IP address of the destination; the metric, or cost, to get a datagram from the host to the destination; the address of the next router in the path to the destination; a flag indicating whether the routing information has been recently updated; and timers.

Routing information is exchanged via RIP packets, shown in Figure 4-14, which are transmitted to/from UDP port number 520. The packet begins with a 32-bit header and may contain as many as 25 messages giving details on specific networks. The first field of the header is 1 octet long and specifies a unique command. Values include:

Command	Meaning
1	Request for routing table information
2	Response containing routing table information
3	Traceon (obsolete)
4	Traceoff (obsolete)
5	Reserved for Sun Microsystems
9	Update Request (from RFC 2091)
10	Update Response (from RFC 2091)
11	Update Acknowledge (from RFC 2091)

The second octet contains a RIP Version Number. Octets 3 and 4 are set equal to zero. The next 2 octets identify the Address Family being transmitted within that RIP packet; RFC 1058 only defines a value for IP with Address Family ID = 2.

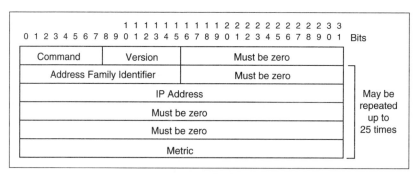

Figure 4-14 Routing Information Protocol (RIP) Packet Format

The balance of the RIP packet contains entries for routing information. Each entry includes the destination IP address and the metric to reach that destination. Metric values must be between 1 and 15, inclusive. A metric of 16 indicates that the desired destination is unreachable. Up to 25 of these entries (from the Address Family Identifier through the Metric) may be contained within the datagram.

An extension to the Routing Information Protocol, called RIP version 2, is defined in RFC 1723 [4-10]. This enhancement expands the amount of useful information carried in RIP messages and also adds a measure of security to those messages. The RIP version 2 packet format is very similar to the original format, containing a four-octet header and up to 25 route entries of 20 octets each in length. Within the header, the Command, Address Family Identifier, IP Address, and Metric fields are identical to their counterparts used with the original RIP packet format. The Version field specifies version number 2, and the two-octet unused field (filled with all zeros) is ignored. The Route Tag field carries an attribute assigned to a route that must be preserved and readvertised with a route, such as information defining the routing information's origin (either intra- or inter-network). Within each route entry, the Subnet Mask field (four octets) defines the subnet mask associated with a routing entry. The Next Hop field (also four octets) provides the immediate next hop IP address for the packets specified by this routing entry. The spaces now occupied by the Subnet Mask and Next Hop fields were previously filled with all zeros.

4.5.2 Open Shortest Path First Protocol

The Open Shortest Path First protocol, defined in RFC 2178 [4-11], is a Link State algorithm that offers several advantages over RIP's Distance Vector algorithm. These advantages include the ability to configure hierarchical (instead of flat) topologies; to quickly adapt to changes within the internet; to allow for large internetworks; to calculate multiple minimum-cost routes that allow traffic load to be balanced over several paths; to authenticate the exchange of routing table information; and to permit the use of variable-length subnet masks. The protocol uses the IP address and Type of Service field for its operation. An optimum path can be calculated for each Type of Service.

4.5.2.1 LINK STATE ALGORITHM OPERATION

OSPF, a Link State algorithm (LSA), improves on RIP, a Distance Vector algorithm (DVA), in several ways. Before considering the improvements, let's review some of the characteristics of Distance Vector algorithms. First, a DVA routes its packets based on the distance, measured in router hops, from the source to the destination. With RIP the maximum hop count is 16, which is a possible limitation for large networks. A DVA-based network is a flat network topology, without a defined hierarchy to subdivide the network into smaller, more manageable pieces. In addition, the hop count measurement does not account for other factors in the communication link, such as the speed of that link or its associated cost. Furthermore, RIP broadcasts its complete routing table to every other router every 30 seconds. Recall that the RIP packet may contain information for up to 25 routes. If a router's table contains more entries, say 100 routes, then transmitting all of these routes would require a total of four RIP packets. This requires considerable overhead at each router for packet processing, and it consumes valuable bandwidth on the WAN links in between these routers.

The improvements obtained with a Link State algorithm come in several areas. First, an LSA is based on type of service routing, not hop counts. This allows the network manager to define the least-cost path between two network points based on the actual cost, delay characteristics, reliability factors, and so on. Second, OSPF defines a hierarchical, not a flat network topology. This allows the routing information to be distributed to only a relevant subset of the routers in the internetwork instead of to all of the routers. This hierarchical structure reduces both the router processing time and the bandwidth consumed on the WAN links.

An *autonomous system* (AS), used with an LSA, is defined as a group of routers that exchange routing information via a common routing protocol. The AS is subdivided into *areas*, which are collections of contiguous routers and hosts that are grouped together, much like the telephone network is divided into area codes. The topology of an area is invisible from outside that area, and routers within a particular area do not know the details of the topology outside of that area. When the AS is partitioned into areas, it is no longer likely (as was the case with a DVA) that all routers in the AS are storing identical topological information in their databases. A router would have a separate topological database for each area it is connected to; however, two routers in the same area would have identical topological databases. A backbone is also defined; it connects the various areas and is used to route a packet between two areas.

Different types of routers are used to connect the various areas. Internal routers operate within a single area, connect to other routers within that area, and maintain information about that area only. An area border router attaches to multiple areas, runs multiple copies of the basic routing algorithm, and condenses the topological information about their attached areas for distribution to the backbone. A backbone router is one that has an interface to the backbone, but it does not have to be an area border router. Lastly, an AS router is one that exchanges information with routers that belong to other autonomous systems.

4.5.2.2 OSPF OPERATION AND PACKET FORMATS

The basic routing algorithm for OSPF provides several sequential functions, as defined in RFC 2178, Section 4: discovering a router's neighbors and electing a Designated Router for the network using the OSPF Hello protocol; forming adjacencies between pairs of routers and synchronizing the databases of these adjacent routers; performing calculations of routing tables; and flooding the area with link state advertisements.

These protocol operations are performed using one of five OSPF packets. The OSPF packets are carried within IP datagrams and are designated as IP protocol = 89. If the datagram requires fragmentation, the IP process handles that function. The five OSPF packet types have a common 24-octet header as shown in Figure 4-15. The first 32-bit word includes fields defining a Version Number (1 octet), an OSPF Packet Type (1 octet), and a Packet Length (2 octets), which measures the length of the OSPF packet including the header. The five packet types defined are:

Type	Packet Name	Protocol Function
1	Hello	Discover/maintain neighbors
2	Database Description	Summarize database contents
3	Link State Request	Database download
4	Link State Update	Database update
5	Link State Acknowledgment	Flooding acknowledgment

The next two fields define the Router ID of the source of that packet (4 octets) and the Area ID (4 octets) that the packet came from. The balance of the OSPF packet header contains a Checksum (2 octets), an Authentication Type (AuType, 2 octets), and an Authentication field (8 octets), which is used to validate the packet.

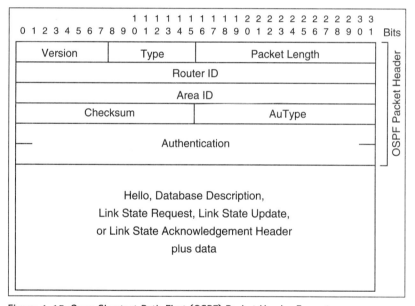

Figure 4-15 Open Shortest Path First (OSPF) Packet Header Format

4.5.3 Exterior Gateway Protocol

Recall from our earlier discussion that there are two general categories of routing protocols: Interior Gateway Protocols and Exterior Gateway Protocols. In short, the interior protocols are concerned with routing within a network. In contrast, exterior protocols are concerned with routing between autonomous systems, which are generally described as a group of routers that all fall within a single administrative domain. In other words, exterior protocols facilitate your communication with networks outside of your router's domain. In this section, we will briefly study the Exterior Gateway Protocol (EGP), defined in RFC 904 [4-12]. In the next section, we will go into greater detail about the Border Gateway Protocol (BGP), defined in RFC 1771 [4-13], which is a higher function replacement for EGP.

EGP is used to convey network reachability information between neighboring gateways (or routers) that are in different autonomous systems. EGP runs over IP and is assigned IP protocol number 8. Three key mechanisms are present in the protocol. The Neighbor Acquisition mechanism allows two neighbors to begin exchanging information using the Acquisition Request and Acquisition Confirm messages. The Neighbor Reachability mechanism maintains real-time information regarding the reachability of its neighbors, using the Hello and I Hear You (I-H-Y) messages. Finally, Update messages are exchanged that carry routing information. The specific messages, as defined in RFC 904, are:

Message	Function
Request	Request acquisition of neighbor and/or initialize polling variables
Confirm	Confirm acquisition of neighbor and/or initialize polling variables
Refuse	Refuse acquisition of neighbor
Cease	Request de-acquisition of neighbor
Cease-ack	Confirm de-acquisition of neighbor
Hello	Request neighbor reachability
I-H-U	Confirm neighbor reachability
Poll	Request net-reachability update
Update	Net-reachability update
Error	Error

The general structure of the EGP messages is shown in Figure 4-16. A common message header precedes each message type. The header consists of the EGP Version number field (one octet); the Type field (one octet), which identifies the message type; the Code field (one octet), which identifies a subtype; the Status field (one octet), which contains message-specific status information; the Checksum field (two octets), used for error control; the Autonomous System Number (two octets), which is an assigned number that identifies the particular autonomous system; and the Sequence Number (two octets), which maintains state variables.

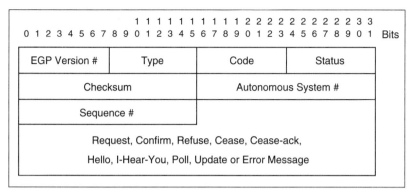

Figure 4–16 Exterior Gateway Protocol (EGP) Message Header Format

Further details on the use and specific formats of the various messages can be found in RFC 904.

4.5.4 Border Gateway Protocol

The Border Gateway Protocol, currently in its fourth version (BGP-4), is defined in RFC 1771 [4-13]. BGP is an inter-autonomous system (AS) protocol, which builds upon and enhances the capabilities of EGP. For example, where EGP runs on IP, BGP runs on TCP, thus ensuring a connection-oriented data flow and greater reliability. BGP is assigned TCP port number 179 (more on TCP port numbers in the next chapter). BGP also supports Classless Domain Routing (CLDR) and the aggregation of routes.

The system running BGP is called a *BGP speaker*. Connections between BGP speakers in different autonomous systems are called *external links*, while connections between BGP speakers in the same autonomous system are called *internal links*. In a similar fashion, a BGP peer in another AS is referred to as an *external peer*, while a peer within the same AS is called an *internal peer*. After the TCP connection has been established in support of BGP, the two BGP systems exchange their entire routing tables. Updates are then sent as those routing tables change. As a result, the BGP speaker will maintain the current version of the routing tables for all of its peers. That routing information is stored within a Routing Information Base, or RIB.

The BGP message consists of a fixed message header that is 19 octets in length, followed by one of four messages: OPEN, UPDATE, NOTIFICATION, or KEEPALIVE. The OPEN, UPDATE, and NOTIFICATION messages add additional information to the BGP message header, while the KEEPALIVE consists of only the annotated message header.

The BGP message header is shown in Figure 4-17, and consists of three fields plus message-specific information. The Marker field (16 octets) contains a value that the receiver can predict. For example, an OPEN message would use a Marker of all ones. Otherwise, the Marker can be incorporated into some authentication mechanism. The Length field (2 octets) indicates the total length of the message, including the header, given in octets. The valid range of the Length field is 19–4,096 octets. The Type field (one octet) specifies the type of the message as follows:

Type	Message	Function
1	OPEN	The first message sent after transport connection is established
2	UPDATE	Transfers routing information between BGP peers
3	NOTIFICATION	Indicates detection of an error and closure of the connection
4	KEEPALIVE	Periodic confirmation of reachability

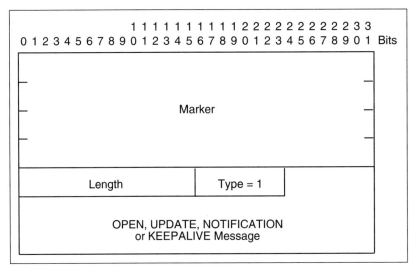

Figure 4-17 Border Gateway Protocol version 4 (BGP-4) Message Header Format

Further details on the operation of BGP-4 can be found in RFC 1771.

4.6 Host Name – Address Translation

The IPv4 and IPv6 addresses and the various classes defined for these addresses provide an extremely efficient way to identify devices on an internetwork. Unfortunately, remembering all of these addresses can be overwhelming. To solve that problem, a system of hierarchical naming known as the Domain Name System was developed. DNS for IPv4 is described in RFCs 1034 [4-14] and 1035 [4-15]. Updates to support DNS for IPv6 are described in RFC 1886 [4-16]. In this section, we will concentrate on the IPv4 case.

DNS is based on several premises. First, it arranges the names hierarchically, like the numbering plan devised for the telephone network. Just as a telephone number is divided into a country code, an area code, an exchange code, and finally a line number, the DNS root is divided into a number of top-level domains, defined in RFC 920. These are:

Domain	Purpose
MIL	U.S. Military
GOV	Other U.S. Government
EDU	Educational
COM	Commercial
NET	NICs and NOCs
ORG	Nonprofit Organizations
CON	Two-letter country code, e.g. US represents the United States, CA represents Canada, and so on.

The second DNS premise is that devices are not expected to remember the IP addresses of remote hosts. Rather, Name Servers throughout the internetwork provide this information. The requesting device thus assumes the role of a client, and the Name Server provides the necessary information, known as a *resource record*, or RR. RRs provide a mapping between domain names and network objects, such as IP addresses. Many different types of RRs are defined in RFCs 1034 and 1035. Examples of RRs include: the A record, which is used to map a host address; the MX record, which provides a mail exchange for the domain and is used with the SMTP; the NS record, which defines the name server for a domain; and the PTR record, which is a pointer to another part of the domain name space.

The format for client/server interaction is a DNS message, shown in Figure 4-18. The message header is 12 octets long and describes the type of message. The next four sections provide the details of the query or response.

The first field within the header is an Identifier (16 bits) that correlates the queries and responses. The QR bit identifies the message type as a Query (QR = 0) or a Response (QR = 1). An OPCODE field (4 bits) further defines a Query. Four Flags are then transmitted to further describe the message, and a Response Code (RCODE) completes the first word. The balance of the header contains fields that define the lengths of the remaining four sections: Question, Answer, Authority, and Additional Records.

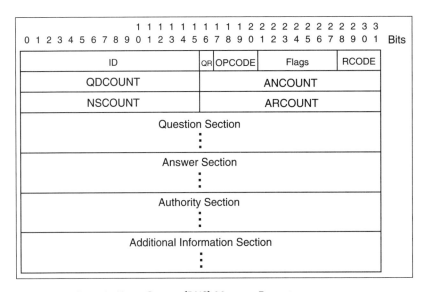

Figure 4-18 Domain Name System (DNS) Message Format

A good resource on DNS is the DNS Resources Directory Web site [4-17].

4.7 End-to-End Reliability: UDP and TCP

Routing the datagram from the source to the destination is only part of the story — the reliability of that transmitted information must be ensured. And since IP provides a connectionless (or unreliable) network service, protocols at a layer above IP are required to ensure reliable delivery of the information between hosts. That reliability is the job of two protocols that will be considered in this section: the User Datagram Protocol (UDP) and the Transmission Control Protocol (TCP).

4.7.1 User Datagram Protocol

UDP provides a connectionless host-to-host communication path for the host's message. A connectionless path is one in which the communication channel is not established prior to the transmission of data. Instead, the network transmits the data in a package called a datagram. The datagram contains all of the addressing information necessary for that message to reach its intended destination. UDP is described in RFC 768 [4-18] and is an ARPA Host-to-Host (or OSI Transport Layer) protocol. UDP assumes that IP, which is also connectionless, is the underlying ARPA Internet (or OSI Network Layer) protocol.

The UDP service requires minimal overhead, and therefore uses the relatively small UDP header shown in Figure 4-19. Note in the figure that each horizontal group of bits, called a word, is 32 bits wide. The first two fields in the UDP header are the Source and Destination Port numbers (each 2 octets in length) that identify the higher layer protocol process that the datagram carries. The Source Port field is optional, and when not used contains all zeros. The Length field (2 octets) is the length of the UDP datagram, which has a minimum value of 8 octets. The Checksum field (2 octets) is also optional, and is filled with all zeros if the upper layer protocol (ULP) process does not require a checksum.

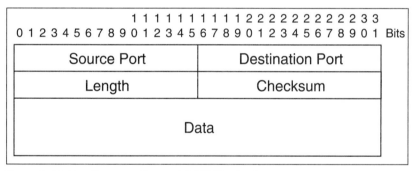

Figure 4-19 User Datagram Protocol (UDP) Header Format

Other host processes that use UDP as the Host-to-Host protocol include the Time protocol, port number 37; the Domain Name Server (DNS), port number 53; the Bootstrap Protocol (BOOTP) server and client, port numbers 67 and 68, respectively; the Trivial File Transfer Protocol (TFTP), port number 69; and the Sun Microsystems Remote Procedure Call (SunRPC), port number 111. All of these applications are designed with the assumption that if the Host-to-Host connection fails, some higher layer process would provide some error notification or error recovery procedures. For example, if a network management message transmission were to fail, a Trap message (defined by the Simple Network Management Protocol, or SNMP) might be sent as a notification of that failure.

However, some applications require more reliable end-to-end data transmissions, and therefore use the more rigorous Transmission Control Protocol (TCP) instead of UDP. As we will see in the next section, TCP provides a number of error control procedures that UDP lacks.

4.7.2 Transmission Control Protocol

TCP is a connection-oriented protocol that is responsible for reliable communication between two end processes, and is defined in RFC 793 [4-19]. The unit of data transferred is called a *stream,* which is simply a sequence of octets. The stream originates at the upper layer protocol process and is subsequently divided into TCP segments, IP datagrams, and Local Network frames.

TCP handles six functions: basic data transfer, reliability, flow control, multiplexing, connections, and precedence/security. These functions are performed by the various fields within the TCP header, which has a minimum length of 20 octets (Figure 4-20). This header contains a number of fields – relating to connection management, data flow control, and reliability – which UDP did not require. The TCP header starts with two Port addresses (2 octets each) to identify the logical host processes at each end of the connection.

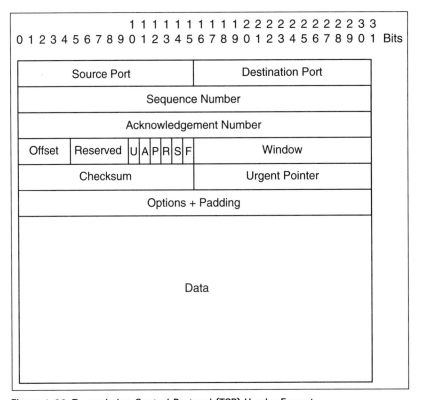

Figure 4-20 Transmission Control Protocol (TCP) Header Format

The Sequence Number field (4 octets) is the sequence number given to the first octet of data. When the SYN flag bit is set, the sequence number indicates the Initial Sequence Number (ISN) selected. The first data octet sent would then use the next sequence number [ISN+1]. (For example, if ISN = 100, then the data would begin with SEQ = 101. If the sequence number was not advanced by one, the process would end up in an endless loop of transmissions and acknowledgements.) The sequence number ensures the sequentiality of the data stream, which is a fundamental component of reliability.

The Acknowledgement Number field (4 octets) verifies the receipt of data. This protocol process is called Positive Acknowledgement or Retransmission (PAR). The process requires that each unit of data (the octet in the case of TCP) be explicitly acknowledged. If it is not, the sender will time-out and retransmit. The value in the acknowledgement is the next octet (i.e., the next sequence number) expected from the other end of the connection. When the Acknowledgement field is in use (i.e., during a connection), the ACK flag bit is set.

The next 32-bit word (octets 13–16 in the header) contains a number of fields used for control purposes. The Data Offset field (4 bits) measures the number of 32-bit words in the TCP header. Its value indicates where the TCP header ends and the upper layer protocol (ULP) data begins. The Offset field is necessary because the TCP header has a variable, not fixed, length; therefore, the position of the first octet of ULP data may vary. Since the minimum length of the TCP header is 20 octets, the minimum value of the Data Offset field would be five 32-bit words. The next 6 bits are reserved for future use and are set equal to zero.

Six flags that control the connection and data transfer are transmitted next. Each flag has its own 1-bit field. These flags include:

◆ URG: Urgent Pointer field significant

◆ ACK: Acknowledgement field significant

◆ PSH: Push function

◆ RST: Reset the connection

◆ SYN: Synchronize Sequence numbers

◆ FIN: No more data from sender

The Window field (2 octets) provides end-to-end flow control. The number in the Window field indicates the quantity of octets, beginning with the one in the Acknowledgement field, that the sender of the segment can accept. Note that, like the Acknowledgement field, the Window field is bidirectional. Since TCP provides a full-duplex communication path, both ends send control information to their peer process at the other end of the connection. In other words, my host provides both an acknowledgement and a window advertisement to your host, and your host does the same for mine. In this manner, both ends provide control information to their remote partner.

The Checksum field (2 octets) is used for error control.

The Urgent Pointer field (2 octets) allows the position of urgent data within the TCP segment to be identified. This field is used in conjunction with the Urgent (URG) control flag and points to the sequence number of the octet that follows the urgent data. In other words, the Urgent pointer indicates the beginning of the routine (nonurgent) data.

Options and Padding fields (both variable in length) complete the TCP header. The Options field is an even multiple of octets in length and specifies options required by the TCP process within the host. The Padding field contains a variable number of zeros that ensure that the TCP header ends on a 32-bit boundary.

4.8 Protocols Supporting VoIP: Multicast IP, RTP, RTCP, RSVP, and RTSP

Thus far in Chapter 4, we have looked at the underlying infrastructure and protocols that are used to route and reliably deliver IP datagrams through an internetwork. These protocols, such as IP, RIP, OSPF, UDP, TCP, and the others we studied, were developed with data applications in mind: email, file transfers, remote terminal access, and so on. In this final section, we will briefly consider some of the additional protocols, primarily at the higher layers, that are required to support real-time and multimedia applications such as VoIP. A summary of these protocols, plus their dependencies, is shown in Figure 4-21.

4.8.1 Multicast IP

The term *multi* is derived from a Latin term that means *much* or *many*. In the case of IP datagrams, the objective is to send one packet and have it be received at many destinations. This *one* to *many* packet transport mechanism can be used in a number of applications, including: audio and video conferencing, news broadcasts, stock quotation distribution, and distance learning.

When datagrams are multicast, instead of individual copies of the message being sent to each recipient, the bandwidth of the communications infrastructure is conserved. A single stream of information from one source is delivered to the destination end stations, instead of multiple streams from that one source being delivered to those end stations (Figure 4-22).

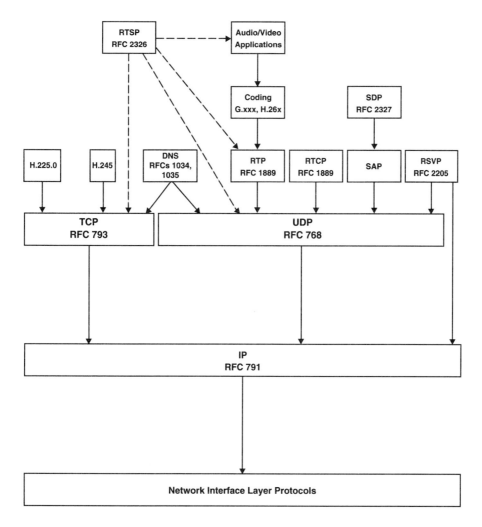

Figure 4-21 Voice over IP Protocols

The concepts of multicast transmission over IP-based internetworks were first described in RFC 1112, "Host Extensions for IP Multicasting," published in 1989 [4-20]. To support multicast applications, the end stations must be able to support the Internet Group Management Protocol (IGMP, also described in RFC 1112), which enables multicast routers to determine which end stations on their attached subnets are members of multicast groups. These groups are identified by special multicast addresses. IPv4 Class D addresses are reserved to support multicast applications, and range in value from 224.0.0.0 through 239.255.255.255.

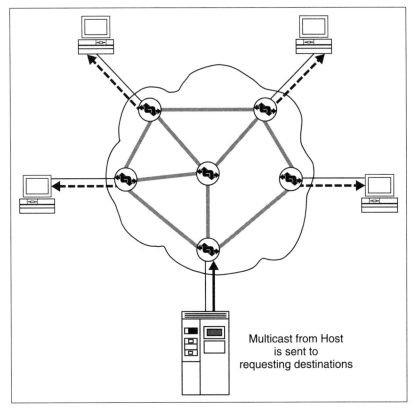

Figure 4-22 IP Multicast Operation

From these values, the Internet Assigned Numbers Authority (IANA) has assigned specific values for particular multicast functions. For example, the range of addresses between 224.0.0.0 and 224.0.0.255, inclusive, is used for routing protocols and other topology and maintenance functions. Within this range, address 224.0.0.1 identifies "all systems on this subnet" and 224.0.0.2 identifies "all routers on this subnet." Other values have been specified RIP2 routers (224.0.0.9), DHCP Server/Relay Agents (224.0.0.12), audio and video transport, and others. Addresses in the range from 239.0.0.0 through 239.255.255.255 are reserved for local applications. A complete listing of the assigned multicast addresses is available in the Assigned Numbers document (currently RFC 1700), and also in Reference [4-21].

In order to propagate these datagrams to multiple destinations, the routers within the network infrastructure operate with modified routing protocols. Two examples of these multicast routing protocols are the Distance Vector Multicast Routing Protocol (DVMRP), described in RFC 1075 [4-22], and the Multicast Extensions to OSPF (MOSPF), described in RFC 1584 [4-23]. These multicast routing protocols construct logical spanning trees, which describe how the multicast traffic flows to the end stations.

Much of the testing of multicast IP protocols and processes has occurred on the Multicast Backbone, or MBONE, which is a virtual multicast network that runs on top of the existing Internet. Further details on the MBONE can be found in Reference [4-24]. A good source of information on multicasting in general is the IP Multicast Initiative (IPMI) [4-25].

4.8.2 Real-Time Transport Protocol

Recall from our earlier discussions that IP networks provide connectionless (CLS) data transport services. One of the main characteristics of CLS networks is their absence of delay characteristics. In other words, you drop a packet into the network, and if all works as planned, it reaches the intended destination. However, you cannot make any statements regarding the timeframe that will be required for that packet to travel from the source to the destination. Perhaps it will travel slowly, or perhaps it will travel quickly (or perhaps it will get clobbered and not get there at all, but we optimists will dismiss that alternative for the moment and assume successful packet delivery).

So the next question becomes, how do we take data from an application, such as voice or video, which is real-time, and send it through a network that cannot (by definition and design) guarantee reliable delivery? The answer is found in the use of the Real-time Transport Protocol (RTP), which is defined in RFC 1889 [4-26]. A companion protocol, the RTP Control Protocol (RTCP), monitors the quality of service and conveys information about the participants in the communication session.

RTP provides end-to-end delivery services for data that requires real-time support, such as interactive audio and video. According to RFC 1889, the services provided by RTP include payload type identification, sequence numbering, timestamping, and delivery monitoring. Applications typically run RTP on top of UDP to make use of UDP's multiplexing and checksum services, and as such both RTP and UDP contribute parts of the transport protocol functionality. Provisions are defined, however, to use RTP with other underlying network or transport protocols.

It is also important to note the functions that RTP does not provide. For example, RTP itself does not provide any mechanism to ensure timely delivery or provide other quality-of-service guarantees, but relies on the lower layer services for these functions. It does not guarantee packet delivery or prevent out-of-order packet delivery, nor does it assume that the underlying network is reliable and deliver packets in sequence. The sequence numbers included in RTP allow the receiver to reconstruct the sender's packet sequence, but sequence numbers might also be used to determine the proper location of a packet, for example in video decoding, without necessarily decoding packets in sequence.

There are two parts of RTP defined in RFC 1889: the real-time transport protocol (RTP), which carries data that has real-time properties, and the RTP control protocol (RTCP), which monitors the quality of service and conveys information about the participants in an on-going session. In addition to the protocol specification given in RFC 1889, a companion document, RFC 1890 [4-27], provides a profile specification that defines a set of payload type codes and their mapping to payload formats, such as various media encodings. For example, RFC 1890 defines a profile specification with minimal session control. In other words, this profile is designed for sessions where no negotiation or membership control is used. Examples of the use of RTP and its profiles are given in both RFC 1889 and RFC 1890.

Before discussing the RTP packet format, a few definitions, taken from RFC 1889, are in order:

◆ RTP payload: The data transported by RTP in a packet, for example audio samples or compressed video data.

◆ RTP packet: A data packet consisting of the fixed RTP header, a possibly empty list of contributing sources (as defined below), and the payload data.

◆ RTCP packet: A control packet consisting of a fixed header part similar to that of RTP data packets, followed by structured elements that vary depending on the RTCP packet type. The formats are defined in RFC 1889, Section 6.

◆ Port: The addressing mechanism that uniquely identifies different applications within a host. For example, the File Transfer Protocol (FTP) and the Simple Network Management Protocol (SNMP) have different port numbers. RTP depends on the lower layer protocol to provide some mechanism such as ports to multiplex the RTP and RTCP packets of a session.

◆ Transport address: The combination of a network address and port that identifies a transport-level endpoint, for example an IP address and a UDP port. Packets are transmitted from a source transport address to a destination transport address.

◆ RTP session: The association among a set of participants communicating with RTP. For each participant, the session is defined by a particular pair of destination transport addresses (one network address plus a port pair for RTP and RTCP). The destination transport address pair may be common for all participants, as in the case of IP multicast, or may be different for each, as in the case of individual unicast network addresses plus a common port pair. In a multimedia session, each medium is carried in a separate RTP session with its own RTCP packets. The multiple RTP sessions are distinguished by different port number pairs and/or different multicast addresses.

◆ Synchronization source (SSRC): The source of a stream of RTP packets, identified by a 32-bit numeric SSRC identifier carried in the RTP header so as not to be dependent upon the network address. All packets from a synchronization source form part of the same timing and sequence number space, so a receiver groups packets by synchronization source for playback. Examples of synchronization sources include the sender of a stream of packets derived from a signal source such as a microphone or a camera, or an RTP mixer (as defined below). A synchronization source may change its data format, for example its audio encoding mechanism, over time.

◆ Contributing source (CSRC): A source of a stream of RTP packets that has contributed to the combined stream produced by an RTP mixer (as defined below). The mixer inserts a list of the SSRC identifiers of the sources that contributed to the generation of a particular packet into the RTP header of that packet. This list is called the CSRC list. An example application is audio conferencing, where a mixer indicates all the talkers whose speech was combined to produce the outgoing packet, allowing the receiver to indicate the current talker even though all the audio packets contain the same SSRC identifier (that of the mixer).

◆ End system: An application that generates the content to be sent in RTP packets and/or consumes the content of received RTP packets. An end system can act as one or more synchronization sources in a particular RTP session, but typically acts only as one.

◆ Mixer: An intermediate system that receives RTP packets from one or more sources, possibly changes the data format, combines the packets in some manner, and then forwards a new RTP packet. Since the timing among multiple input sources will not generally be synchronized, the mixer will make timing adjustments among the streams and generate its own timing for the combined stream. Thus, all data packets originating from a mixer will be identified as having the mixer as their synchronization source.

◆ Translator: An intermediate system that forwards RTP packets with their synchronization source identifier intact. Examples of translators include devices that convert encodings without mixing, replicators from multicast to unicast, and application-level filters in firewalls.

◆ Monitor: An application that receives RTCP packets sent by participants in an RTP session, in particular the reception reports, and estimates the current quality of service for distribution monitoring, fault diagnosis, and long-term statistics.

◆ Non-RTP: Protocols and mechanisms that may be needed in addition to RTP to provide a usable service. In particular, for multimedia conferences, a conference control application may distribute multicast addresses and keys for encryption, negotiate the encryption algorithm to be used, and define dynamic mappings between RTP payload type values and the payload formats they represent for formats that do not have a predefined payload type value.

Given the above functional definitions, we will now consider the RTP message header format which is shown in Figure 4-23. The first twelve octets are present in every RTP packet, while the list of CSRC identifiers is present only when inserted by a mixer.

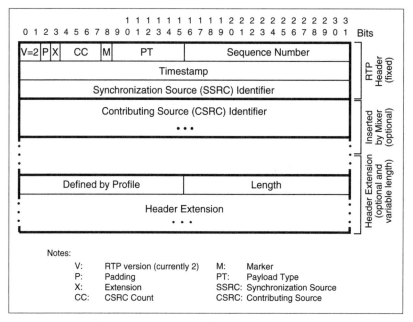

Figure 4-23 Real-Time Transport Protocol (RTP) Message Header

The fields of the RTP header are:

◆ Version (V, 2 bits): Identifies the version of RTP, currently 2.

◆ Padding (P, 1 bit): If the padding bit is set, the packet contains one or more additional padding octets at the end that are not part of the payload. The last octet of the padding contains a count of how many padding octets should be ignored. Padding may be needed by some encryption algorithms with fixed block sizes or for carrying several RTP packets in a lower layer protocol data unit.

◆ Extension (X, 1 bit): If the extension bit is set, the fixed header is followed by exactly one header extension, with a format defined in RFC 1889, Section 5.3.1.

◆ CSRC count (CC, 4 bits): The CSRC count contains the number of CSRC identifiers that follow the fixed header.

◆ Marker (M, 1 bit): The interpretation of the marker is defined by a profile. It is intended to allow significant events such as frame boundaries to be marked in the packet stream.

◆ Payload type (PT, 7 bits): Identifies the format of the RTP payload and determines its interpretation by the application.

◆ Sequence number (16 bits): The sequence number increments by one for each RTP data packet sent, and may be used by the receiver to detect packet loss and to restore packet sequence. The initial value of the sequence number is random (unpredictable) to make known-plaintext attacks on encryption more difficult, even if the source itself does not encrypt (because the packets may flow through a translator that does).

◆ Timestamp (32 bits): The timestamp reflects the sampling instant of the first octet in the RTP data packet. The sampling instant must be derived from a clock that increments monotonically and linearly in time to allow synchronization and jitter calculations.

◆ SSRC (32 bits): The SSRC field identifies the synchronization source. This identifier is chosen randomly, with the intent that no two synchronization sources within the same RTP session will have the same SSRC identifier.

◆ CSRC list (0 to 15 items, 32 bits each): The CSRC list identifies the contributing sources for the payload contained in this packet. The number of identifiers is given by the CC field. If there are more than 15 contributing sources, only 15 may be identified. CSRC identifiers are inserted by mixers, using the SSRC identifiers of contributing sources. For example, for audio packets the SSRC identifiers of all sources that were mixed together to create a packet are listed, allowing correct talker indication at the receiver.

◆ RTP Header Extension (variable length): An optional extension mechanism is provided with RTP to allow individual implementations to experiment with new functions that require additional information in the RTP header.

Specific details regarding the use of these header fields is given in RFC 1889.

4.8.3 Real-Time Control Protocol

The RTP control protocol (RTCP) is also defined in RFC 1889 and is based on the periodic transmission of control packets to all participants in the session, using the same distribution mechanism as the data packets. The underlying protocol must provide multiplexing of the data and control packets, such as using separate port numbers with UDP. The following RTCP functions are identified in RFC 1889:

1. Providing feedback on the quality of the data distribution. This is an integral part of RTP's role as a transport protocol and is related to the flow and congestion control functions of other transport protocols. The feedback may be directly useful for control of adaptive encodings, but experiments with IP multicasting have shown that it is also critical to get feedback from the receivers to diagnose faults in the distribution. Sending reception feedback reports to all participants allows one who is observing problems to evaluate whether those problems are local or global. With a distribution mechanism like IP multicast, it is also possible for an entity such as a network service provider that is not otherwise involved in the session to receive the feedback information and act as a third-party monitor to diagnose network problems. This feedback function is performed by the RTCP sender and receiver reports, described in RFC 1889, Section 6.3.

2. Carrying a persistent transport-level identifier for an RTP source called the canonical name or CNAME. Since the SSRC identifier may change if a conflict is discovered or a program is restarted, receivers require the CNAME to keep track of each participant. Receivers also require the CNAME to associate multiple data streams from a given participant in a set of related RTP sessions, for example to synchronize audio and video.

3. The first two functions require that all participants send RTCP packets, therefore the rate must be controlled in order for RTP to scale up to a large number of participants. By having each participant send its control packets to all the others, each can independently observe the number of participants.

4. An optional function of conveying minimal session control information, for example participant identification to be displayed in the user interface. This is most likely to be useful in "loosely controlled" sessions where participants enter and leave without membership control or parameter negotiation. RTCP serves as a convenient channel to reach all the participants, but it is not necessarily expected to support all the control communication requirements of an application.

RFC 1889 defines five different RTCP packet formats:

- ◆ SR or Sender Report: for transmission and reception statistics from participants that are active senders

- ◆ RR or Receiver Report: for reception statistics from participants that are not active senders

- ◆ SDES or Source Description Items: includes CNAME

- ◆ BYE: indicates the end of participation

- ◆ APP: application-specific functions

Each RTCP packet begins with a fixed part similar to that of RTP data packets, followed by structured elements that may be of variable length according to the packet type but always end on a 32-bit boundary. The alignment requirement and a length field in the fixed part are included to make RTCP packets "stackable." Multiple RTCP packets may be linked together without any intervening separators to form a compound RTCP packet that is sent in a single packet of the lower layer protocol, for example UDP. There is no explicit count of individual RTCP packets in the compound packet since the lower layer protocols are expected to provide an overall length to determine the end of the compound packet.

The formats of these RTCP packets vary by function and are rather complex. Interested readers are referred to RFC 1889, section 6, for these details.

Details on the operation of RTP can be found in RFC 1889 [4-26] and RFC 1890 [4-27]. Reference [4-28] is an excellent resource for RTP information.

4.8.4 Resource Reservation Protocol

As more time-sensitive applications have been developed for the Internet, the need to define a Quality of Service (QoS), and the mechanisms to provide that QoS, have become requirements. The Resource Reservation Protocol (RSVP), defined in RFC 2205 [4-29], is designed to address those requirements. When a host has an application such as real-time video or multimedia, it may use RSVP to request an appropriate level of service from the network in support of that application. But for RSVP to be effective, every router in that path must support that protocol – something that some router vendors and ISPs are not yet equipped to do. In addition, RSVP is a control protocol, and therefore works in collaboration with – not instead of – traditional routing protocols. In other words, the routing protocol, such as RIP or OSPF, determines *which* datagrams are forwarded, while RSVP is concerned with the *QoS* of those datagrams that are forwarded.

RSVP requests that network resources be reserved to support data flowing on a simplex path, and that reservation is initiated and maintained by the receiver of the information. Using this model, RSVP can support both unicast and multicast applications. Reviewing Figure 4-6, RSVP messages may be sent directly inside IP datagrams (using IP Protocol = 46) or encapsulated inside UDP datagrams, using Ports 1698 and 1699.

RSVP defines two basic message types: Reservation Request (or Resv) messages and Path messages (Figure 4-24). A receiver transmits Resv messages upstream toward the senders. These Resv messages create and maintain reservation state information in each node along the path or paths. A sender transmits Path messages downstream toward the receivers, following the paths prescribed by the routing protocols that follow the paths of the data. These Path messages store path state information in each node along the way.

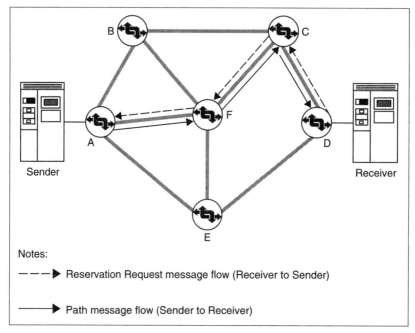

Figure 4-24 Resource Reservation Protocol (RSVP) Operation

The RSVP message consists of three sections: a Common Header (8 octets), an Object Header (4 octets), and Object Contents (variable length), as shown in Figure 4-25. The Version field (4 bits) contains the protocol version (currently 1). The Flags field (4 bits) is reserved for future definition. The Message Type field (1 octet) defines one of seven currently defined RSVP messages:

Message Type	Message Name	Function
1	Path	Path message, from sender to receiver, along the same path used for the data packets.
2	Resv	Reservation message with reservation requests, carried hop-by-hop from receiver to senders.
3	PathErr	Path error message; reports errors in processing Path messages, and travels upstream toward senders.

Message Type	Message Name	Function
4	ResvErr	Reservation error message; reports errors in processing Resv messages, and sent downstream toward receivers.
5	PathTear	Path teardown message, initiated by senders or by a timeout, and sent downstream to all receivers.
6	ResvTear	Reservation teardown message, initiated by receivers or by a timeout, and sent upstream to all matching senders.
7	ResvConf	Reservation confirmation message, acknowledges reservation requests.

The RSVP Checksum field (2 octets) provides error control. The Send_TTL field (1 octet) is the IP Time to Live field value with which the message was sent. The RSVP length field (2 octets) is the total length of the RSVP message, given in octets.

Every object consists of one or more 32-bit words with a 1-octet Object Header. This second header includes a Length field (2 octets), which is the total length of the object (with a minimum of 4 octets, and also a multiple of 4 octets); a Class Number (1 octet), which defines the object class; and a C-Type field (1 octet), which is an object type that is unique with the Class Number. The Object Contents complete the message.

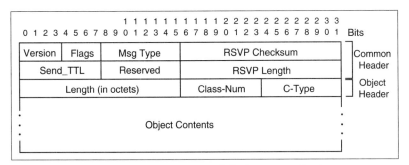

Figure 4-25 Resource Reservation Protocol (RSVP) Message Header

Details on the operation of RSVP can be found in RFC 2205 [4-29]. Reference [4-30] is a good resource for RSVP information.

4.8.5 Real-Time Streaming Protocol

The Real-Time Streaming Protocol, defined in RFC 2326 [4-31], is an Application Layer protocol that controls the delivery of data that has real-time properties, such as audio and video. RTSP does not typically deliver the continuous streams itself, although interleaving of the continuous media stream with the control stream (such as RTCP) is possible. In effect, RTSP acts as a "network remote control" for multimedia servers.

There is no notion of an RTSP connection; instead, a server maintains a session labeled by an identifier. An RTSP session is in no way tied to a transport-level connection such as a TCP connection. During an RTSP session, an RTSP client may open and close many reliable transport connections to the server to issue RTSP requests. Alternatively, it may use a connectionless transport protocol such as UDP.

The streams of information controlled by RTSP may use RTP; however, RTSP's operation is independent of the underlying transport mechanism. RTSP is intentionally similar in syntax and operation to the Hypertext Transfer Protocol (HTTP), version 1.1, defined in RFC 2068 [4-32], so that extension mechanisms to HTTP can in most cases also be added to RTSP. However, RTSP differs in a number of important aspects from HTTP, including its client/server operation, protocol identifier, and typical out-of-band data transport.

RFC 2326 defines the following operations that RTSP supports:

◆ Retrieval of media from media server: The client can request a presentation description via HTTP or some other method. If the presentation is being multicast, the presentation description contains the multicast addresses and ports to be used for the continuous media. If the presentation is to be sent only to the client via unicast, the client provides the destination for security reasons.

◆ Invitation of a media server to a conference: A media server can be "invited" to join an existing conference, either to play back media into the presentation or to record all or a subset of the media in a presentation. This mode is useful for distributed teaching applications. Several parties in the conference may take turns "pushing the remote control buttons."

◆ Addition of media to an existing presentation: Particularly useful for live presentations, the server can tell the client about additional media becoming available.

Details of RTSP operation can be found in RFC 2326. An excellent reference for additional RTSP information is Reference [4-33].

4.8.6 Session Description Protocol

The Session Description Protocol (SDP), defined in RFC 2327 [4-34], is used to describe a multimedia session for the purposes of session announcement, session invitation, and other forms of session-related initiation. SDP conveys information about media streams in multimedia sessions to allow the recipients of a session description to participate in that session. One of the applications for SDP is the session directory tool used on the MBONE, which advertises multimedia conferences on that network. Thus, SDP provides a means to communicate the existence of the session, and also conveys sufficient information to enable another station to join and participate in that session.

A conference session is announced by periodically multicasting an announcement packet to a well-known address and port using the Session Announcement Protocol, or SAP, which is transmitted using UDP. The payload of the SAP packet is the SDP session description, which includes:

- ◆ Session name and purpose.

- ◆ Time(s) the session is active.

- ◆ The media comprising the session.

- ◆ Information to receive those media, such as addresses, ports, formats, and so on.

- ◆ Information about the bandwidth to be used by the conference.

- ◆ Contact information for the person responsible for the session.

4.9 Looking Ahead

In this chapter, we have looked at the ARPA protocol suite in general, and the protocols that support VoIP services in particular. A summary of what we have learned is shown in Figure 4-26, a composite Voice over IP packet, which includes the IPv4 header, the UDP header, the RTP header, and a 20 millisecond sample of packetized voice information. We will return to this composite figure in the following chapters to better understand how this information is originated at the sender, transmitted through an IP network, and eventually sent to the ultimate destination.

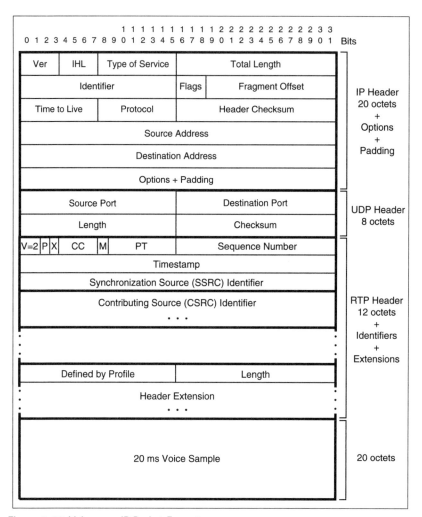

Figure 4-26 Voice over IP Packet Format

In the next chapter, we will bring the wide area transport into the equation and consider a number of WAN systems that support the transmission of the Internet Protocol.

4.10 References

[4-1]   Leiner, B. M., et al. "The ARPA Internet Protocol Suite."
            RS-85-153, included in the *DDN Protocol Handbook*, Volume 2:
            2-27–2-49.

[4-2]   Padlipsky, M. A. "A Perspective on the ARPANET Reference
            Model." RFC 871, The Mitre Corp., September 1982.

[4-3]   Postel, J. "Internet Protocol." RFC 791, September 1981.

[4-4]   Reynolds, J., and J. Postel. "Assigned Numbers." RFC 1700,
            October 1994.

[4-5]   Postel, J. "Internet Control Message Protocol." RFC 792,
            September 1981.

[4-6]   Deering, S., and R. Hinden. "Internet Protocol, Version 6 (IPv6)
            Specification." RFC 2460, December 1998.

[4-7]   Further information on IPv6 standards and implementations is
            available at the IPv6 Home Page: http://www.playground.
            sun.com/pub/ipng/ipng-main.html.

[4-8]   Hinden, R., and S. Deering. "IP Version 6 Addressing
            Architecture." RFC 2373, July 1998.

[4-9]   Hedrick, C. "Routing Information Protocol." RFC 1058,
            June 1988.

[4-10]   Malkin, G. "RIP Version 2 – Carrying Additional Information."
            RFC 1723, November 1994.

[4-11]   Moy, John. "OSPF Version 2." RFC 2178, March 1994.

[4-12]   Mills, D. L. "Exterior Gateway Protocol Frame Specification."
            RFC 904, April 1984.

[4-13]   Rekhter, Y., and T. Li. "A Border Gateway Protocol 4 (BGP-4)."
            RFC 1771, March 1995.

[4-14]   Mockapetris, P. "Domain Names: Concepts and Facilities."
            RFC 1034, November 1987.

[4-15]   Mockapetris, P. "Domain Names: Implementation and
            Specification." RFC 1035, November 1987.

[4-16]   Thomas, S., and C. Huitema. "DNS Extensions to Support IP -ver-
            sion 6." RFC 1886, December 1995.

[4-17]   A good resource for directory information is:
            http://www.dns.net/dnsrd.

[4-18]   Postel, J. "User Datagram Protocol." RFC 768, August 1980.

[4-19]   Postel, J. "Transmission Control Protocol." RFC 793,
                August 1980.

[4-20]   Deering, S. "Host Extensions for IP Multicasting." RFC 1112,
                August 1989.

[4-21]   A complete listing of IP multicast addresses can be found at:
                ftp://ftp.isi.edu/in-notes/iana/assignments/
                multicast-addresses.

[4-22]   Waitzman, D., et al. "Distance Vector Multicast Routing
                Protocol." RFC 1075, November 1988.

[4-23]   Moy, J. "Multicast Extensions to OSPF." RFC 1584, March 1994.

[4-24]   Information about the MBONE can be found at
                http://www.mbone.com.

[4-25]   A good resource for IP Multicast information is the IP Multicast
                Initiative's Web site: http://www.ipmulticast.com.

[4-26]   Schulzrinne, H., et al. "A Transport Protocol for Real-Time
                Applications." RFC 1889, January 1996.

[4-27]   Schulzrinne, H. "RTP Profile for Audio and Video Conferences
                with Minimal Control." RFC 1890, January 1996.

[4-28]   A good resource for RTP information is http://www.cs.
                columbia/~hgs/rtp/papers.html.

[4-29]   Braden, R., editor. "Resource Reservation Protocol (RSVP)
                Version 1 Functional Specification." RFC 2205, September 1997.

[4-30]   Agood resource for RSVP information is the RSVP Project at
                http://www.isi.edu/div7/rsvp/rsvp-home.html.

[4-31]   Schulzrinne, H., et al. "Real Time Streaming Protocol (RTSP)."
                RFC 2326, April 1998.

[4-32]   Fielding, R., et al. "Hypertext Transfer Protocol – HTTP/1.1."
                RFC 2068, January 1997.

[4-33]   A good resource for RTSP information is http://www.real.
                com/devzone/library/fireprot/rtsp/faq.html.

[4-34]   Handley, M., and V. Jacobson. "SDP: Session Description
                Protocol." RFC 2327, April 1998.

Chapter 5

WAN Transport for Converged Networks

In the previous chapters, we have discussed the principles of converged networks from several perspectives: the end user's objectives, the applications, the business and financial considerations, and the protocols that comprise an IP-centric network architecture.

In this chapter, we will extend our discussion to the operation and protocols of the wide area network (WAN) transport, which connects end user systems and provides a transmission mechanism between the end users and the applications that those end users are running. In the previous chapters, this issue was cleverly avoided by using what are called cloud diagrams (Figure 5-1). The WAN transport is shown as a big cloud, with the end users on the outside and the carriers on the inside. The end users are depicted as being on the outside looking in – they are users of the WAN's service, but do not know the intimate details of how that service operates. The conventional cloud diagram places the carriers on the inside looking out – they are the providers of the WAN service, but do not necessarily know the details of the systems that their customers are using to connect to the network. Thus, the cloud diagram obscures both the details of the users' network and the internal operation of the WAN.

This chapter aims to lift the fog surrounding the internal workings of the WAN cloud. We will briefly consider a number of WAN transport alternatives, including digital leased lines such as T1 or T3 lines, Integrated Services Digital Network (ISDN) connections, frame relay, and asynchronous transfer mode (ATM).

The information in this chapter is primarily aimed at readers who may have come from the local area networking side of the data communications industry, and who may not be familiar with all of the WAN transport alternatives that are available. However, readers that *are* experienced with the many wide area alternatives currently available may find this information useful. Specifically, an existing WAN transport – be that ISDN, Frame Relay, ATM or some other technology – was probably installed to support a singular application, such as voice *or* data, and is now under consideration to support both voice *and* data. A reasonable question is whether or not that existing infrastructure is capable of doing both, or if a higher capacity alternative should be deployed. To better answer that question, consideration of all of the available alternatives, as overviewed in this chapter, would be appropriate.

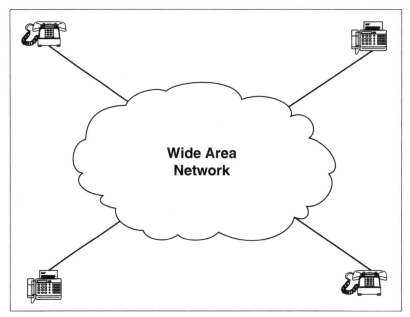

Figure 5-1 The Wide Area Network Cloud

In Chapter 6 we will consider the other side of the cloud, and examine end user equipment used for VoIP networks.

5.1 WAN Transport Alternatives

Perhaps the greatest challenge in navigating through the fog of the WAN cloud is sorting through all of the transmission alternatives presented by carriers. As you might expect, some of these alternatives are used for very specialized applications and are not good fits for converged network applications.

Consider Figure 5-2, which shows the various WAN alternatives organized into a hierarchy. The first distinction defines the transmission format, either analog or digital. Generally, analog lines have a lower bandwidth, and are more susceptible to noise and other error-causing disturbances than digital lines. Analog lines come in two types: switched (or dialup) and dedicated (or leased). Switched telephone lines are used to access the Public Switched Telephone Network (PSTN), and provide service for pay telephones, fax machines, low-speed modems, and the like. Since the local telephone loops vary in their quality (some are decades old), PSTN transmission characteristics can be somewhat random. In other words, sometimes you get a good connection, and sometimes you don't. When you don't, your best alternative is to hang up and redial, and hope for better luck next time.

Dedicated analog lines are archaic by today's standards, but met some specific requirements in the early days of data communications (circa 1970). Since the dedicated line provided a fixed path between two points, that line could be conditioned through the use of filters, amplifiers, and other electronic devices to optimize its transmission characteristics. Nevertheless, most analog leased line configurations were designed to support modems in the 2.4 to 9.6 Kbps range, which by today's standards is inadequate. For VoIP applications we would only want to use analog circuits for connections from a single end user into the network via the PSTN, but not for the transport of any multi-user or higher speed data.

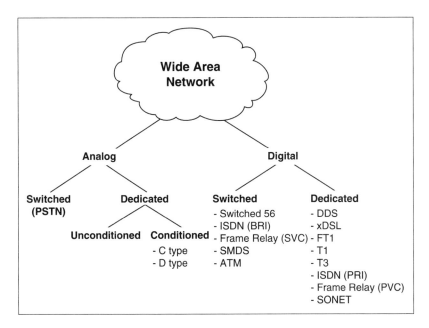

Figure 5-2 Wide Area Network Options

In contrast to their problematic analog cousins, digital lines are designed for high-speed data applications and will serve as the primary transport mechanisms for voice, fax, data, and video over IP applications. Like analog lines, digital lines can be divided into switched or dedicated connections. In addition, the fundamental building block for these digital circuits is called a DS0 channel, which provides a bandwidth of either 56 or 64 Kbps. Multiple DS0 channels can be multiplexed together to satisfy the requirements for greater amounts of bandwidth. We will discuss these multiplexing processes later in this chapter.

A number of switched digital lines have been developed, although not all of these may be available from each Local Exchange Carrier (LEC) or Inter-exchange Carrier (IXC). Switched 56 service provides a 56 Kbps link between two locations, and provides one DS0 of bandwidth. The next step up is Integrated Services Digital Network (ISDN) service, with a Basic Rate Interface (BRI). The ISDN-BRI provides two DS0 channels that operate at 64 Kbps, plus an additional D channel that supplies a lower rate (typically 16 Kbps, although 9.6 Kbps is provisioned in some areas). Frame relay service may operate in two modes: Switched Virtual Connections (SVCs), where calls are established and terminated using call setup procedures, and Permanent Virtual Connections (PVCs), where connections are established on an end-to-end basis and appear to the end user like a leased line. Frame relay service is provided at a number of transmission rates, ranging from 64 Kbps to 45 Mbps. Switched Multimegabit Data Service (SMDS) is a high speed data transmission that was developed by Bell Communications Research, Inc. (Bellcore, now Telcordia Technologies, Inc.). SMDS operates at 1.5 Mbps or 45 Mbps, but is only available in limited areas. Asynchronous Transfer Mode (ATM) is a cell-based switched network architecture that was designed to carry a wide range of traffic types: packet switched data, circuit switched data, voice, video, and so on. ATM can operate at a wide variety of data rates, beginning at 1.5 Mbps.

A number of dedicated digital lines have also been developed. The lowest speeds are typically called DDS (Digital Data Service) lines. DDS lines operate at 2.4, 4.8, 9.6, 19.2, 56, and 64 Kbps, and are typically used for terminal-to-host applications such as point-of-sale terminals. The Digital Subscriber Line (xDSL) services are available in some areas, which access rates in the hundreds of kilobits per second rate, with even higher rates planned in some areas. Various carriers support different versions (and therefore various transmission rates) of DSL services, hence the "x" in the xDSL acronym. T1 lines operate at a rate of 1.544 Mbps, which is known as the Digital Signal Level 1, or DS1 rate. The T1 line has a capacity of 24 DS0 channels. In many areas, customers are given the option of subscribing to only a portion of a T1, known as a Fractional T1 or FT1 service. Thus, if you only need the equivalent of six DS0 channels (384 Kbps data rate), you do not have to pay for a complete T1 connection. T3 lines operate at a rate of 44.736 Mbps, which is known as the Digital Signal Level 3, or DS3 rate. A T3 line is equivalent to 28 T1 lines, or 672 DS0 channels. Primary Rate Interface ISDN service (ISDN-PRI) operates at the same transmission rate (1.544 Mbps) as a T1 line, but divides its information carrying channels into 23 B channels for information transfer and one D channel for call setup and control purposes. The individual ISDN-PRI B and D channels are equivalent to a DS0 channel. Synchronous Optical Network (SONET) services are available in larger metropolitan areas and provide fiber-optical based transmission at the DS1 and DS3, and in some cases, higher, rates.

In the next few sections, we will look at the specific WAN infrastructures that are most likely to be used to carry IP traffic on converged networks, and consequently the types of interfaces that are likely to be found on converged network components such as VoIP gateways. The WAN technologies that we will discuss in the next sections are: T1 and T3 lines, ISDN, frame relay, and ATM.

5.2 T1/T3 Digital Lines

The T-carrier system was developed to multiplex voice signals onto a digital transmission line. It was designed in response to the "one pair – one conversation" problem, which limited telephone conversations to the number of physical copper pairs between two points. As the usage of the telephone network grew, and as services such as dial-up modem applications became more widespread, the telephone network started running out of available copper pairs to provide those circuits. And since those copper pairs were in cables (which, in turn, were likely buried in conduits under city streets), a practical limit on how many physical pairs could be installed between two locations was reached. The solution, which was called a *pair-gain system*, was to deploy digital instead of analog transmission, and to use two pairs for the transmission system – one pair for transmit and one pair for receive. For T1 lines, two pairs carry 24 voice or data channels, which results in a pair-gain of twelve.

Thus, the T1 circuit is a digital, full-duplex transmission facility operating at 1.544 Mbps, and is part of a hierarchy of multiplexed digital signals. The fundamental building block of this hierarchy is called the Digital Signal Level 0 (DS0) channel, which carries 64 Kbps of bandwidth. (As an aside, the 64 Kbps is derived from the analog to digital conversion process that is used to create the digital telephone signal. The analog signal is sampled (or measured) 8,000 times per second. Each sample is then converted into an 8-bit code. The resulting digital signal – 8 bits times 8,000 times per second – yields a data rate of 64 Kbps.) Also note the distinction between the T1 *circuit* and the DS1 *signal*. The T1 designation refers to the technology (such as a digital telephone system over copper pairs). The DS1 designation refers to the format of the data that is sent over that circuit. This digital multiplexing hierarchy includes the following:

Signal Level	Carrier System	Equivalent DS0 Channels	Equivalent DS1 Channels	Data Rate (Kbps)
DS0	N/A	1	N/A	64
DS1	T1	24	1	1,544
DS1C	T1C	48	2	3,152
DS2	T2	96	4	6,312
DS3	T3	672	28	44,736
DS4	T4	4,032	168	274,760

The multiplexing hierarchy is illustrated in Figure 5-3. Of the various signal rates noted, the DS0, DS1, and DS3 signals are the ones most likely to be used for customer-provided network equipment, such as VoIP gateways and IP routers. The DS1C, DS2, and DS4 signals are typically reserved for internal carrier circuits only. Also note that there are rather large steps in bandwidth capacity between the DS0, DS1, and DS3 signals that end users employ. In other words, if a T1 line (operating at 1.544 Mbps) is insufficient, your next step is a T3 line (operating at 44.736 Mbps), which is a 28-fold increase in capacity – a rather large jump!

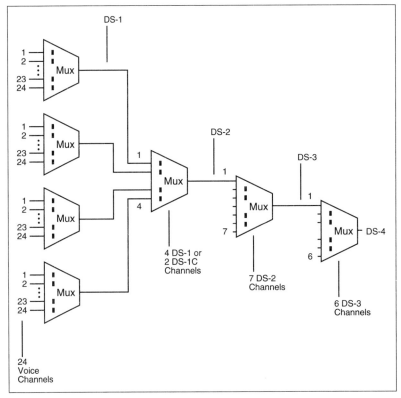

Figure 5-3 Digital Signal Multiplexing Hierarchy

After the format of the data is specified, a method of distinguishing between the individual channels (which may be distinct telephone conversations or data circuits) must be established. For DS1 signals, this framing is accomplished by adding one additional bit, dubbed the 193rd bit, to each frame, as illustrated in Figure 5-4. This extra bit adds 8,000 bps to the DS1 signal bandwidth. Thus, the DS1 data rate of 1.544 Mbps is derived from: 24 DS0 channels at 64 Kbps or 1,536 Kbps, plus 8 Kbps (the framing bit) yielding 1,544 Kbps or 1.544 Mbps.

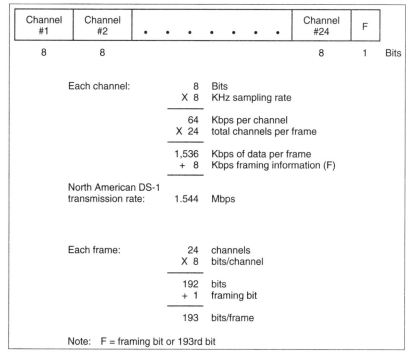

Figure 5-4 DS1 Frame Format

DS1 frames are typically delivered to the end-user equipment in a larger format that allows more efficient use of the framing bits. This larger delivery package is called a *superframe*. There are two superframe formats defined: the D4 superframe and the extended superframe, or ESF.

D4 framing uses the 193rd bit strictly for framing purposes (Figure 5-5). A total of 12 individual frames are combined into the D4 superframe. A pattern of the sampled 193rd bits (bit numbers 193, 386, 579, etc.) is used to identify individual DS0 channels within each DS1 frame. This framing pattern (100011011100) is repeated every 12 frames (or superframe). Signaling information (used for central office–to–central office messages) appears in bit 8 of frames 6 and 12. When this signaling information is present, the effective throughput of that channel is reduced to 56 Kbps. (This is because only 7 bits are available to carry end-user information. With each bit having a capacity of 8 Kbps, the resulting channel capacity is 56 Kbps. And since you don't know if the carrier has inserted these signaling bits in the data stream after that data has left your premises, it is only wise to count on 56 Kbps of capacity per channel, instead of the 64 Kbps that would normally be available.)

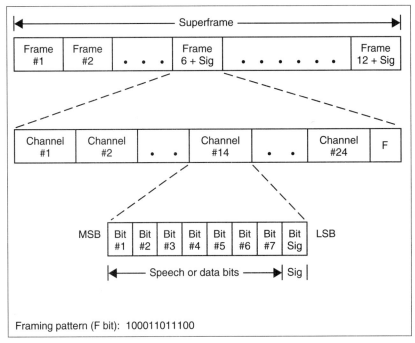

Figure 5-5 D4 Superframe Format
(Source: ANSI T1.107)

The extended superframe format (ESF) is illustrated in Figure 5-6. ESF extended the superframe from 12 to 24 DS1 frames, which resulted in a total of 24 of the framing (or 193rd) bits. With 24 bits instead of 12 to work with, two additional capabilities became available (see Figure 5-7). The signaling capabilities were expanded to four options (T, 2, 4, 16) and are shown in the traffic and signaling columns in Figure 5-7. Signaling information (if used) is present in frames 6, 12, 18, and 24.

There are three uses for the framing function (shown as F in Figure 5-6): Framing itself (Fe); Data Link (DL); and Block Check (BC). The Data Link function provides a 4 Kbps communications link between circuit end points. Transmissions on this data link would typically consist of maintenance and performance messages. The Block Check framing function (BC) provides a six-bit Cyclic Redundancy Check (CRC-6), which is used to verify the accuracy of the entire superframe. Any individual line errors would cause a violation of the CRC-6, thus alerting the intermediate transmission equipment of the problem. The advantage of the ESF framing format over that of the D4 is its ability to monitor the network and then notify a network management console of any difficulties.

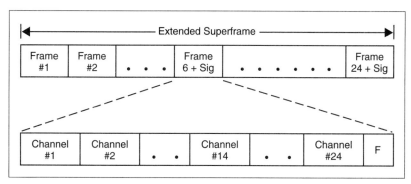

Figure 5-6 Extended Superframe Format
(Source: ANSI T1.107)

Frame Number	Information Coding Bits	Signaling Bit	ESF Signaling Options			
			T	2 State	4 State	16 State
1	1-8					
2	1-8					
3	1-8					
4	1-8					
5	1-8					
6	1-7	8	—	A	A	A
7	1-8					
8	1-8					
9	1-8					
10	1-8					
11	1-8					
12	1-7	8	—	A	B	B
13	1-8					
14	1-8					
15	1-8					
16	1-8					
17	1-8					
18	1-7	8	—	A	A	C
19	1-8					
20	1-8					
21	1-8					
22	1-8					
23	1-8					
24	1-7	8	—	A	B	D

Notes:
Option T: Transparent (bit 8 used for information coding).
Option 2 State: Two state Option provides one 1,333 bps signaling channel (A).
Option 4 State: Four state option provides two 667 bps signaling channels (A and B).
Option 16 State: Sixteen state option provides four 333 bps signaling channels (A, B, C, and D).

Figure 5-7 Extended Superframe Format Coding
(Source: ANSI T1.107)

It is important to ask the carrier if D4 or ESF formats are used on the DS1 circuits being provided. If these superframe formats are used, and network signaling is required, then there is a good possibility that the effective data rate of each DS0 channel (or at least the capacity that can be assured) is 56 Kbps instead of 64 Kbps. This is a useful bit of information to know when planning the capacities of access lines between your network and the carrier.

As a final note, a different multiplexing hierarchy is used in Europe. This hierarchy is sometimes referred to as the CEPT hierarchy, which stands for the Conference of European Postal and Telecommunications Administrations. The CEPT hierarchy defines different rates from the North American (DS) hierarchy. These include E1 (2.048 Mbps), E2 (four multiplexed E1 channels with a transmission rate of 8.448 Mbps), and E3 (16 multiplexed E1 channels with a transmission rate of 34.368 Mbps). The E1 channel is based on 32 DS0 channels, where 30 of these channels carry end-user information, one carries framing information, and one carries signaling information.

Further technical details on the digital signal hierarchy can be found in ITU-T G.704 [5-1] and ANSI T1.107 [5-2].

5.3 ISDN Connections

Integrated Services Digital Network, or ISDN, service is available in many areas. There are two standard interfaces for ISDN service: the Basic Rate Interface, or BRI, and the Primary Rate Interface, or PRI. ISDN service has been standardized by both the International Telecommunications Union – Telecommunications Standards Sector (ITU-T), for international connections, and the American National Standards Institute (ANSI), for use within the United States. Both the BRI and the PRI provide serial, synchronous, full duplex connections (Figure 5-8).

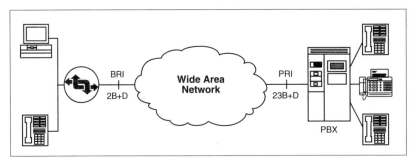

Figure 5-8 ISDN Interfaces

The BRI is defined in ITU-T I.430 [5-3] and transmits with a line rate of 192 Kbps. Some of that information is devoted to timing, framing, and other control overhead; as a result, 144 Kbps of bandwidth is delivered to the end user. This bandwidth is divided into two B-channels at 64 Kbps each (equivalent to a DS0), plus a D-channel at 16 Kbps. The B (or Bearer) channels transport end-user information. The D-channel carries signaling information or packet switched data. The BRI may be configured for either point-to-point or multipoint connections, and is typically used for residential and small business applications. ISDN BRI service is provided by the Local Exchange Carrier (LEC) and is typically delivered to the end user on a 4-pin modular (RJ-11) or 8-pin modular (RJ-45) connector. For applications with converged networks and VoIP service, the ISDN BRI is most likely to be used in small office–home office (SOHO) applications for access to a headquarters location.

The PRI is defined in ITU-T I.431 [5-4] and transmits at one of two rates: 1.544 Mbps, which is used in North America, Japan, and some of the Pacific Rim countries; and 2.048 Mbps (the E1 channel), which is used in Europe. The PRI definition is based on the T1/E1 standards that were discussed in Section 5.2. The PRI is configured for point-to-point connections only, and is typically used for high capacity trunks between PBXs or between the carrier's access point and a PBX. As such, this interface would be optionally available on most routers and VoIP gateways that connect the customer's premises to the WAN, and is also found on digital PBXs that integrate premises voice and data communication functions.

5.4 Transmitting IP Datagrams over Serial Lines

Two protocols have been developed to support TCP/IP-based data transmission over switched and dedicated serial lines: the Serial Line IP (SLIP) and the Point-to-Point Protocol (PPP).

Serial Line IP (SLIP), described in RFC 1055 [5-5], frames IP datagrams on a serial line. SLIP is not an Internet Standard protocol; therefore, specific implementations may vary. SLIP defines two characters: END (C0H or octal 300 or decimal 192) and ESC (DBH or octal 333 or decimal 219), as shown in Figure 5-9. To transmit, the SLIP host begins sending the IP datagram (see Figure 5-9). It replaces any data octet equivalent to the END character with the 2-octet sequence of ESC plus octal 334 (DB DCH). It replaces any octet equal to the ESC character with the 2-octet sequence of ESC plus octal 335 (DB DDH). After completing the datagram transmission, it sends an END character. (Note that the ESC character used with SLIP is not the ASCII escape character.) SLIP does not have a defined maximum packet size; however, many systems adhere to the maximum packet size used by the Berkeley UNIX SLIP of 1,006 octets (excluding the SLIP framing characters). An enhancement to SLIP, known as Compressed SLIP or CSLIP, compresses the TCP/IP header for transmission over low speed serial lines. CSLIP is defined in RFC 1144 and is often referred to as Van Jacobson header compression. This technique minimizes the protocol overhead being sent, thus partially compensating for the lower speed of the transmission system.

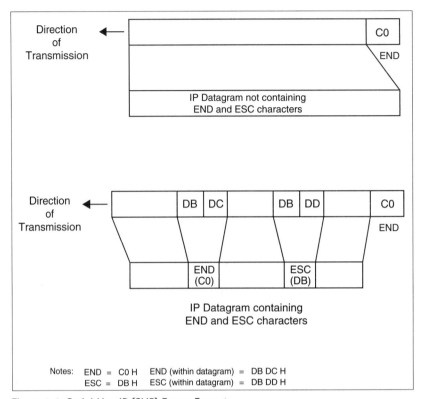

Figure 5-9 Serial Line IP (SLIP) Frame Format

The Point-to-Point Protocol (PPP), described in RFC 1661 [5-6], is the second protocol used for serial line connections. Unlike SLIP, PPP is an Internet standard protocol for use over asynchronous or synchronous serial lines. RFC 1661 describes three main components of PPP: a method of encapsulating multiprotocol datagrams, a Link Control Protocol (LCP), and a family of Network Control Protocols (NCPs). LCP packets initialize the Data Link Layer of the communicating devices. NCP packets negotiate the Network Layer connection between the two endpoints. Once the LCP and NCP configuration is complete, datagrams may be transmitted over the link.

The PPP frame is based on the ISO High Level Data Link Control (HDLC) protocol (known as ISO 3309), which has been implemented by itself and has also been incorporated into many other protocol suites, including X.25, Frame Relay, and ISDN. (The 1979 HDLC standard addresses synchronous environments; the 1984 modification extends the usage to asynchronous environments. When asynchronous transmission is used, all octets are transmitted with 1 start bit, 8 data bits, and 1 stop bit.)

The PPP frame (see Figure 5-10) includes fields for beginning and ending Flags (set to 07H); an Address (set to FFH, the all-stations address); Control (set to 03H, for Unnumbered Information); Protocol (a one- or two-octet field identifying the higher layer protocol in use); Information (the higher layer information, with a default maximum length of 1,500 octets); and a Frame Check Sequence (2 octets). RFC 1662 describes the details of the HDLC-like framing.

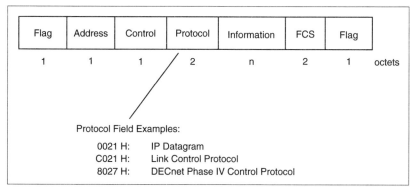

Figure 5-10 Point-to-Point Protocol Frame

The Protocol field is used to distinguish multiprotocol datagrams, with the value contained in that field identifying the datagram encapsulated in the Information field of the packet. RFC 1661 specifies values for the Protocol field that are reserved; the Assigned Numbers document (currently RFC 1700) contains specific Protocol field assignments.

The Protocol field is 2 octets (or 4 hex characters) in length, with possible values from 0000–FFFFH. Values in the 0xxx–3xxx range identify the Network Layer protocol of specific packets, and values in the 8xxx–Bxxx range identify packets belonging to the associated Network Control Protocols (NCPs), if any. Protocol Field values in the 4xxx–7xxx range are used for protocols with low volume traffic that have no associated NCP. Protocol field values in the Cxxx–Fxxx range identify packets as link layer Control Protocols (such as LCP). For example, the value of 0021H would identify an IPv4 datagram.

PPP's second component is the Link Control Protocol (LCP), which deals with Data Link Layer issues. LCP defines five steps for link control. The process begins with the Link Dead phase, which indicates that the Physical Layer is not ready. When the Physical Layer is ready to be used, the process proceeds with the Link Establishment phase. In the Link Establishment phase, the Link Control Protocol (LCP) is used to establish the connection through the exchange of Configure packets between the two ends of the link. The Authentication Phase, which is optional, allows the peer at the other end of the link to authenticate itself prior to exchanging Network Layer protocol packets. In the Network Layer Protocol Phase, each Network Layer in operation, such as IP, Novell's IPX, or AppleTalk, is configured by the Network Control Protocol (NCP). The final step, the Link Termination Phase, uses LCP to close the link.

PPP's third objective is to develop a family of NCPs to transmit Network Layer information. A number of NCPs have been defined, each addressing a particular Network Layer protocol. These include DECnet Phase IV, defined in RFC 1762; Banyan VINES, defined in RFC 1763; and Xerox Network Systems (XNS) Internet Datagram Protocol (IDP), defined in RFC 1764. Each of these protocols would be defined by a distinct value of the Protocol field.

The IETF Assigned Numbers document, which is available online, contains all the current assignments for the PPP fields [5-7].

5.5 IP over Frame Relay Networks

Frame Relay (FR) was developed by the International Telecommunications Union — Telecommunications Standards Sector (ITU-T), and derived from earlier work on Integrated Services Digital Networks (ISDNs). As such, the FR protocol is similar to the ISDN protocols, and, for that matter, also similar to the 1970s era X.25 packet switching technologies that preceded ISDN. Frame relay improves on both X.25 and ISDN by streamlining the protocol processing. For example, both X.25 and ISDN are implemented at the three lower layers of the OSI model, that is the Physical, Data Link, and Network layers. A significant part of the Data Link and Network layer functions deal with error control — what to do when the transmission is corrupted. In today's environments, with very reliable networks that are often fiber optic based (and therefore less susceptible to transmission errors caused by electromagnetic interference), much of this error control is no longer necessary. The architects of frame relay recognized this change and reduced the complexity of the frame relay protocols accordingly.

Thus, frame relay is implemented at only the Physical and Data Link Layers. Frame relay eliminates the Network Layer (i.e., packet) processing and performs only a few Data Link Layer functions. For example, FR checks the frame for errors, but it does not automatically request a retransmission if it discovers one. Should an error occur, the processes within the sender and receiver take responsibility for that function.

Frame relay provides a logical connection, either a switched virtual circuit (SVC) or a permanent virtual circuit (PVC), between end-user systems (Figure 5-11). A virtual circuit is a logical communication channel between the end-user equipment, or Terminal Equipment (DTE), and the frame relay network, or Data Circuit-Terminating Equipment (DCE). In most cases, the DTE is called a Frame Relay Access Device, or FRAD, and the DCE is called a Frame Relay Network Device, or FRND. The frame relay network interface, called the User Network Interface, or UNI, is defined as the physical communication line between the FRAD and the FRND. For frame relay implementations in the United States, the ANSI T1.606 [5-8] standard provides the technical details. Other implementation guidelines are provided by documents produced by a trade organization, the Frame Relay Forum [5-9].

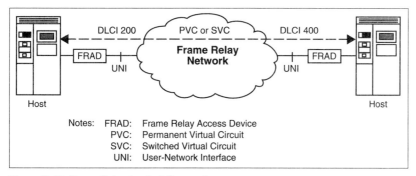

Figure 5-11 Frame Relay Logical Connections

The data to be transmitted across those connections is contained within a frame relay frame, as shown in Figure 5-12. The first two octets of the frame relay frame comprise the frame relay header and are followed by the higher layer information, such as an IP datagram.

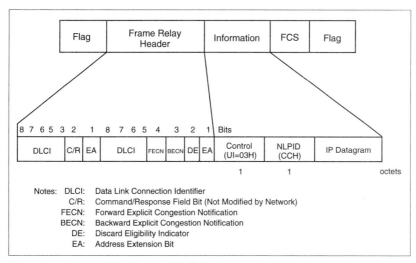

Figure 5-12 Frame Relay Frame with IP Datagram
(Source: ANSI T1.618)

The FR header contains a number of subfields. The longest of these is the Data Link Connection Identifier (DLCI), which identifies the virtual circuit used for any particular communication path. Multiple virtual circuits may exist at this interface. For example, if a router is the FRAD, it may serve 50 workstations on a LAN, which could each conceivably have a virtual circuit (identified with the DLCI field) into the frame relay network. The DLCI field (10 bits in length when the default two-octet frame relay header is used) allows up to 1,024 virtual circuits, although some are reserved for network diagnostic purposes. These circuits are further defined as Permanent Virtual Circuits (PVCs) and are established when the FRAD is attached to the frame relay network.

When a frame enters the frame relay network, the FRND examines the Frame Check Sequence (FCS) at the end of the frame for errors. If an error is present, the frame is discarded. If the FCS passes, the FRND examines the DLCI field and a table lookup determines the correct outgoing link. If a table entry does not exist for a particular frame, the frame is discarded. The frame relay header contains 3 bits to indicate congestion on the frame relay network. The first 2 bits are known as Explicit Congestion Notification (ECN) bits. Any node within the frame relay network can send an ECN bit in two directions: downstream using the Forward ECN (or FECN) bit and upstream using the Backward ECN (or BECN) bit. The third bit used for congestion control is the Discard Eligibility (DE) bit. The DE bit indicates which frames should be discarded to relieve congestion. ANSI T1.617a [5-10] discusses these congestion management principles. The Command/Response (C/R) and Extended Address (EA) complete the frame relay header. The C/R bit was defined for LAPD, but is not used with frame relay networks. The EA bits allow the frame relay header to extend to 3 or 4 octets in length to accommodate more DLCI addresses.

The Internet standard for frame relay support is RFC 1490 [5-11], which provides specifics for implementing multiprotocol traffic over frame relay networks. Several variations are presented in that document; however, consistent among all the variants are the Control field and the Network Level Protocol ID (NLPID). The Control field may either specify Unnumbered Information (UI) with a field value of 03H or Exchange Identification (XID) with a field value of AF or BFH. ISO and ITU-T administer the NLPID and identify the type of protocol used within the Information field. RFC 1490 defines the value of NLPID = CCH to designate IPv4 datagrams. Other formats for routed and bridged frames have been defined as well; consult RFC 1490 for specific details.

5.6 Voice over Frame Relay Networks

The transmission of voice and fax traffic over frame relay networks is addressed in a Frame Relay Implementation Agreement, FRF.11.1, published by the Frame Relay Forum [5-12]. The technical characteristics of that document address several key functions, including: the transport of compressed voice payloads within frame relay frames, multiplexing of up to 255 sub-channels on a single frame relay DLCI, and support for a number of voice compression algorithms.

To support these services, a Voice Frame Relay Access Device (VFRAD) is defined, which would likely be positioned between a voice concentrator (such as a PBX or key system) and the frame relay network if it were a stand-alone device, or possibly integrated into some other system that supported both voice traffic and a frame relay interface. The VFRAD accesses the frame relay service across the UNI, but provides additional functions to the end users, as noted above. For example, the VFRAD may provide voice/data sub-channel multiplexing, as shown in Figure 5-13. Multiple voice and data connections can be supported over a single PVC. This multiplexing function becomes specific to a single PVC, as illustrated by DLCI 16 in Figure 5-14. Note that other PVCs, such as DLCI 17, could use other frame relay supported services (such as data transport) across the same frame relay physical interface.

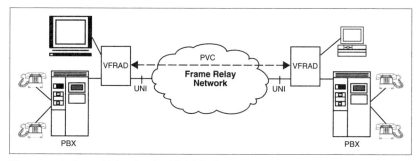

Figure 5-13 Frame Relay Service Multiplexing
(Source: Frame Relay Forum FRF.11.1)

The multiplexing of these various payloads requires an additional level of protocol encapsulation, as illustrated in Figure 5-15. Each voice or data payload is packaged as a distinct sub-frame, and then multiple sub-frames are carried within the Information field of the frame relay frame. The sub-frames may be combined within a single frame to increase the efficiencies of the protocol processing and transport functions of the end-user equipment. For example, Figure 5-15 shows three voice channels and one data channel that are all supported over a single DLCI.

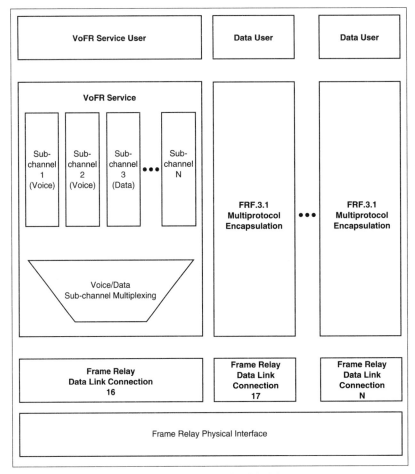

Figure 5-14 Voice over Frame Relay Multiplexing Model
(Source: Frame Relay Forum FRF.11.1)

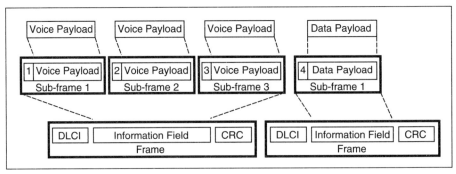

Figure 5-15 Relationship between Frames and Sub-frames
(Source: Frame Relay Forum FRF.11.1)

Each sub-frame consists of a variable length header plus a payload. The sub-frame header carries the multiplexing functions that identify the specific voice/data channels (Figure 5-16a). The sub-frame header consists of six fields. The Extension Indication (EI) and Length Indication (LI) determine the length of the sub-frame header and its functions, which are further defined in Figure 5-16b. The Sub-channel Identification (CID) specifies the particular sub-channel (one of up to 256) in use. The Payload Type field indicates the payload contained in that sub-frame, such as dialed digits, fax information, and so on. The Payload Length field specifies the number of payload octets that follow the header. Finally, the payload itself, as defined by the Payload Type, completes the sub-frame.

8	7	6	5	4	3	2	1	Octets
EI	LI	Sub-channel Identification (CID) (Least significant 6 bits)						1
CID (msb)		0 Spare	0 Spare	Payload Type				1a (Note 1)
Payload Length								1b (Note 2)
Payload								P

Notes: 1. When the EI bit is set, the structure of Octet 1a given in Figure 5-16b applies.

2. When the LI bit is set, the structure of Octet 1b given in Figure 5-16b applies.

3. When both the EI bit and the LI bit are set to 1 both Octet 1a and 1b are used.

Figure 5-16a Subframe Format
(Source: Frame Relay Forum FRF.11.1)

Further details regarding the transport of voice over frame relay networks, plus the various coding options for the VFRAD implementations, are given in FRF.11.1 [5-12].

Extension indication (octet 1)

The extension indication (EI) bit is set to indicate the presence of octet 1a. This bit must be set when a sub-channel identification value is > 63 or when a payload type is indicated. Each transfer syntax has an implicit payload type of zero when the EI bit is cleared.

Length indication (octet 1)

The length indication (LI) bit is set to indicate the presence of octet 1b. The LI bit of the last sub-frame contained within a frame is always cleared and the payload length field is not present. The LI bits are set for each of the sub-frames preceeding the last sub-frame.

Sub-channel identification (octets 1 and 1a)

The six least significant bits of the sub-channel identification are encoded in octet 1. The two most significant bits of the sub-channel identification are encoded in octet 1a. A zero value in the two most significant bits is implied when octet 1a is not included in the VoFR header (EI bit cleared). Sub-channel identifiers 0000 0000 through 0000 0011 are reserved in both the short and long format.

Payload type (octet 1a)

This field indicates the type of payload contained in the sub-frame.

Bits				
4	3	2	1	
0	0	0	0	Primary payload transfer syntax
0	0	0	1	Dialed digit transfer syntax
0	0	1	0	Signalling bit transfer syntax
0	0	1	1	Fax relay transfer syntax
0	1	0	0	Silence Information Descriptor

A zero value for the payload type is implied when octet 1a is not included in the header (EI bit cleared).

Payload length (octet 1b)

Payload length contains the number of payload octets following the header. A payload length indicates the presence of two or more sub-frames packed in the information field of the frame.

Payload (octet p)

The payload contains octets as defined by the applicable transfer syntax assigned to the sub-channel or as indicated by the payload type octet 1a.

Figure 5-16b Subframe Format Details
(Source: Frame Relay Forum FRF.11.1)

5.7 IP over ATM Networks

Asynchronous Transfer Mode, or ATM, is a transmission technology that was originally conceived to meet the transport requirements for local, metropolitan, and wide area network applications. As such, ATM technologies operate over a wide range of transmission rates, currently defined from 1.5 Mbps (DS1) to 622 Mbps (Optical Carrier Level 12, or OC12), with higher rates under development. From a practical perspective, however, ATM technologies have been primarily deployed in MAN and WAN environments for backbone transmission. Many other high speed alternatives exist for LANs, such as Fast Ethernet and Gigabit Ethernet, that are often more cost effective than an ATM implementation. As a result, the desktop-to-desktop ATM service that was originally conceived is not frequently implemented.

The ATM architecture is connection-oriented, and is based on high speed switches that direct the 53-octet cells of information from their source to the ultimate destination. ATM has a four layer architecture. This includes the Physical Layer, which handles bit timing and transmission-related issues; the ATM layer, which is responsible for the transfer of the 53-octet cells; the ATM Adaptation layer (AAL), which supports the transport of higher layer information by dividing that information into 53-octet cells and incorporating appropriate error control mechanisms; and the Higher layers, which contain user information.

The 53-octet ATM cell is comprised of a 5-octet header and a 48-octet payload. The format of the cell is a standard across all AALs; however, the format of the 48-octet payloads, the various protocol processes, such as segmentation and reassembly, and so on, vary with the AAL type in use. At the present time, five AALs have been defined:

◆ AAL0: is the null AAL, where the entire 48-octet payload carries end-user information.

◆ AAL1: is typically used for circuit emulation service, which would include both voice and video applications that operate with a constant bit rate. With AAL1, the 48-octet payload is divided into a 1-octet field that contains sequence and error control information, and a 47-octet payload that carriers end-user information.

◆ AAL2: is intended for delay-sensitive applications with a variable bit rate, such as voice and video. AAL2 is still in its early stages of development.

◆ AAL3/4: is used for connectionless applications and others that need extensive error control capabilities, such as Switched Multimegabit Data Service (SMDS). With AAL3/4, the 48-octet payload carries 4 octets of sequencing and error control information, plus 44-octets of end-user information.

◆ AAL5: provides a straightforward mechanism to send connection-oriented traffic, such as frame relay or X.25. With AAL5, a short header is appended to the original end-user message, and then that message is divided into 48-octet payloads for transmission via ATM cells.

A thorough study of ATM is beyond the scope of this text. However, readers interested in an in-depth study of ATM and its protocols are referred to a companion text, *Analyzing Broadband Networks* [5-13].

Despite the differences between the original ATM architecture and the realities of the marketplace, the transport of IP traffic over ATM infrastructures has been the topic of much research. Much of this research has been under the guidance of The ATM Forum, a consortium of users, vendors, and carriers who have joined together to further develop the technology [5-14]. The Internet Engineering Task Force (IETF) has also played key roles in the publication of RFC documents that detail how IP-based and ATM-based internetworks can coexist. Four related alternatives for TCP/IP internetworking with ATM have been developed: Multiprotocol Encapsulation over AAL5 (defined in RFC 1483), Classical IP and ARP over ATM (defined in RFC 1577), LAN Emulation – LANE (defined by the ATM Forum), and Multiprotocol over ATM – MPOA (defined by the ATM Forum).

Multiprotocol Encapsulation over ATM Adaptation Layer 5 is documented in RFC 1483 [5-15]. This document describes two encapsulation techniques for carrying network interconnect traffic over ATM AAL5: Logical Link Control (LLC) encapsulation and Virtual Circuit (VC)–based multiplexing. The LLC encapsulation method allows multiplexing of multiple protocols over a single ATM virtual circuit, and is typically used when it is not feasible to have a separate VC for each protocol. With the VC-based multiplexing technique, each protocol is carried on a separate VC. This method is used when it is feasible and economical to dynamically create large numbers of virtual circuits.

The LLC encapsulation method is shown in Figure 5-17. Information contained within an IEEE 802.2 LLC header and an IEEE 802.1a SNAP header identifies the protocol carried within that PDU. Of particular interest within the SNAP header is the Protocol Identifier (PID) field, which would have the value 08 00H for IP traffic. The Protocol Data Unit (PDU) that would follow these headers contains up to 65,527 octets of higher layer information, such as an IP datagram.

RFC 1577, "Classical IP and ARP over ATM" [5-16], considers the application of ATM as a direct replacement for the physical transmission technologies (such as cables and routers) that have heretofore been employed. In this case, the network is assumed to be configured as a Logical IP Subnetwork (LIS), where members of that LIS that have the same IP network/subnet number and address mask, are directly connected to the ATM network, and meet other protocol requirements. Hosts connected to ATM communicate directly to other hosts within the same LIS. To communicate with a host outside of the local LIS requires an IP router. Figure 5-18 illustrates such a LIS, where all members have a consistent IP network and subnet address [N.S.x] and use a router for communication outside of the LIS.

For two LIS members to communicate, they must know each other's IP and ATM addresses. IP over ATM uses an enhanced version of the Address Resolution Protocol (ARP) called ATMARP to provide translation between ATM and IP addresses. ATMARP runs on a server that exists at an ATM address that all LIS members are aware of. The IP datagram is encapsulated within an ATM Adaptation Layer 5 (AAL5) message, and is then further subdivided into cells for transmission over the ATM network.

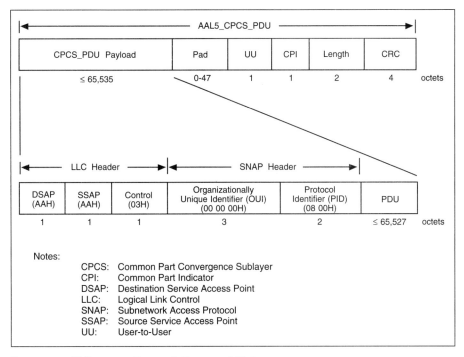

Figure 5-17 IP Datagram Encapsulation over AAL 5

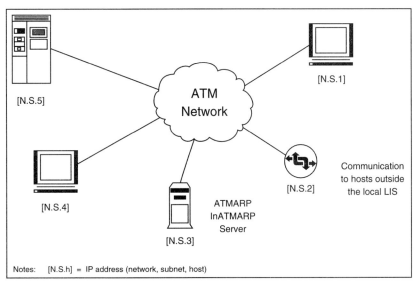

Figure 5-18 Logical IP Subnetwork

LAN Emulation, or LANE as it is commonly known, is a service that allows existing end-user applications to access an ATM network. More importantly, this access appears to the application as if it were using more traditional protocols, such as TCP/IP or Novell's Internetwork Packet Exchange (IPX), and as if it were running over more traditional LANs such as Ethernet or token ring. One of the design constraints is to account for the differences in protocol design – ATM is connection oriented, whereas IP and IPX are connectionless. A number of functions, including setting up the ATM connection and translating LAN to ATM addresses, must be hidden from the upper layers, thus making the application think that it is operating over a traditional network.

The ATM Forum's LAN Emulation version 2.0 specification [5-17] defines two scenarios that are applicable. In the first, an ATM network may be used to interconnect Ethernets to Ethernets, an Ethernet to an ATM device, or an ATM device to another ATM device. The second scenario replaces Ethernet LANs with token ring LANs under similar conditions. The ATM-to-LAN converter sits at the edge of the network, running dual protocol stacks: one that communicates with the LAN (on one side) and another that communicates with the ATM switch (on the other side). Note that this ATM-to-LAN converter is functioning as a bridge, operating independently of the Network and higher layer protocols. The ATM switch (or switches) do not participate in LAN Emulation other than to switch the ATM connections, as would be the case with any other ATM-based network scenario.

An evolution of the ATM Forum's LAN Emulation work is a process known as Multiprotocol over ATM (MPOA) [5-18]. While LANE operates at the MAC layer (OSI Data Link Layer), MPOA operates at the OSI Network layer. MPOA is designed to integrate with LAN Emulation, and to support the traditional routing functions of protocol filtering with enhanced security through firewalls, while handling both Data Link and Network layer operations.

MPOA is designed with a client/server architecture, with the MPOA Client (MPC) residing in an edge device or MPOA host, and the MPOA Server (MPS) residing in an MPOA router. Both the MPC and the MPS contain a LAN Emulation Client (LEC) function. The MPC includes a Layer 3 forwarding function, but it does not run internetwork routing protocols. The primary function of the MPC is to act as the initiation and termination points (source and sink, respectively) of internetwork shortcuts. When the MPC recognizes a data flow that could benefit from a shorter path, or shortcut, it requests the establishment of a shortcut to the destination. When the shortcut path is used, performance gains should result, especially for the transmission of stream-oriented traffic such as voice and video.

With this introduction into the transmission of IP over ATM networks, let us next consider some of the research regarding the transmission of voice traffic over ATM networks.

5.8 Voice over ATM Networks

Recall that one of the original design objectives of ATM technology was to incorporate voice, data, video, and other types of media into a cohesive stream of 53-octet cells. The ATM Forum has developed a number of documents that describe the various technologies and the protocols involved in these technologies, which go by the acronym VTOA, *Voice and Telephony over ATM*. These documents, which are all available from the ATM Forum's Web site [5-14], include:

◆ **Circuit Emulation Service 2.0 (af-vtoa-0078.000):** Addresses the need to carry constant bit rate (CBR) or circuit-oriented traffic over ATM networks. One of the goals of the Circuit Emulation Service (CES) is that the performance realized over ATM should be comparable to that experienced with currently available digital technologies, such as DS1 and DS3 lines.

◆ **Voice and Telephony over ATM to the Desktop (af-vtoa-0083.001):** Specifies the particular features required to provide voice and telephony service in Broadband ISDN networks, such as ATM. Issues discussed include interworking between Narrowband ISDN (ISDN-BRI or ISDN-PRI) and Broadband ISDN (ATM) environments, along with signaling systems that are required to complete those calls.

◆ **Dynamic Bandwidth Utilization in 64 Kbps Time Slot Trunking over ATM – Using CES (af-vtoa-0085.000):** Provides methods for detecting which time slots of a given trunk are active and which are inactive, which will optimize the bandwidth utilization of the ATM network.

◆ **ATM Trunking Using AAL1 for Narrowband Services v. 1.0 (af-vtoa-0089.000):** Describes interworking functions between Narrowband services, such as 64 Kbps channels, and ATM trunks for PBX-like applications.

◆ **ATM Trunking Using AAL2 for Narrowband Services (af-vtoa-0113.000):** Describes trunking arrangements for transport of voice, voice-band data, circuit mode data, frame mode data, and fax traffic. The document specifies the use of ATM virtual circuits with AAL2 to transport bearer information and ATM virtual circuits with AAL2 or AAL5 to transport signaling information.

◆ **Low Speed Circuit Emulation Service (af-vtoa-0119.000):** Discusses the transport of constant bit rate (CBR) traffic over ATM networks, with specific emphasis on the support of low speed applications (less than 64 kbits). This document supports interfaces of both Data Terminal Equipment (DTE) and Data Circuit Terminating Equipment (DCE) for applications using EIA-449, EIA-530, and V.35 interfaces.

◆ **ICS for ATM Trunking Using AAL2 for Narrowband Services (af-vtoa-0120.000):** This document provides an Implementation Conformance Statement (ICS) for the ATM Trunking using AAL2 for Narrowband Services. The ICS is a statement of which capabilities and options have been implemented; its purpose is to evaluate conformance of a particular implementation.

As might be expected, these technologies are in their early stages of development. Readers are therefore advised to follow the progress of this work on the ATM Forum's Web site.

5.9 Carriers Providing IP Transport Services

Now that we have examined the various transport alternatives – T1 lines, frame relay circuits, ATM switched connections, and so on – below is a listing of some of the carriers that provide these IP-based transport alternatives.

Carrier	Contact	Notes
Access Power Gateway Network, Inc.	www.accesspower.com	Serves North and South America
AT&T Jens	www.attjens.co.jp	Serves Japan
.comfax, Inc.	www.comfax.com	Worldwide fax service
Concentric Network Corporation	www.concentric.com	Serves Australia, Germany, the Netherlands, New Zealand and U.S.
Delta Three, Inc.	www.deltathree.com	Worldwide phone-to-phone and PC-to-phone service
DotCom Technologies	www.dotcomtech.net	Serves North America and U.K.
efusion, Inc.	www.efusion.com	Worldwide Internet Call Waiting and Push to Talk service
FaxSav, Inc.	www.faxsave.com	International internet fax service

Carrier	Contact	Notes
Fnet Corporation	www.fnet.net	Worldwide phone/fax service
Global Exchange Carrier Co.	www.gcubed.com	Serves Canada, Germany, Italy, Japan, Korea, the Netherlands, Spain, U.K., U.S.
GlobalNet Telecom, Inc.	www.globalnettelecom.com	Worldwide fax service
Glocalnet AB	www.glocalnet.com	Serves Sweden
GRIC Communications, Inc.	www.gric.com	Serves Europe, U.S. and other countries
GTE Internetworking	www.bbn.com	Fax network service
IBasis	www.ibasis.net	Serves Far East and U.S.
Iscom, Inc.	www.iscom.net	Worldwide service
ISPTel	www.isptel.com	Worldwide Service
ITXC Corporation	www.itxc.com	Serves Australia, Hong Kong, Japan and Mexico
Justice Technology Corporation	www.justicecorp.com	Voice and fax service for U.S., Europe, Far East and South America
Level Three	www.level3.com	Servicing U.S.
MCI Worldcom	www.mci.com	Servicing U.S.
Net Communications, Inc. (NCI)	www.nciglobal.com	Worldwide fax and VoIP service
Net2phone	www.net2phone.com	U.S., Korea and Spain phone-to-phone; Worldwide PC-to-phone
NeTrue Communications, Inc.	www.concentric.com	Worldwide data, voice, and fax service
NetVoice Technologies	www.netvoice.net	Serves Texas and Southern U.S.

Continued

Continued

Carrier	Contact	Notes
Networks Telephony Corporation	www.networkstelephony.com	Serves Europe and U.S.
NKO, Inc.	www.nko.com	Worldwide fax and voice service
Ozemail Interline Pty Ltd.	www.ozemail.com.au	Serves Australia, New Zealand, U.K., U.S.
Poptel GmbH	www.poptel com	Serves Germany, France, Switzerland, U.S.
Qwest Communications	www.qwest.net	U.S. phone/fax service
Telecom Finland Ltd.	www.tele.fi	Serving Finland
World Interactive Network	www.win-inc.com	Worldwide fax and voice service

With so many alternatives available—T1/T3 lines, frame relay circuits, ATM connections, and the like—there are a number of opinions regarding which of these methods is the optimum transport for IP-based services. These various alternatives have been written about extensively in the trade press. References [5-19] through [5-23] provide perspectives on the new carrier services; References [5-24] through [5-27] discuss voice over frame relay networks; References [5-28] through [5-34] discuss voice over ATM networks; References [5-35] and [5-36] discuss voice over cable networks; and References [5-37] through [5-38] look at other alternatives, including mobile IP services.

5.10 Looking Ahead

In this chapter, we considered the WAN infrastructures that are used to transport IP-based traffic, be that voice, fax, data, or video traffic. In the next chapter, we will deal with the customer-premises equipment, such as VoIP gateways, that prepares the end-users' information for transmission over the infrastructures we have just examined.

5.11 References

[5-1]   International Telecommunication Union – Telecommunications
          Standardization Sector. General Aspects of Digital Transmission Systems –
          Terminal Equipments – Synchronous Frame Structures Used at Primary
          and Secondary Hierarchical Levels. *Recommendation G.704,* 1991.

[5-2]   American National Standards Institute. Telecommunications –
          Integrated Services Digital Network (ISDN) – Digital Hierarchy –
          Formats Specifications. *ANSI T1.107,* 1995.

[5-3]   International Telecommunication Union – Telecommunications
          Standardization Sector. Integrated Services Digital Network (ISDN) –
          ISDN User-Network Interfaces – Basic User-Network Interface – Layer 1
          Specification. *Recommendation I.430,* March 1993.

[5-4]   International Telecommunication Union – Telecommunications
          Standardization Sector. Integrated Services Digital Network (ISDN) –
          ISDN User-Network Interfaces – Primary User-Network Interface –
          Layer 1 Specification. *Recommendation I.431,* March 1993.

[5-5]   J. Romkey. "A Nonstandard For Transmission of IP Datagrams Over
          Serial Lines: SLIP." RFC 1055, June 1988.

[5-6]   W. Simpson. "The Point-to-Point Protocol (PPP)." RFC 1661, July 1994.

[5-7]   The IETF Assigned Numbers document is available online at
          `ftp://ftp.isi.edu/in-notes/iana/assignments/`.

[5-8]   American National Standards Institute. *Integrated Services Digital
          Network (ISDN) – Architectural Framework and Service Description for
          Frame-Relaying Bearer Service. T1.606,* 1990.

[5-9]   The Frame Relay Forum may be contacted at:

          Frame Relay Forum North American Office
          39355 California Street, Suite 307
          Fremont, CA 94538
          Tel: (510) 608-5920
          Fax: (510) 608-5917
          Email: `frf@frforum.com`
          `http://www.frforum.com`

[5-10]   American National Standards Institute. *Integrated Services Digital
          Network (ISDN) – Signaling Specification for Frame Relay Bearer
          Service for Digital Subscriber Signaling System Number 1 (DSS1)
          (Protocol Encapsulation and PICS). ANSI T1.617a,* 1994.

[5-11]   T. Bradley, C. Brown, and A. Malis. "Multiprotocol Interconnect over Frame Relay." RFC 1490, July 1993.

[5-12]   Frame Relay Forum. Voice over Frame Relay Implementation Agreement. *FRF.11.1*. December, 1998.

[5-13]   Miller, Mark A. *Analyzing Broadband Networks*, second edition. M&T Books, Inc. (New York, NY), 1997.

[5-14]   The ATM Forum may be contacted at:

ATM Forum Worldwide Headquarters
2570 W. El Camino Rio, Suite 304
Mountain View, CA 94440
Tel: (650) 949-6700
Fax: (650) 949-6705
Email: info@atmforum.com
http://www.atmforum.com

[5-15]   Heinanen, Juha. "Multiprotocol Encapsulation over ATM Adaptation Layer 5." RFC 1483, July 1993.

[5-16]   Laubach, M. "Classical IP and ARP over ATM." RFC 1577, January 1994.

[5-17]   The ATM Forum. *LAN Emulation Over ATM Version 2 – LUNI Specification*, document AF-LANE-00084.000, July 1997.

[5-18]   The ATM Forum. *Multiprotocol over ATM (MPOA) Specification 1.0*, Document AF-MPOA-0087.000, July 1997.

[5-19]   Gareiss, Robin. "Voice Over IP Services: The Sound Decision." *Data Communications* (March 1998): 75–84.

[5-20]   Masud, Sam "Transforming the PSTN." *Telecommunications* (July 1999): 22–31.

[5-21]   Carden, Philip. "Meet the New-Age Carriers." *Network Computing* (July 12, 1999): 40–51.

[5-22]   Greene, Tim. "Carriers to Debut Innovative IP Services." *Network World* (July 26, 1999).

[5-23]   Kennard, Linda. "Packet Voice – Because We Need to Talk." *NetWare Connection* (August 1999): 6–18.

[5-24]   Lee, Wei Wei. "Voice Over Frame Relay: And They Said It Couldn't Be Done." *CTI* (October 1997): 110–112.

[5-25]   Greene, Tim. "Talk is Cheap with Frame Relay." *Network World* (January 18, 1999): 37–38.

[5-26]   Flanagan, William. "Convergence? Try Voice over Frame." *Network World* (June 7, 1999): 53.

[5-27]   Wexler, Joanie. "Speaking in Frames." *Sounding Board* (August 1999): 38–42.

[5-28]   Wright, David J. "Voice over ATM: An Evaluation of Network Architecture Alternatives." *IEEE Network* (September/October 1996): 22–27.

[5-29]   Karve, Anita. "ATM Gets a Dial Tone." *Network Magazine* (January 15, 1998): 46–49.

[5-30]   Steinke, Steve. "ATM and Alternatives in the Wide Area Backbone." *Network Magazine* (July 1999): 36–42.

[5-31]   Nolle, Tom. "Is It Time to Reconsider ATM?" *Network Magazine* (July 1999): 34.

[5-32]   Willis, David. "The Year of the ATM WAN?" *Network Computing* (July 26, 1999): 53–56.

[5-33]   "The ATM Report Guide to Public ATM Services." *Broadband World* (Volume 1, Number 1, 1999): 39–46.

[5-34]   Information on the ATM Local Telephony Alliance (ALTA) can be obtained from www.altainfo.org.

[5-35]   Galitzine, Greg. "Cable: A Brilliant Broad (Band) Horizon." *Internet Telephony* (May 1999): 65–66.

[5-36]   Komanecky, Mark. "The New Paradigm for Delivery of IP-Based Services Over Cable." *Telecommunications* (July 1999): 37–39.

[5-37]   Lambert, Peter. DSL Advances Packet Voice, Video Cause. *Sounding Board* (August 15, 1999): 30–33.

[5-38]   Oliphant, Malcolm W. "The Mobile Phone Meets the Internet." *IEEE Spectrum* (August 1999): 20–28.

Chapter 6

Hardware Systems for Converged Networks

Converged networks are comprised of a number of elements (Figure 6-1). Suppose you wish to communicate with a colleague over an IP-based infrastructure. On your end, the communications path includes a Voice over IP client application, a local network that supports IP, and a wide area network that supports IP, such as an ISDN or a T1 line. Likewise, your colleague requires a similar connection on their end. We studied these three elements in Chapters 2, 4, and 5, respectively.

But there is one more element of this network topology that needs to be considered – some additional equipment on the customer's premises that coordinates between the applications, the LAN, and the WAN. Let's suppose that you decide to use your network for an audio/video teleconference. Does sufficient bandwidth exist on the LAN to support this application? What about your existing voice communication systems, such as the Private Branch Exchange (PBX) or your voice mail system? How will the new converged network incorporate these existing systems and allow for legacy investment? What effects will additional traffic have on the WAN circuits?

These issues are addressed by the customer premises equipment, which includes Gateways, Gatekeepers, and interfaces to legacy equipment such as digital PBXs. We will study these converged network-specific devices in this chapter. In Chapter 7, we will consider issues like quality of service, network latency, and interoperability, which are concerns that arise once the network equipment is in place.

We will begin by examining various converged network environments and their component parts. Then we will turn our attention to the fundamental standard, ITU-T H.323, that governs multimedia networks.

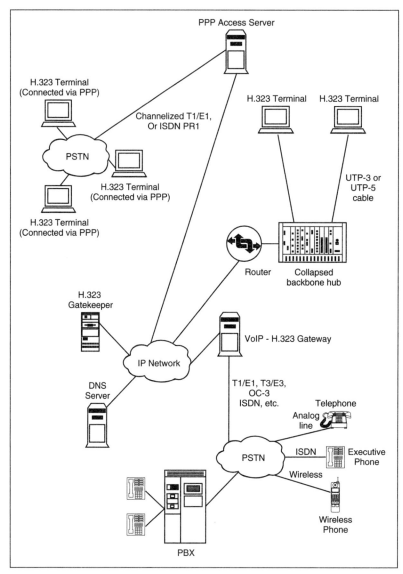

Figure 6-1 Voice over IP Network Elements
(Courtesy of the IMTC Conferencing over IP (CoIP) activity group)

6.1 Converged Network Environments

As we have seen, environments for converged networks contain a number of elements that encompass both local and wide area network infrastructures. The IMTC Conferencing over IP (CoIP) activity group, which is part of the International Multimedia Teleconferencing Consortium (IMTC), has developed an Implementation Agreement (IA) that describes three possible connectivity configurations for converged networks [6-1]. All three of these configurations use some combination of an IP-based network and the PSTN to provide the communication infrastructure required.

In the first configuration, two multimedia-equipped PCs (with microphone and speakers) communicate over an IP network (Figure 6-2a). Communication to this IP network could use a number of dial-up or dedicated connections, or a higher speed connection over a LAN. Two other required elements that will be discussed later in this chapter are: the H.323 Gatekeeper, which provides network management functions, and a Domain Name Service (DNS) Server, which provides address translation functions.

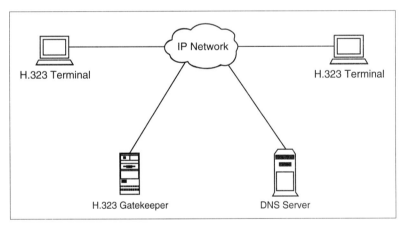

Figure 6–2a Network Elements Used for the PC to PC Connection
(Courtesy of the IMTC Conferencing over IP (CoIP) activity group)

The second alternative brings in the PSTN connection (Figure 6-2b). In this example, one user is accessing the network via a telephone and the PSTN, while another user receives access from an H.323 terminal. This configuration introduces another element into the mix – an H.323 Gateway between the PSTN and the IP network. We will discuss the operation of this Gateway in the following section. As before, the H.323 Gatekeeper and DNS Server are also required. Note that since the telephone is assumed to be an audio (not audio/video) device, this configuration would be limited to telephone-like conversations, not multimedia streams as was the case in the previous example.

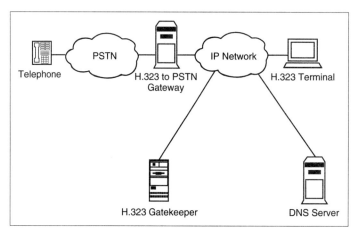

Figure 6-2b Network Elements Used for the PC to Phone Connection (Courtesy of the IMTC Conferencing over IP (CoIP) activity group)

The final scenario deploys two connections to the PSTN, and also two Gateways (Figure 6-2c). In this configuration, two end users can communicate over their standard telephones, with an IP network carrying the traffic between the two PSTN connections. Two analogies can be drawn from this topology. First, this appears to be very similar to the current telephone network in the United States, where the end users connect to Local Exchange Carriers (LECs), and those carriers are interconnected via an Interexchange Carrier (IXC). For example, my offices are located in Colorado. If I want to call a colleague in Chicago, the local access on my end is through US West Communications, and the local access on his end is provided by Ameritech. We can select from a number of Interexchange Carriers (AT&T, MCI Worldcom, Sprint, and so on) for the long distance connection. Second, this PSTN–IP Network–PSTN topology is very similar to the service provided by many Internet Telephony Service Providers (ITSPs), such as OzEmail Interline that we considered in Section 2.3. By using an international ITSP, like OzEmail's Interline service, the end user circumvents expensive international toll charges. Recognizing this threat to their revenue base, the IXCs in the United States are beginning to offer IP-based services along with their more standard offerings such as T1 lines and frame relay connections.

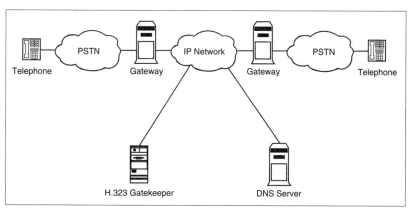

Figure 6–2c Network Elements Used for the Phone to Phone Connection
(Courtesy of the IMTC Conferencing over IP (CoIP) activity group)

All the network elements in these varied topologies – the end-user terminals, the Gateways, the miscellaneous network devices – share one major feature. They all adhere to the ITU-T H.323 multimedia standard.

6.2 The H.323 Multimedia Standard

The original title of the ITU-T H.323 standard was lengthy, but described its purpose: *Visual Telephone Systems and Equipment for Local Area Networks Which Provide a Non-guaranteed Quality of Service* (The new title [6-2] is also more succinct!). If we dissect the title, we see two key elements: visual telephone systems (in contrast to just audio telephone systems), and their use over LANs that do not provide a guaranteed quality of service, or QoS. To better understand the scope of this standard, it helps to put it in context with other ITU-T Series H Recommendations that deal with audiovisual and multimedia systems. These other standards include:

◆ **H.320:** Narrowband visual telephone systems and terminal equipment (used with narrowband ISDN services).

◆ **H.321:** Adaptation of H.320 terminals to broadband ISDN (ATM) environments.

◆ **H.322:** Visual telephone systems and equipment for local area networks that provide a guaranteed quality of service.

◆ **H.323:** Visual telephone systems and equipment for local area networks that provide a nonguaranteed quality of service.

◆ **H.324:** Terminal for low bit rate multimedia communication (used for PTSN and wireless applications).

H.323 assumes that the transmission media is a LAN that does not provide guaranteed packet delivery. A typical Ethernet would be a good example – if two Ethernet workstations transmit at the same time, a collision occurs. Since the probability of such a collision is difficult to predict, defining a specific quality of service is also difficult. Other standards in this family address other network types, such as H.320 (ISDN), H.321 (ATM), and H.324 (low bit rate connections), or in the case of H.324, networks that provide QoS guarantees. Thus, the H.323 standard is designed to work with the local and wide area network types that are most commonly found – those that do not provide guarantees on the QoS provided.

In addition to the network implementation standards noted above, there are other standards that fall within the umbrella of the H.323 recommendation. These include:

◆ **H.225.0:** Terminal to Gatekeeper signaling functions.

◆ **H.245:** Terminal control functions that are used to negotiate channel usage, capabilities, and other functions.

◆ **Q.931:** Call signaling functions to establish and terminate the call.

◆ **T.120:** Data conferencing, which might include shared whiteboarding and still image transfer applications.

Before delving into the H.323 standard in greater detail, a few terms, as defined in that standard, should be mentioned:

◆ **Call:** A point-to-point multimedia communication between two H.323 endpoints, which begins with the call set-up procedure and ends with the call termination procedure.

◆ **Endpoint:** An H.323 terminal, Gateway (GW), Gatekeeper (GK), or Multipoint Control Unit (MCU). The endpoint can call and be called, and generates and/or terminates streams of information.

◆ **Gatekeeper (GK):** An entity on the LAN that provides address translation and controls access to the LAN for other devices, such as terminals, Gateways, and MCUs.

◆ **Gateway (GW):** An endpoint on the LAN that provides real-time, two-way communications between H.323 terminals on the LAN and other ITU terminals on a WAN, or to another H.323 Gateway.

◆ **H.323 Entity:** Any H.323 component, which includes terminals, Gateways, Gatekeepers, Multipoint Controllers (MCs), Multipoint Processors (MPs), and Multipoint Control Units (MCUs).

◆ **Multipoint Control Unit (MCU):** An endpoint on the LAN that provides the capability for three or more terminals and Gateways to participate in a multipoint conference. The MCU includes a mandatory MC and optional MPs.

◆ **Multipoint Controller (MC):** An entity on the LAN that provides for the control of three or more terminals participating in a multipoint conference.

◆ **Multipoint Processor (MP):** An H.323 entity on the LAN that provides for the centralized processing of audio, video, and/or data streams in a multipoint conference.

◆ **Terminal (Tx):** An endpoint on the LAN that provides for real-time, two-way communications with another H.323 terminal, Gateway, or Multipoint Control Unit.

◆ **Zone:** A collection of all Terminals, Gateways, and Multipoint Control Units managed by a single Gatekeeper.

The various building blocks that comprise a typical H.323 network are illustrated in Figure 6-3. Note that the building blocks imply that each of these functions is in a distinct box. However, one physical box often contains more than one functional element. For example, both MCU and Gatekeeper functions could be located in the same physical device. A typical H.323 environment might include Gateways to other networks, such as the PSTN or ISDN, as shown in Figure 6-4.

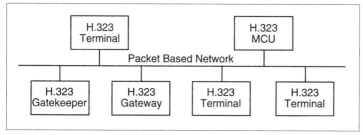

Figure 6-3 H.323 Building Blocks
(Source: ITU-T Recommendation H.323)

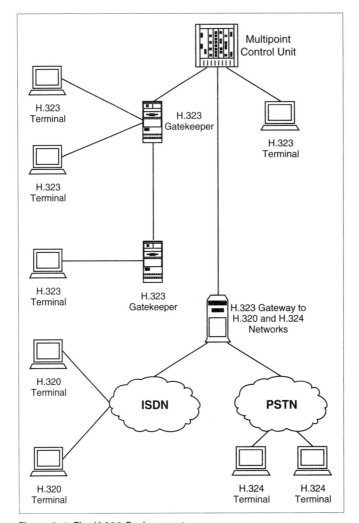

Figure 6-4 The H.323 Environment

Multimedia networks must support a number of different end-user applications; therefore, H.323 must support different streams of information. These are:

◆ **Audio:** Digitized and coded speech signals. The audio signal is accompanied by an audio control signal.

◆ **Video:** Digitized and coded motion video. The video signal is accompanied by a video control signal.

◆ **Data:** Still pictures, facsimile, computer files, and so on.

◆ **Communications Control:** Information that passes control data between
like functional elements (such as terminal-to-terminal control) to
exchange capabilities between these devices, to open and close logical
channels, to control transmission modes, and to perform other functions.

◆ **Call Control:** Information that includes call establishment and call disconnect functions.

In the following sections, we will consider in greater detail the various elements
of H.323 that support these five different information stream types. In addition, we
will consider the related protocols, such as H.245 [6-3], Q.931 [6-4] and H.225.0
[6-5], that are used for control and communication functions between the network
elements. References [6-6] through [6-9] provide additional insight into the various
applications for the H.323 standard.

6.3 Terminals

The end users interact with an H.323 terminal, which provides real-time, two-way
communication with another H.323 device. On that terminal, support for voice
communications is required, and support for video and data communications is
optional. This results in two important implementation factors. First, by requiring
support for voice communication, H.323 terminals can be used as packet-based
replacements for plain old telephone service (POTS) over the PSTN.

Second, by making support for video and data communication optional, the
standard opens the door to interoperability problems. On a practical level this
means two manufacturers can have products that meet the H.323 standard yet are
very different in their capabilities. For example, one H.323 terminal product may be
a voice client software package, available without charge. Another H.323 terminal
may be a very sophisticated video conferencing system that supports voice, video,
and data communication, and costs tens of thousands of dollars. Both products are
compliant with the H.323 standard, but may not be interoperable with each other
because of the vast difference in their capabilities. But H.323 is a multimedia standard and is designed to address a variety of end-user requirements, so a difference
in terminal capabilities exists both by design and necessity.

An example of an H.323 terminal and its capabilities is illustrated in Figure 6-5.
Note that the video, audio, and data information streams are shown on the left-
hand side of the figure, and that the interface to the LAN is shown on the right-
hand side. The center of the figure illustrates the scope of H.323. There are five
elements that comprise the H.323 implementation. The first two of these employ
Coding/Decoding (codec) algorithms that convert the analog signal into a digital
format and further optimize that signal for transmission. The video codec encodes
the information for transmission from the video source, such as a camera, and
decodes the received video information for display. The audio codec encodes the

information for transmission from the audio source, such as a microphone, and decodes the received audio for output to a loudspeaker. Video codec standards, such as H.261, and audio codec standards, such as G.711, as well as the issue of delays in codec processing, will be discussed in the following section.

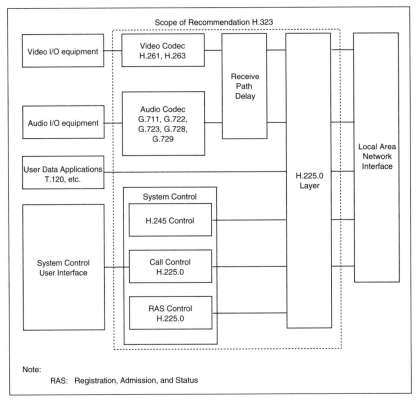

Figure 6-5 H.323 Terminal Equipment
(Source: ITU-T Recommendation H.323)

The data channel supports standardized data conferencing applications, such as file exchange, database access, still image transmission, and electronic whiteboards, as defined in the ITU-T T.120 series of recommendations.

The System Control unit provides signaling functions that are required for the proper operation of the terminal, such as call control, the exchange of terminal capabilities, and so on. The H.245 Control functions allow the terminals to negotiate channel usage and other capabilities. These functions are defined in ITU-T Recommendation H.245 [6-3]. Part of this control is a channel known as the RAS channel, which stands for Registration, Admission, and Status. The Call Control functions are used for call establishment and call termination functions. These functions are derived from a well-known signaling protocol, Q.931 [6-4], that has influenced work in ISDN, frame relay, and ATM network signaling. The RAS channel is used for communication between terminals and Gatekeepers. Finally, the H.225.0 Layer formats transmit and receive information [6-5]. For example, this layer sends the information to be transmitted to the network interface, and retrieves the received information from that network interface. In conjunction with transmit and receive operations, sequence numbering, error detection, and other functions may also be provided by the H.225 Layer.

6.4 Audio and Video Codecs

Reviewing Figure 6-5, note that the input for the audio and video signals is a codec, which stands for *coder/decoder*. We will look at voice and video codecs separately in the following sections.

6.4.1 Voice Codecs

The origins of voice encoding devices can be traced back several decades to the development of digital telephony. Recall from our discussion in Chapter 5 that WAN connections can be divided into two general categories: analog lines and digital lines. Digital lines were developed for several reasons, but one of the key reasons was to pack more information content into the cable pairs that were available. Bell System researchers discovered that they could send 24 voice conversations over two pairs of wire, thus yielding a pair gain of 12 from the older, analog technology.

In order to transport the analog voice signal using a digital transmission line, the voice signal first needs to be processed, which takes several steps. First, the analog signal is *sampled* (or measured) at a periodic rate. The sampling rate that is most frequently used is 8,000 samples per second. Next these samples (or measurements) are converted from an analog value into an equivalent digital value, which is called *quantizing*. In most cases, an 8-bit scale is used, which yields 256 (2^8) distinct quantization levels. Thus, the basic bit rate becomes:

8,000 samples/second * 8 bits/sample = 64,000 bits/second

This basic rate is known as the DS0 rate, which, as we discussed in Section 5.2, has become the fundamental building block for all digital telephony worldwide (Figure 6-6).

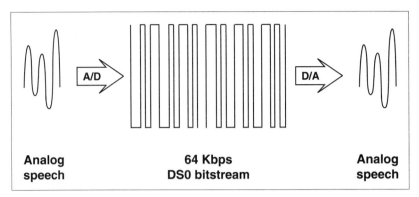

Analog | **64 Kbps** | **Analog**
speech | **DS0 bitstream** | **speech**

Figure 6-6 Channelized Telephony
(Courtesy of Netrix Corporation)

However, by current technology standards, voice channels do not need to consume 64,000 bits/second of bandwidth because additional signal processing can be applied after the analog-to-digital conversion (Figure 6-7). This additional process is known as *coding*; it may involve a number of mathematical functions, including data compression, voice activity detection, silence suppression, and so on. A reverse process, aptly called *decoding*, occurs at the receiver. When the coding/decoding is added to the signal processing, much less than 64,000 bits/second is required for each voice channel (Figure 6-7). As a result, more channels can be included in each WAN link, and the overall network costs should decrease.

There are two general categories of voice coders: those that have been approved by a standards body, such as the ITU-T, and those that are proprietary to a particular vendor. Some vendors choose standardized codecs in their terminals, Gateways, and other devices, thus making their products more interoperable with other vendors' designs. Other vendors may have developed a coding algorithm that they feel has superior performance to those that are standardized, and for a number of reasons (market share certainly being one) choose to keep that algorithm proprietary. As a result, the likelihood that one vendor's products will interoperate with another vendor's devices is low (close to zero in some cases). As one might expect, there are a number of differing opinions regarding the use of proprietary vs. standardized codecs, and the reader can determine individually which of these two options is best suited to their networking environment.

In any event, most coding algorithms are actually implemented on a Digital Signal Processor, or DSP integrated circuit. As References [6-10] and [6-11] detail, DSP technology has made extensive advances in the last few years, which has enabled both the processing complexity and the processing density to increase dramatically. Thus, with more signals being processed per chip, and with more complex algorithms employed, the resulting bandwidth consumption of a typical voice conversation has been dramatically decreased from the benchmark 64,000 bits/second. This decrease means more conversations per circuit, which lowers the telecommunications costs of organizations and allows them to purchase more terminals and Gateways. In summary, DSPs have become one of the most significant technologies that have fueled the growth of converged networks.

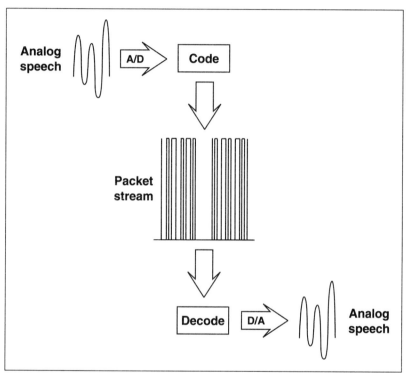

Figure 6-7. Packet Telephony
(Courtesy of Netrix Corporation)

Listed below is a brief summary of the capabilities of the coding algorithms that have been standardized:

◆ **G.711 (1972):** This algorithm operates at 64 Kbps. It uses Pulse Code Modulation (PCM) and produces a frame that contains 125 microseconds of speech. This is the original encoding standard. It produces a high quality of speech against which all other algorithms are compared, but it also has the highest bandwidth consumption, as no compression is involved.

◆ **G.722 (1988):** This algorithm operates at 48, 56, or 64 Kbps, and is often referred to as the wideband coder.

◆ **G.723.1 (1995):** This algorithm operates at 5.3 and 6.4 Kbps. It uses Algebraic Code Excited Linear Prediction (ACELP) for the low rate coder, and Multipulse Maximum Likelihood Quantization (MP-MLQ) for the high rate coder. The algorithm produces a frame with 30 milliseconds of speech and a total delay of 37.5 milliseconds. It has been adopted by the International Multimedia Teleconferencing Consortium's (IMTC) Conferencing IP (CoIP) activity group in their Implementation Agreement and, as a result, is used in a number of converged network equipment applications.

◆ **G.726 (1990):** This algorithm operates at 16, 24, 32, and 40 Kbps. It uses Adaptive Differential Pulse Code Modulation (ADPCM). The algorithm produces a frame with 0.125 milliseconds of speech and a total delay of 0.125 milliseconds. It was originally designed to optimize bandwidth consumption over T1 networks.

◆ **G.728 (1994):** This algorithm operates at 16 Kbps. It uses Low Delay Code Excited Linear Prediction (LD-CELP). The algorithm produces a frame with 0.625 milliseconds of speech and a total delay of 0.625 milliseconds.

◆ **G.729 (1995):** This algorithm operates at 8 Kbps. It uses Conjugate Structure Algebraic Code Excited Linear Prediction (CS-ACELP). The algorithm produces a frame with 10 milliseconds of speech and a total delay of 15 milliseconds. It was originally designed for wireless environments.

◆ **G.729A (1996):** This algorithm operates at 8 Kbps. It uses a less complex version of the CS-ACELP algorithm implemented in G.729. The algorithm produces a frame with 10 milliseconds of speech and a total delay of 15 milliseconds. It was adapted for integrated voice and data applications, and has been adopted by the International Multimedia Teleconferencing Consortium's Interoperability NOW! Activity Group.

We will revisit the selection of coding algorithms and their associated delay characteristics when we discuss converged network implementations in Chapter 7.

6.4.2 Video Codecs

Two codecs have been defined by the ITU-T for use with H.323 systems. These are:

◆ **H.261:** This algorithm operates at a multiple of p x 64 Kbps, where p can range in value from 1 to 30. The resulting video bit rate ranges from approximately 40 Kbps to 2 Mbps. H.261 is a required element of H.323.

◆ **H.263:** This algorithm is based on H.261, with additional compression. It contains negotiable options and can operate with a number of different video information formats. H.263 is an optional element of H.323.

In most cases, equipment designers, not network managers, select the encoding scheme that will be used in a particular product. Therefore, some knowledge about codec characteristics is valuable; however, the intricate details of the algorithms should be left to the designers. The ITU-T Recommendations regarding voice codecs, (References [6-12] through [6-14]), and regarding video codecs (Reference [6-15]), provide details for those readers wishing to dig deeper.

6.5 Client Software

A number of firms have developed client software that supports voice and video over IP applications. Some of this software is available for free download over the Internet, and some of it comes with a cost. As might be expected, the capabilities, ease of use, and other features of these products vary. A sample client package is on the CD-ROM that accompanies this text. As with all software, thorough testing in a lab environment, prior to more widespread enterprise deployment, is advised.

Company	Product	Notes
DigiPhone Internet Communications Software www.digiphone.com/download	DigiPhone	DOS, Windows 3.1, 95, Macintosh compatible
eRing Solutions, Inc. www.eRing.net	eRing Client	Windows 95, 98, NT compatible
FreeTel Communications, Inc. www.freetel.com/#dnld	FreeTel	Windows 95/98, NT compatible
Intel Corporation www.intel.com/pccamera	Internet Video Phone	Windows 95/98 compatible
IRIS Systems http://irisphone.com/download1.htm	IRIS Phone	Windows 3.1, 95, NT compatible
MediaRing, Inc. www.mediaring.com/door/next.html	MediaRing Talk	Windows 95/98 compatible
Microsoft Corporation www.microsoft.com/windows/netmeeting	NetMeeting	Windows 95/98, NT compatible
Netscape Communications Corp. http://shareware.netscape.com Sun OS compatible	CoolTalk (16-bit)	Windows 3.x, Macintosh System 7,

Continued

Continued

Company	Product	Notes
NetSpeak Corporation www.webphone.com/product/ webphone/download.html	WebPhone	Windows 3.1, 95/98 NT compatible
Net2Phone, Inc. www.net2phone.com	Net2Phone	DOS, Windows 3.1, 95/98 compatible
OnLive, Inc. www.onlive.com	OnLive! Talker	Windows 95/98, NT compatible
Open Source Software www.speakfreely.org	Speak Freely for Unix	Unix compatible
SilverSoft Network www.pak.net/softfone.htm	Softfone for the Internet	DOS, Windows compatible, includes video capabilities
VocalTec Communications www.vocaltec.com/dnls/ download_frame.htm compatible	InternetPhone	Windows 95/98, NT compatible Macintosh
ZeroPlus.com www.zeroplus.com/download.asp	ZeroPlus.com	Windows 95/98, NT compatible

Reference [6-16] provides additional details on PC-based multimedia communication.

6.6 Gateways

The Gateway provides a communication and connection path between an endpoint on the LAN and the switched circuit network (SCN). If two H.323 endpoints are on the same network, they can communicate directly without Gateway intervention. Similarly, two endpoints on the SCN (that are not on the network) can also communicate without Gateway intervention. When communication between these two networks is required, however, the Gateway translates between the transmission formats and the communication procedures that are used on each side. Gateways can be provided as stand-alone devices or integrated into other systems, such as a PBX.

Four different types of Gateways are defined in H.323; they provide for two different network types (H.323 Terminal and H.323 MCU), and two different SCN types (SCN Terminal and SCN MCU), as shown in Figure 6-8. The SCN side of the

Gateway communicates with the appropriate network type, such as H.320 (ISDN) or H.324 (PSTN). The Conversion Function provides the necessary conversions of the transmission format, control, audio, video, and data signal streams between the two different networks. In addition, the Gateway may also provide for conversion of any signaling messages between the Network side (which uses H.225.0) and the SCN side (which might use Q.921, Q.2931, or some other signaling scheme).

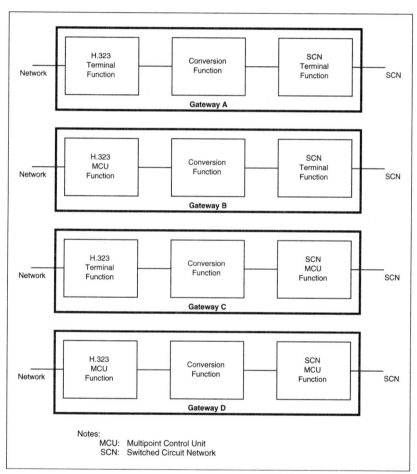

Figure 6-8 H.323 Gateway Configurations
(Source: ITU-T Recommendation H.323)

As illustrated in Figure 6-9, the Gateway performs a very critical function that allows H.323 systems to coexist with other (legacy) systems, such as ISDN and PTSN video conferencing equipment.

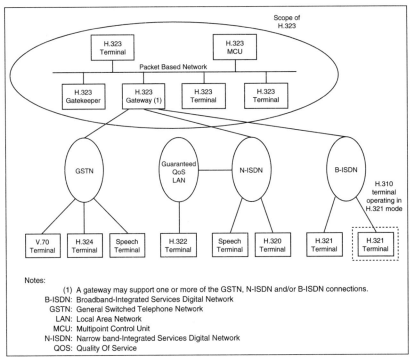

Figure 6-9 Interoperability of H.323 Terminals
(Source: ITU-T Recommendation H.323)

The architecture of a Gateway includes three key elements: an interface for the voice side of the network, an interface for the packet side of the network, and the necessary signal processing between these two sides [6-17] as shown in Figure 6-10. The signal processing is most likely performed on a Digital Signal Processor (DSP) integrated circuit, which has been optimized for the processing speed required to support real-time voice and video connections. Signal processing functions include: canceling any echoes that exist on the telephone line (thus optimizing the intelligibility of the conversation); encoding/decoding of the analog signal, typically using one of the algorithms discussed above, such as G.711 or G.723.1; adapting the digitally encoded information into a series of IP datagrams (Review Figure 4-26); and transmitting those datagrams via a network, such as an Ethernet, to the ultimate destination.

As most of these Gateway functions are software-related, many manufacturers opt to purchase specialized communication software that can be embedded into their products, rather than develop their own code. One of the developers of this software is Telogy Networks, Inc., of Germantown, Maryland. Telogy's software module is designed for general Voice over Packet applications, which includes transport using ATM, frame relay, and IP-based networking environments [6-18]. The Telogy software is representative of H.323 Gateway design and operation.

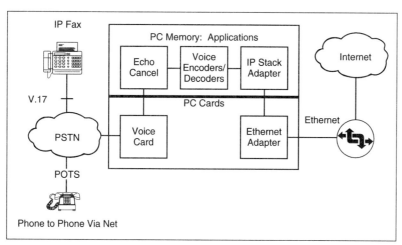

Figure 6-10. IP Telephony Gateway Architecture (Courtesy of Natural Microsystems)

The Telogy software functions can be divided into four general areas: a Voice Packet Module, a Telephony Signaling Module, a Network Protocol Module, and a Network Management Module (Figure 6-11). The Voice Packet Module interacts with the voice signal. It typically runs on a DSP and prepares the voice samples for transmission over the packet network. The Telephony Signaling Module interacts with the telephone network equipment and translates signaling indications (such as on- and off-hook signals) into state changes that can be interpreted by the Network Protocol Module. The Network Protocol Module processes that signaling information and converts it into a format that is compatible with the packet network. Finally, the Network Management Module supports the Simple Network Management Protocol (SNMP), providing management of the operations.

The Voice Packet Module contains a number of functions (Figure 6-12). The Pulse Code Modulation (PCM) interface interacts with the voice samples, and includes a tone generator to generate the Dual Tone Multifrequency (DTMF) tones as necessary. The Echo Canceler is compliant with the ITU-T G.165/G.168 echo cancelation standards, which improve the clarity of the received signal. The Voice Activity Detector monitors the received signal for voice activity. If no activity is detected, the silence is suppressed, yielding additional savings in transport bandwidth. The Tone Detector receives the DTMF tones and reports them to the host system. The Voice Codec software includes algorithms for many of the codecs (discussed above in Section 6.4), which compress the voice signal. A Fax Interface unit is also included; it allows facsimile information to be transmitted and received. The Adaptive Playout Unit provides timing information in both transmit and receive directions, thus controlling packet jitter and packet loss. The Packet Protocol function encapsulates the compressed voice or fax information into a packet for transmission over the network. Finally, the Message Processing Unit controls the exchange of monitoring and control information between this software module and the host equipment that it resides in.

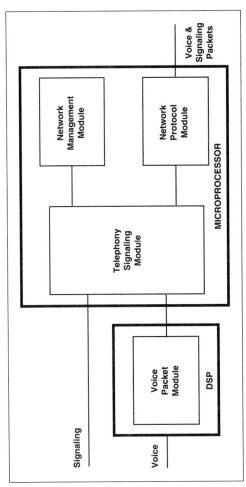

Figure 6-11 VoP Software Architecture
(Courtesy of Telogy Networks, Inc.)

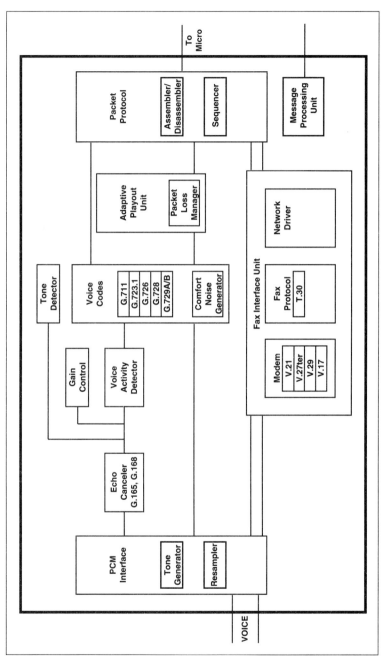

Figure 6-12 Voice Packet Module
(Courtesy of Telogy Networks, Inc.)

The Telephony Signaling Module detects the presence of a new call, and collects the destination address information (via the dialed digits) that will route that call to the intended destination (Figure 6-13). This module's functions include interfaces for various types of channel-associated signaling (CAS) circuits such as Foreign Exchange Station (FXS), Foreign Exchange Office (FXO), Loop Start, Ground Start, Pulse Dialing, and Ear and Mouth (E & M). In addition, various types of common channel signaling (CCS) are supported, including ISDN Primary Rate Interface (PRI) and Basic Rate Interface (BRI) connections, plus other signaling schemes based on the ITU-T Q-series of recommendations (QSG). The Address Translation function maps the telephone or fax number to a number that can be used by the packet network, such as an IP Address, a frame relay Data Link Connection Identifier (DLCI), or an ATM Virtual Path Identifier/Virtual Channel Identifier (VPI/VCI). Also included in this module are control functions for the DSP.

The Network Management Module includes processes that allow the software implementation to be managed effectively. This includes an SNMP Agent, plus Management Information Bases (MIBs) supporting both telephone and network protocol functions.

The Network Protocol Module implements three network options: H.323 for VoIP networks; ATM Adaptation Layers 1, 2, or 5 for Voice Telephony over ATM (VTOA); and the Frame Relay Forum's Voice over Frame Relay (VoFR) Implementation Agreement, specified in the Frame Relay Forum's FRF.11.1 Implementation Agreement (review Reference [5-12]).

Further information on Telogy's software is available in Reference [6-19]. References [6-20] through [6-26] describe and compare various vendors' Gateway implementations.

6.7 Terminal-to-Gateway Communication

As we have studied, terminals support end-user applications, and Gateways provide access to other networks, such as an ISDN or the PSTN. Procedures are defined in H.225.0 that specify the communication between the terminal and the Gateway. These protocols are illustrated in Figure 6-14, with the terminal functions on the left and the Gateway functions on the right. Note that the H.225.0 architecture includes a number of protocols that provide specific communication functions between the terminal and Gateway.

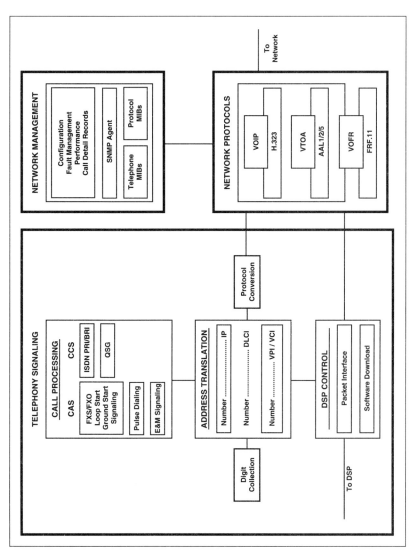

Figure 6-13 Signaling Module
(Courtesy of Telogy Networks, Inc.)

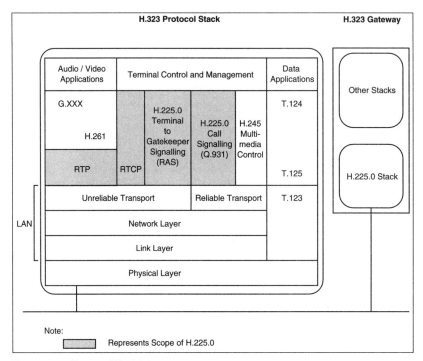

Figure 6-14 Scope of H.225.0
(Source: ITU-T Recommendation H.225.0)

Three types of information streams are shown at the top of the terminal side of the figure: audio and video applications, terminal control and management functions, and data applications. The scope of the H.225.0 is shown in the shaded boxes in the center of the figure. The lower layers (Transport through Physical) illustrate the local network connection and reliability functions.

The Real Time Transport Protocol (RTP) and the Real Time Control Protocol (RTCP), which we studied in Section 4.8, are used to convey and control the audio/video application information. Note that there are two transport options: an unreliable transport and a reliable transport. As we studied in Section 4.7, the User Datagram Protocol (UDP) provides unreliable (or datagram) service, while the Transmission Control Protocol (TCP) provides reliable (or stream-oriented) service. UDP and TCP are two examples of protocols that could be used within the H.225.0 architecture for the unreliable and reliable service, respectively. However, H.225.0 leaves open the option of using other transport protocols, and specifically states that the use of the RTP/RTCP is not specifically tied to the use of IP, UDP, or TCP.

Four control protocols are defined within the H.225.0 architecture for terminal control and management functions. The Real Time Control Protocol (RTCP) provides feedback regarding the quality of the data distribution, identification of the RTP data source, and control of the rate of RTP packet transmission; it conveys minimal session control information. A terminal-to-Gatekeeper signaling protocol, known as the Registration, Admission, and Status (RAS) protocol, is also defined. Note that RTP, RTCP, and RAS run over unreliable transport. The H.225.0 Call Signaling, which was developed from the Q.931 signaling protocol, provides call establishment and call termination functions. The H.245 protocol (which is outside the scope of H.225.0) is a protocol for terminal information messages that control terminal procedures at the start of or during communication. Note that both the signaling and the call control protocols run over reliable transport.

Data applications include support for the ITU-T T.123 (network-specific data protocol stacks for multimedia conferencing), T.124 (generic conference control), and T.125 (multipoint communication service protocol) standards.

6.8 Gatekeepers

A Gatekeeper (GK) manages all activities in a *zone*. A zone, as illustrated in Figure 6-15, is a collection of at least one (or more) terminal(s), Gateways, and multipoint control units that are managed by a single Gatekeeper. From a logical standpoint, the GK is separate from other H.323 entities. From a physical standpoint, however, the GK may coexist with a terminal, GW, MCU, or other device. Thus, the Gatekeeper should be thought of as a *logical function,* instead of as a distinct, physical box.

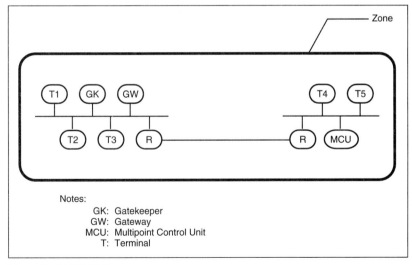

Figure 6–15 H.323 Zone
(Source: ITU–T Recommendation H.225.0)

According to ITU-T H.323, the Gatekeeper is an optional entity in the H.323 environment. From a practical implementation perspective, however, the GK is an essential network element [6-27]. When present in a system, the functions of the GK can be divided into two categories: those services that the GK must perform, and those services that the GK may optionally perform.

When the GK is present in a system, it must perform the following functions:

♦ **Address Translation:** Provides a translation between an alias (such as a name or email address for a Terminal or a Gateway) and a transport address.

♦ **Admissions Control:** Authorizes access to the network based on call authorization, bandwidth availability, or some other manufacturer-specified criteria. Messages specified in ITU-T H.225.0 are used for this purpose.

♦ **Bandwidth Control:** Monitors and controls the network bandwidth, such that the available network bandwidth limits are not exceeded. Messages specified in ITU-T H.225.0 are used for this purpose.

♦ **Zone Management:** Provides the three services noted above for Terminals, Gateways, and Multipoint Control Units that are registered with that Gatekeeper.

Optional functions that the GK may perform include:

♦ **Call Control Signaling:** Where the GK processes the call control signaling with the endpoints.

♦ **Call Authorization:** Where the GK rejects a terminal's call because of an authorization failure, such as access restrictions to a particular terminal or Gateway or access restrictions during a certain time period.

♦ **Bandwidth Management:** Where the GK controls the number of H.323 terminals that are permitted to access the network simultaneously, and rejects access if sufficient bandwidth does not exist.

♦ **Call Management:** Where the GK maintains a list of ongoing H.323 calls, and is able to indicate if a particular called terminal is busy.

♦ **Other Functions:** A GK management information data structure, bandwidth reservation for terminals, and directory services are functions that have been proposed for further study.

These key services provided by Gatekeepers allow functions such as billing for bandwidth-specified services, interoperability between PBX dialing plans and IP-based terminals, and automatic call routing and call distribution features for multimedia call centers. Further details on the services and functions that Gatekeepers provide are given in Reference [6-27].

6.9 Multipoint Control Units

The Multipoint Control Unit (MCU) manages conferences between three or more H.323 terminals and/or Gateways. The MCU may also connect two terminals in a point-to-point configuration initially, and then a multipoint conference developed subsequently. The MCU consists of two parts: a Multipoint Controller (MC), which is mandatory, and Multipoint Processors (MPs), which are optional. For example, a typical MCU may contain one MC and three MPs, each of which would support audio, video, and data traffic.

The MC provides the function of capability negotiation, using the ITU-T H.245 protocol, to ensure that all of the terminals have a common level of communication. The MC may also control resources of the conference, such as the particular terminal that is currently multicasting video. An MC may be located within a terminal, Gateway, Gatekeeper, or the MCU.

The MP provides for the centralized processing of audio, video, and/or data streams of information in a multipoint conference. These processing functions include mixing and switching of that information under the control of the MC. Depending on the type of conference supported, the MP may process single or multiple streams of media.

Four types of multipoint conferences are defined in H.323: centralized multipoint, decentralized multipoint, hybrid multipoint with centralized audio, and hybrid multipoint with centralized video. In the centralized multipoint case, the endpoints communicate with the MC in a point-to-point manner on the H.245 control channel, and with the MP on the audio, video, and data channels. The MC performs the multipoint control functions using H.245, and the MP transmits the resulting information streams back to the communicating endpoints. With the decentralized multipoint capability, the endpoints communicate with the MC in a point-to-point mode, and optionally communicate with the MP on the data channels. The endpoints have the capabilities to multicast their information to all other endpoints in the conference. Figure 6-16 illustrates both the centralized and decentralized cases, which can both be managed by the MCU.

Hybrid multipoint conferences combine the features of the centralized and decentralized cases. With the hybrid multipoint-centralized audio case, the endpoints multicast their video channels to other endpoints on the conference under the control of the MC. The endpoints transmit their audio channels to the MP, which performs audio mixing functions and outputs the resulting audio streams to the various endpoints. In the hybrid multipoint-centralized video case, the endpoints multicast their audio channels to other endpoints on the conference under the control of the MC. The endpoints transmit their video channels to the MP, which performs the video switching, mixing, or format conversion functions, and outputs the resulting video streams to the various endpoints.

Details regarding MCU operation are provided in H.323 and H.245.

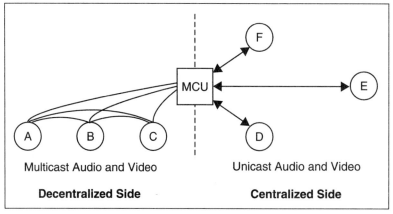

Figure 6-16 Mixed Multipoint Conference
(Source: ITU–T Recommendation H.323)

6.10 Call Processing Examples

In Chapters 4 and 5 we looked at IP-based network infrastructures. We considered the VoIP packet format that included headers from the Internet Protocol (IP), the User Datagram Protocol (UDP), and the Real Time Protocol (RTP) that precede the sample of the voice information (Figure 6-17). The voice information would come from one of the voice encoding algorithms that we considered in Section 6.4. Also recall from that previous discussion that the transport of this voice sample is not very efficient, since at least 40 octets of overhead is required to transmit 20 octets of voice information. As we discussed in Chapter 4, this overhead is required to reliably transmit the real-time voice signal, which is connection oriented, over an IP-based network infrastructure, which is connectionless. In a sense, we are force-fitting an application (voice) onto a network that was designed for data. In order for that voice information to be perceived by a human as if it had been transmitted over a conventional telephone network, we have to pay the price of additional overhead.

In this chapter, we have discussed a number of H.323-defined entities, such as Terminals, Gateways, Gatekeepers, and Multipoint Control Units. We have also considered a number of related protocols, including H.225.0, H.245, and Q.931. But now there is one more element of the big picture that we need to put in place. We need to understand how all of these functions work together to process a VoIP call.

In other words, how do we take a sample of human voice, encode that information and put it into an IP datagram, establish a connection with the end user, and then exchange these IP datagrams with the intended recipient?

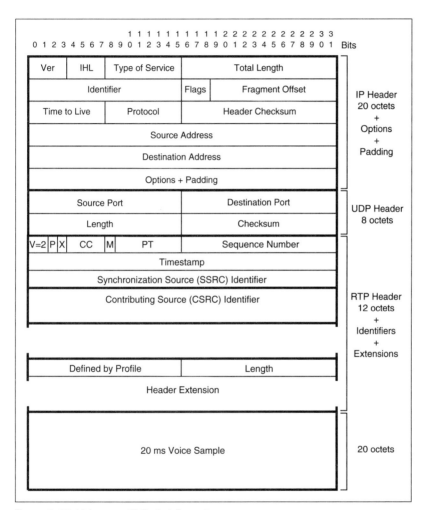

Figure 6-17 Voice over IP Packet Format

To guide us, we will look at three examples, all relating to H.323, but increasing in their complexity, taken from the IMTC Conferencing over IP (CoIP) activity group's Interoperability document [6-1]. To keep the illustrations manageable, we will restrict our discussion to point-to-point calls. Section 8 of H.323 discusses the multipoint case for readers who wish to explore further.

Remember that two endpoints can communicate directly, without the benefit of a Gatekeeper. But since Gatekeepers provide many useful functions, like admission control and bandwidth management, most large network installations include one. Also, recall that Terminals communicate with Gatekeepers using the Registration, Admission, and Status (RAS) channel defined in H.225.0.

In the first example, an H.323 terminal (Bill) wants to contact another H.323 terminal (Bob), as shown in Figure 6-18. Bill sends an Admission Request (an ARQ message, from H.225.0 standard) to the Gatekeeper. The GK responds with an Admission Confirm (ACF) message, which includes the address to be used to contact Bob. In this case, the GK returns Bob's address. It might, however, return the address of a Gateway to be used to access Bob. Thus, in its response, the GK both approves that call (admission to the network) and provides an address to access Bob (address translation) in a single step.

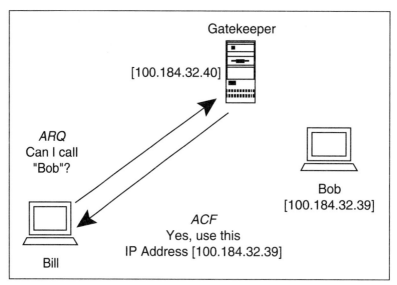

Figure 6-18 H.323 Gatekeeper Messaging
(Source: IMTC Conferencing over IP (CoIP) activity group)

Once the terminals have been admitted to the network, a second step is involved that establishes the call and sets up the communication channels (Figure 6-19). At this point other protocols enter the process: Q.931 manages call establishment, H.245 sets logical channel establishment and negotiates terminal capabilities, and RTP/RTCP conveys the information, or media, between the terminals.

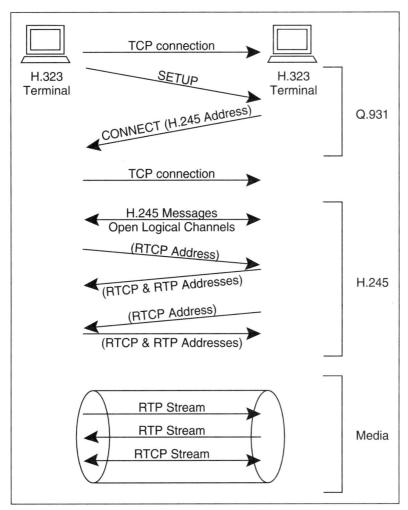

Figure 6-19 H.323 Message Flow
(Source: IMTC Conferencing over IP (CoIP) activity group)

The details of Gatekeeping Protocols are illustrated in Figure 6-20. A description of the various processes, as specified in Appendix D of Reference [6-1], is as follows:

1. Terminal #1 requests permission of the H.323 Gatekeeper to call Terminal #2, and it requests the IP address for Terminal #2 as well. Terminal #1 sends an Admission Request (ARQ), and receives an Admission Confirm (ACF).

2. Terminal #1 initiates the opening of the TCP connection for Q.931. Also, it sends the H.323 Terminal #2 a Q.931 Setup.

3. Upon receiving the Q.931 Setup, Terminal #2 requests permission of the H.323 Gatekeeper to communicate with Terminal #1. It sends an (ARQ) to the Gatekeeper, and receives back an (ACF).

4. Terminal #2 sends a Q.931 Connect back to Terminal #1. Inside of the Q.931 Connect is the H.245 TCP port address that the Terminal #2 wishes to use.

5. Terminal #1 initiates the opening of the H.245 TCP connection between itself and Terminal #2.

6. Terminal #1 and Terminal #2 exchange H.245 Terminal Capabilities.

7. Sometime before Audio channels are opened, Terminal #1 and Terminal #2 use H.245 Master Slave Determination messages to determine who is the master and who is the slave.

8. Terminal #1 sends an H.245 Open Logical Channel requesting that an audio channel be opened. Inside of the H.245 Open Logical Channel are the characteristics of the channel, as well as the UDP port that it wishes to receive the RTCP receiver reports on.

9. Terminal #2 sends an H.245 Open Logical Channel Ack and indicates the UDP ports that it wishes to use for the RTP audio stream as well as the RTCP sender reports.

10. Terminal #2 sends an H.245 Open Logical Channel requesting that an audio channel be opened. Inside of the H.245 Open Logical Channel are the characteristics of the channel, as well as the UDP port that it wishes to receive the RTCP receiver reports on.

11. Terminal #1 sends an H.245 Open Logical Channel Ack and indicates the UDP ports that it wishes to use for the RTP audio stream as well as RTCP sender reports.

12. Audio flows between the two terminals.

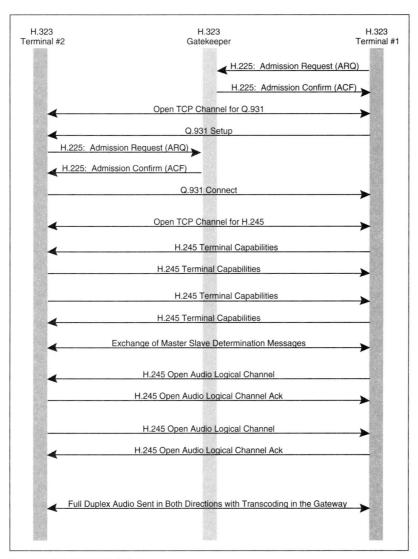

Figure 6-20 H.323 Call Setup
(Source: IMTC Conferencing over IP (CoIP) activity group)

6.11 Looking Ahead

In this chapter, we considered the customer premises equipment that comprises a converged network, such as client terminals, Gateways, Gatekeepers, and so on. In many cases, these elements are embedded into existing systems, such as PBXs, as References [6-28] through [6-30] describe. For implementers, however, key questions remain: how will all of these new elements integrate into the existing network, and are there any design constraints that should be considered? These questions will be discussed in Chapter 7.

6.12 References

[6-1]   Voice over IP Forum. "IMTC Voice over IP Forum Service
            Interoperability Implementation Agreement 1," December 1997.
            Available from ftp://ftp.imtc-files.org/imtc-site/
            VoIPAG/incoming/VIPIA1.doc.

[6-2]   International Telecommunications Union – Telecommunications
            Standardization Sector. Packet-based Multimedia Communication
            Systems. ITU-T H.323, 1998.

[6-3]   International Telecommunications Union – Telecommunications
            Standardization Sector. Control Protocol for Multimedia
            Communication. ITU-T H.245, 1996.

[6-4]   International Telecommunications Union – Telecommunications
            Standardization Sector. Digital Subscriber Signaling System No.
            1 (DSS 1) – ISDN User-Network Interface Layer 3 Specification
            for Basic Call Control. ITU-T Q.931, 1993.

[6-5]   International Telecommunications Union – Telecommunications
            Standardization Sector. Call Signaling Protocols and Media
            Stream Packetization for Packet-based Multimedia
            Communication Systems. ITU-T H.225.0, 1998.

[6-6]   Thom, Gary A. "H.323: The Multimedia Communications
            Standard for Local Area Networks." *IEEE Communications*
            (December 1996): 52–56.

[6-7]   DataBeam Corporation. *A Primer on the H.323 Series Standard.*
            March 1997. Available from http://www.databeam.com/.

[6-8]   Wallman, Roger. "The Case for H.323 in Video Conferencing."
            Internet Telephony (June 1999): 78–79.

[6-9]   Brown, Dave. "Videoconferencing 2000: H.323's Year?" *Network Computing* (September 6, 1999): 79–94.

[6-10]   Krapf, Eric. "DSPs – Powering the Packet-Voice Revolution." *Business Communication Review Voice 2000 Supplement* (October 1998): 2–9.

[6-11]   Eyre, Jennifer, and Jeff Bier. "DSPs Court the Consumer." *IEEE Spectrum* (March 1999): 47–53.

[6-12]   Cox, Richard V. "Three New Speech Coders from the ITU Cover a Range of Applications." *IEEE Communications* (September 1997): 40–47.

[6-13]   Henderson, Khali. "Building A Good Fit." *Sounding Board* (August 15, 1999): 34–38.

[6-14]   IEEE Communication Society. *G.723.1 Tutorial.* Available from http://www.comsoc.org.mx/std_7231.htm.

[6-15]   Rijkse, Karel. "H.263: Video Coding for Low-Bit-Rate Communication." *IEEE Communications* (December 1996): 42–45.

[6-16]   D'Hooge, Herman. "The Communicating PC." *IEEE Communications* (April 1996): 36–42.

[6-17]   Natural Microsystems. "IP Telephony: Powered by Fusion," 1997. Available at http://www.nmss.com.

[6-18]   Telogy Networks, Inc. "Voice over Packet White Paper," 1997. Available from http://www.telogy.com.

[6-19]   Additional information on Telogy Networks, Inc.'s products is available at http://www.telogy.com.

[6-20]   Keating, Tom. "Extending the PSTN: Voice Over IP Gateways." *CTI* (February 1998): 114–118.

[6-21]   Shapiro, Jeffrey. "Buyer's Guide: Voice over IP Gateways." *Network World* (June 29, 1998): 67–75.

[6-22]   Carlino, Peter. "Carrier-Grade Voice over IP Gateways: Meeting the Needs of the Public Networks." *Internet Telephony* (September 1998): 64–69.

[6-23]   Greenstreet, Debbie. "Next-Generation Integrated VoIP Gateways Development – Issues." *Internet Telephony* (September 1998): 66–68.

[6-24]   Cray, Andrew. "Voice Over IP Gateway Three for IP." *Data Communications* (January 1999): 60.

[6-25]   Rizzetto, Daniele, and Claudio Catania. "A Voice over IP Service Architecture for Integrated Communications." *IEEE Network* (May/June 1999): 34–40.

[6-26]   Newman, David. "VoIP Gateways: Voice Doubts?" *Data Communications* (September 1999): 71–78.

[6-27]   RADVision, Inc. *H.323 Handbook Library Volume I: H.323 Gatekeepers*. Available from http://www.radvision.com.

[6-28]   Burton, Jim, Dave Robertson, Brian Allain, Steve Mullaney, and Kurt Jacobs. "Next Generation PBXs from the Incumbents and Their Challengers." *Networld+Interop 1999* CommUnity Conference Notes (May 1999).

[6-29]   Jessup, Toby. "Porting the PBX." *Data Communications* (July 1999): 72–76.

[6-30]   Machi, Jim. "An IP-PBX and CT Server Enable Smooth Internet Telephony Transitions." *Internet Telephony* (August 1999): 76–78.

Chapter 7

Implementing the Converged Network

Time for a review. We have studied converged network applications, infrastructures, WAN transport options, and premises equipment. We have also examined the business aspects of the converged network, assuming that someone will be asking for a cost benefit analysis of the proposal. So now that you've done your homework, and have a grasp of all the technical and financial issues, you are ready to begin installing your converged network.

In this concluding chapter, we will turn our attention to the steps required to begin the implementation phase of a converged network. But before we can get to that point, there are some additional technical issues to be considered, which transcend the topics of applications, local and wide area networks, protocols, and systems that have been addressed in previous chapters. These include the topics of interoperability between converged networks and other systems, alternative protocols to the very popular H.323 that may be incorporated into some vendor's products, Application Programming Interfaces (APIs) that may be included in systems for the benefit of software developers, and Quality of Service (QoS) factors that affect the satisfaction of the end users of these networks. We will begin by looking at one of the biggest challenges facing network managers, the interoperability between various network components, and then we'll move on to examine a number of other implementation-related topics.

7.1 Interoperability Frameworks

Interoperability is one of those terms with a fairly simple meaning, but widespread implications. If we look at the root terms, we see *inter* (between) *operate* (to perform a function). So in other words, *interoperability* defines whether or not two systems work with each other.

With communication networks, interoperability can take on several dimensions: connectivity or configuration, functionality, and performance. For example, will a gateway from Vendor A work with a gateway from Vendor B? Perhaps more importantly, what about the interoperability between legacy network equipment and the new converged network equipment? Or, put another way, will a gateway from Vendor A work with your PBX from Vendor B?

Fortunately, the consortia concerned with network convergence are addressing these challenges head on. The International Multimedia Teleconferencing Consortium (IMTC) [7-1] has sponsored much research into the issue of interoperability. The results of this research, two new interoperability frameworks, will be the focus of the following sections.

7.1.1 The IMTC Conferencing over IP (CoIP) activity group's Service Interoperability Implementation Agreement

The IMTC Conferencing over IP (CoIP) activity group, affiliated with the IMTC, developed their Service Interoperability Implementation Agreement so that it "combines, clarifies and complements existing standards to provide a complete Internet telephony interoperability protocol." The Implementation Agreement (IA) is based on H.323 and related standards, but it is not intended to replace H.323. Instead, it makes the jobs of the hardware and software developers charged with implementation easier, as it removes some of the inherent ambiguities in all data networking standards.

Thus, by reaching some consensus regarding the interpretation of various elements defined in H.323 prior to product development, the likelihood of vendor-specific interpretations, which could lead to implementations that will not interoperate, is (hopefully) reduced. One could draw an analogy from an old riddle: if you put ten engineers in a room, and ask them to read and interpret the same document, how many unique interpretations will you get? The IA is designed to simplify the answer to this question: only one interpretation.

One of the most significant parts of the Interoperability Profile is a recommended protocol stack to be included in each product implementation (Figure 7-1). As we have studied in Chapters 4, 5, and 6, multimedia networks encompass many protocol layers ranging from Physical Layer infrastructures to specific applications. For many of these layers, several protocols can be chosen. For example, there are a number of voice encoding algorithms, including ITU G.711, G.723.1, G.728, G.729, and others. If one vendor chooses one algorithm (such as G.723.1) and a second vendor chooses another (such as G.728), these two devices will not communicate. They may be able to exchange bits, but there will be no meaningful communication. With choices like this at every level of the protocol stack, the chances that a given vendor's product will operate with any other vendor's product rapidly diminish.

The VoIP Protocol Stack presents specific guidelines organized by functional layer that, if followed, will increase interoperability. Starting at the top of the stack, the Call Establishment and Control function determines the connection setup and disconnect procedures, and controls the H.323 session after it's been established. The Presentation function interprets the audio signal and any other audible control information, such as the comfort noise (the background white noise that assures us that the telephone connection is still active) and the Dual Tone Multi-frequency (DTMF) signals, or touchtones, that are used for end-user signaling functions. For example, you may use DTMF signals to enter a password to retrieve your voicemail, to navigate your way through an interactive voice response (IVR) system, such as a bank's automated teller system, and so on. The IA specifies two different audio codecs to be used with the Presentation Layer and DTMF: the G.711 codec (64 Kbps) and the G.723.1 codec (5.3 or 6.4 Kbps).

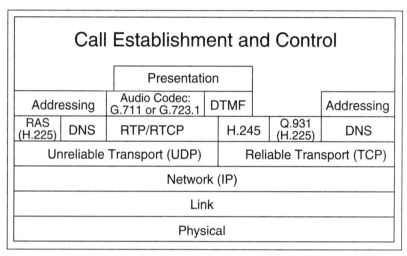

Figure 7-1 The VoIP Protocol Stack
(Courtesy of the IMTC)

The addressing function deals with two issues. First, H.323 terminals may need to locate other terminals by using an H.323 Gatekeeper and the Registration, Admission, and Status (RAS) protocol. Second, an H.323 endpoint may need to initially locate an H.323 Gatekeeper using the Domain Name System, or DNS. Recall that DNS provides a method of associating domain names with IP addresses. Since DNS can operate over both unreliable and reliable transports, it is shown twice in the VoIP Protocol Stack. The Real Time Transport Protocol (RTP) and the Real Time Control Protocol (RTCP) provide control over the digitally encoded analog signals. Recall that both RTP and RTCP are IETF standards, but they are also adopted in the ITU-T H.225.0 recommendation. The H.245 protocol defines control procedures for multimedia communication, such as terminal-to-terminal parameter negotiation messages. Signaling messages, defined in ITU-T Q.931, are also an element of H.225.0. The Q.931 signaling protocol is used with many connection-oriented networks, including ISDN and frame relay. A version of Q.931, known as Q.2931, defines ATM signaling procedures.

Two different transport protocols are specified in the IA. For unreliable transport (connectionless functions) including RAS, DNS, and audio information transfer, the User Datagram Protocol (UDP) is specified. For reliable (connection-oriented functions), including terminal parameter negotiation, call signaling, and DNS, the Transmission Control Protocol (TCP) is specified. For both of these cases, the Internet Protocol (IP) is employed at the Network Layer, with the Data Link and Physical Layers left as implementation-independent options.

For those readers wanting to dig deeper, protocol-specific details are described in the IA [7-2].

7.1.2 The iNOW! Standards-Based IP Telephony Interoperability Profile

The Interoperability NOW! (iNOW!) efforts, which are also affiliated with the IMTC, are an extension of the IMTC Conferencing over IP (CoIP) activity group's Service Interoperability IA research. The IMTC iNOW! Activity Group was formed to serve the needs of both equipment vendors and service providers interested in developing interoperable solutions. ITXC, an Internet Service Provider, spearheaded the formation of the group in 1998 to ensure the interoperability of two of its gateway suppliers, Lucent and VocalTec. After some initial research and development, the partnership demonstrated its interoperabilty solutions at trade shows, generating interest among other equipment vendors. Presently, a number of equipment manufacturers, carriers, embedded systems developers, and independent testing laboratories have joined iNOW!.

A significant result of this effort is the iNOW! Standards-based IP Telephony Interoperability Profile, version 2 [7-3]. Five key interoperability issues are addressed in this document:

◆ Gateway-to-Gateway interoperability (Manufacturer A to/from Manufacturer B)

◆ Gatekeeper-to-Gatekeeper interoperability (Manufacturer A to/from Manufacturer B)

◆ Gatekeeper-to-exchange carrier interoperability (Manufacturer A and Manufacturer B to/from exchange carrier)

◆ Phone-to-phone service

◆ Fax-to-fax service

The Interoperability Profile extends the work of the IMTC Conferencing over IP (CoIP) activity group's Implementation Agreement with a specific set of interoperability requirements. These include support for the G.729A (preferred) and G.723.1 (secondary) codecs, as well as support for the T.38 fax protocol. Support for other standards, such as the IETF TCP/IP and UDP/IP protocols, plus the ITU-T V.21, V.27ter, V.29, and V.17 standards, is also required.

Reference [7-3] describes the iNOW! objectives and conclusions in greater detail. Reference [7-4] considers interoperability issues surrounding Gatekeeper design and implementation.

7.2 Alternatives to H.323

While the ITU-T H.323 standard has received widespread support within the networking and telephony industries, two other multimedia frameworks, both supported by the IETF, are in various stages of deployment and are worth mentioning. These are the Session Initiation Protocol (SIP) and the Media Gateway Control Protocol (MGCP). Support for these architectures may be found in various vendors' networking products, and may be a factor in the implementation of a converged network.

7.2.1 Session Initiation Protocol

The Session Initiation Protocol is a signaling protocol used to create, modify, and terminate sessions between one or more participants. These communication sessions may include Internet telephone calls, multimedia conferences, distance learning, and other multimedia distribution. Session members may communicate using either unicast or multicast operations, or some combination of both. SIP may invite both persons and robots, such as media storage devices, to participate in sessions.

SIP is part of the IETF multimedia data and control architecture, which includes protocols such as RTP/RTCP, RSVP, SAP, and SDP (review Section 4.8). SIP supports five different facets of multimedia communication: user location, user capabilities, user availability, call setup, and call handling. With SIP, the operation of these five integrated functions is not as complex as the ITU-T H.323 standard, since H.323 also employs other protocols, such as RTP/RTCP (data transport), H.225.0 and Q.931 (call signaling and call setup), and H.245 (terminal format negotiation), for specific protocol operations. To simplify the multimedia communications process, SIP is designed with a client/server architecture using text-based messages, similar to the Hypertext Transfer Protocol (HTTP).

The SIP message set is not as complex as with H.323, and has a minimal set of fundamental messages: INVITE, ACK, OPTIONS, BYE, CANCEL, and REGISTER. The INVITE indicates that the user or service is being invited to participate in a session. The ACK confirms that the client has received a final response to an INVITE request. The OPTIONS is used to query the server as to its capabilities. The BYE is an indication from the client to the server that it wishes to release the call. The CANCEL request cancels a pending request. The REGISTER is used by the client to register an address with a server. All clients must be able to generate the INVITE and ACK requests. All servers must understand the INVITE, ACK, OPTIONS, and BYE requests, and proxy servers must understand the CANCEL request.

Further details on SIP are found in RFC 2543 [7-5] and also in References [7-6] through [7-9].

7.2.2 Media Gateway Control Protocol

The Media Gateway Control Protocol (MGCP) is designed as a simple mechanism to control gateways. Other signaling protocols, such as H.323 and SIP, may be used in conjunction with MGCP for connection establishment, disconnects, and so on. The function of MGCP is to control the gateway, while relying on external call control intelligence for more complex functions. Examples of gateways that could be controlled with MGCP include: trunking gateways that are managing a large number of digital circuits; voice over ATM gateways; residential gateways, such as cable modem, xDSL, and broadband wireless devices; PBX-based gateways; and others. With the MGCP model, the gateways focus on the audio signal translation functions while a Call Agent, external to the gateway, handles the signaling and call processing functions. By separating out the internal gateway functions from the external signaling functions, the implementation, upgrade, and maintenance of gateways is simplified, increasing the likelihood of widespread use of these technologies.

MGCP is an IETF initiative based on work combined from two other protocol developments: the Simple Gateway Control Protocol (SGCP) and the Internet Protocol Device Control (IPDC). Much of this early work was done at Telcordia Technologies (formerly Bell Communications Research, or Bellcore) and Level 3 Communications. Further details on MGCP are found in Reference [7-10]. Current work on MGCP is under the sponsorship of the IETF Media Gateway Control (MEGACO) Working Group [7-11].

7.3 Application Programming Interfaces

The interoperability frameworks and protocols, which we studied in the previous sections, primarily deal with the networking infrastructure. In order for an application, such as a voice call between two multimedia workstations, to function, there must be some mechanism for that application to access the networking infrastructure. This is known as the Application Programming Interface, or API. A number of APIs have been proposed within the computer-telephony industry in the past few years, with two of these being widely supported within the industry: Microsoft's Telephony API version 3.0 (TAPI 3.0) and Sun Microsystems' Java Telephony API (JTAPI), as discussed in Reference [7-12]. We will briefly explore these APIs in the following sections.

7.3.1 Microsoft TAPI 3.0

The convergence of the telephony and computing worlds implies that the functions of the desktop appliances, such as telephones and personal computers, will also converge. As a result, a telephony interface is necessary that enables applications to access the telephony options that are available on a computer. Microsoft Corporation's TAPI 3.0 is designed to provide methods for establishing connections between two or more computers and accessing any data streams that flow between those devices. In addition to supporting standard telephone functions, TAPI 3.0 supports both IP multicast and H.323 conferencing, makes use of the Windows 2000 Active Directory service, and also supports various quality of service (QoS) features.

The TAPI 3.0 architecture is illustrated in Figure 7-2, and consists of four major components. The TAPI 3.0 COM API provides access to call, media control, and directory functions. The TAPI Server may connect with a number of functions across the Telephony Provider Interface, including access to PSTN, ATM, and ISDN networks. The Telephony Service Providers (TSPs) resolve the protocol-independent call model of TAPI into a protocol-specific call control model. Two key TSPs ship with TAPI 3.0: the H.323 TSP, and the IP Multicast Conferencing TSP. Finally, the Media Stream Providers allow the telephony service to access data streaming functions.

TAPI 3.0 is a key element in Microsoft's networking architecture, and has been widely documented. References [7-13] and [7-14] are examples of white papers and journal articles that discuss TAPI architecture and applications.

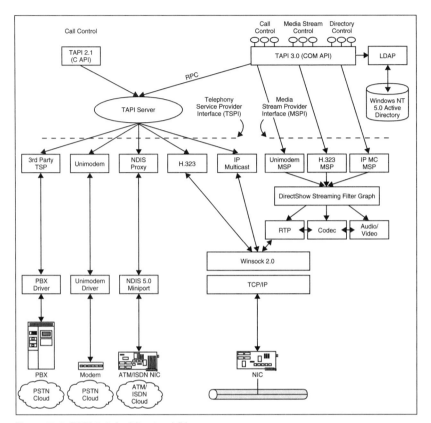

Figure 7-2 TAPI 3.0 Architectural Diagram
(Courtesy of Microsoft Corporation)

7.4 Quality of Service

ITU-T Recommendation E.800 [7-18] defines Quality of Service (QoS) as follows:

> *"The collective effect of service performance, which determines the degree of satisfaction of a user of the service."*

In other words, QoS will be significantly influenced by the end users and their perceptions of how well one network service performs in comparison with other network services. Almost everyone has experience with telephone calls over the PSTN and knows what level of quality to expect from that network. Therefore, one of the significant challenges that must be addressed is ensuring that the QoS the end user experiences with the converged network is on par with their previous experience with the PSTN.

Multimedia applications, such as voice and video, are connection-oriented. In contrast, IP-based internetworks are connectionless. Thus, one would expect some difficulties when transmitting voice or video signals over a network that was not originally designed for that application. As we discussed in Chapter 4, the use of the Real Time Transport Protocol (RTP) and the User Datagram Protocol (UDP) provide some error and sequence control functions that IP lacks. However, other factors inherent in packet data transmission can affect the QoS that the end user perceives. And since the satisfaction of that community of end users may significantly impact the career of the network manager, a discussion of these factors is in order. But first, we should discuss the measurement of QoS.

7.4.1 Measuring Quality of Service

For many years, the telephone industry has employed a very subjective rating system, known as the Mean Opinion Score, or MOS, to measure the quality of telephone connections. These measurement techniques are defined in ITU-T P.800 [7-19], and are based on the opinions of many testing volunteers who listen to a sample of voice traffic and rate the quality of that transmission. In doing so, they consider a number of factors that could degrade the quality of transmission, including loss, circuit noise, sidetone, talker echo, distortion, propagation time (or delay), and other transmission problems.

The most well known test, described in Annex A of P.800, is called the Conversation Opinion Test. The volunteer subjects are asked to provide their opinion of the connection they have just been using, based on a five point scale:

Quality	Rating
Excellent	5
Good	4
Fair	3
Poor	2
Bad	1

Since the test subjects are human, some variation in the scores is expected. For that reason, a large number of people are used in the test, and their individual scores are averaged (hence the term "Mean" in Mean Opinion Score). A MOS of 4 is considered "toll quality" within the telephone industry.

Other tests are also defined in P.800. The listening test rates the ability of the tester to understand speech over the connection. The noise, fading, and disturbances test rates these problems from inaudible to intolerable. The comparison category rating compares a nonprocessed speech sample with a processed speech sample with ratings from "much better" to "much worse."

Readers needing further information can also consult a companion standard, P.861, that defines quality measurements for speech codecs [7-20].

7.4.2 Factors Affecting the Quality of Service

In an ideal environment, voice and fax over IP signals move through seven steps in their journey from source to destination via the IP-based infrastructure (see Figure 7-3 and Reference [7-18]). These seven steps include:

1. Conversion of the analog signal into a digital signal at the Central Office, PBX, or Gateway.

2. Communication to a Gateway, which may further process the signal by compressing the data, suppressing silence on the circuit, and canceling echos.

3. The Gateway may communicate with one or more Gatekeepers for admission to the network, translation of telephone numbers to IP addresses, and other management-related functions.

4. The processed signal will then be placed into IP datagrams and transmitted over the IP-based network.

5. At the receiving end, the IP datagrams will be converted back into a digital bit stream at the destination Gateway.

6. The digital bit stream is decompressed and sent to a receiving Central Office or PBX.

7. The digital signals are converted into an analog signal and sent to the intended recipient.

In an ideal case, where transmission bandwidth is either plentiful or has been reserved using some mechanism such as the Resource Reservation Protocol (RSVP), this packet-based (connectionless) transmission proceeds as if it were a connection-oriented network operation (Figure 7-4). (Packet delay, which is present even under the most ideal conditions, will have a small but measurable effect on the MOS.)

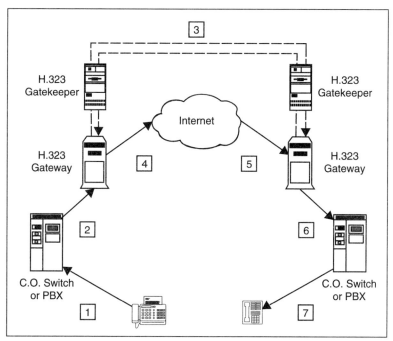

Figure 7-3 Voice and Fax over IP Call Processing
(Courtesy of U.S. Bancorp Piper Jaffray)

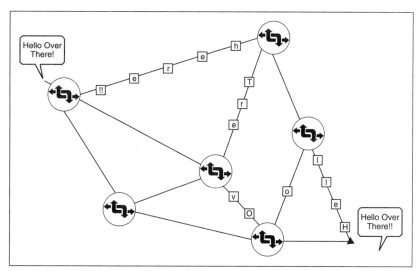

Figure 7-4 IP Telephony Transmission (with RSVP)
(Courtesy of U.S. Bancorp Piper Jaffray)

Unfortunately, not all packet transmission follows the ideal model. Some packets may be lost due to difficulties in the routing infrastructure, collisions on the local Ethernet, transmission impairments such as noisy lines, and so on. The result is a received message that is missing some of its components (Figure 7-5).

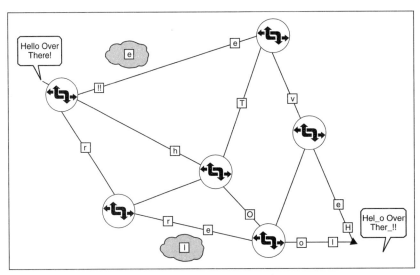

Figure 7-5 IP Telephony Transmission (with Packet Loss)
(Courtesy of U.S. Bancorp Piper Jaffray)

Delay, or latency, can also affect the quality of the transmission (Figure 7-6). The delay is the difference in time between when the signal is transmitted and when it is received. Delay is typically characterized by two components: a fixed delay and a variable delay. The fixed delays are found within the signal processing elements, such as the processing delays inherent in the voice codecs, and also within the physical transmission systems, such as the copper pairs. The variable delays result from queuing times at packet processing points, such as switches and routers, as well as transmission variables, such as the specific route that a particular packet took and any difficulties, such as congestion, that might be experienced on that route. Some of these delays can be controlled by the network manager with thoughtful network engineering decisions. For example, voice gateways containing codecs with lower processing delays could be selected, or additional bandwidth could be provisioned on the wide area network to lower the likelihood of network congestion. There are delay elements that cannot be optimized, such as the physical propagation delay. Electromagnetic signals propagate at approximately 1 nanosecond per foot on copper transmission facilities — a principle of physics that must be dealt with.

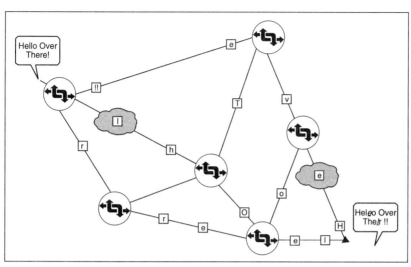

Figure 7-6 IP Telephony Transmission (with Packet Delay)
(Courtesy of U.S. Bancorp Piper Jaffray)

Packet jitter is the variation in arrival rates between individual packets (Figure 7-7). With packet networks, it is possible that a sequence of packets that enter the network at a constant rate will reach the intended destination by a number of routes. Since each of these routes may have unique delay characteristics, it is possible for the arrival rates of the packets to vary. For non-real-time signals, such as an email transmission, this signal would not be an issue. However, for real-time signals such as voice, which are dependent upon a continuous flow of data, jitter affects the signal quality. To correct for jitter, the packets are buffered, or delayed, at the receiver, and then played out at a continuous rate. Unfortunately, this buffering adds to the overall latency of the packet transmission.

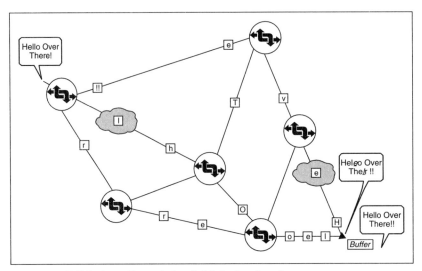

Figure 7-7 IP Telephony Transmission (with Packet Jitter)
(Courtesy of U.S. Bancorp Piper Jaffray)

7.4.3 Signal Echo and Echo Cancellation

The block diagram of a typical full-duplex hardware implementation is shown in Figure 7-8. Both the transmitter and the receiver have connections from the telephone sets to a transformer called a *hybrid*. The hybrid performs 2-wire to 4-wire conversions, such that the connection from the central office to your premises (2-wire) can be divided into both transmit and receive paths (total of 4 wires). Most transformers have some degree of inefficiency; in other words, they do not pass all of the energy that is applied to their primary winding onto the secondary winding(s). Some of that energy is reflected back to the source. That reflected energy is called an *echo*. The Echo Canceller subtracts (or cancels) out the energy that was reflected from the distant end of the connection prior to delivering that signal to the other client processes, such as the speech encoding, packet transmission, and other functions.

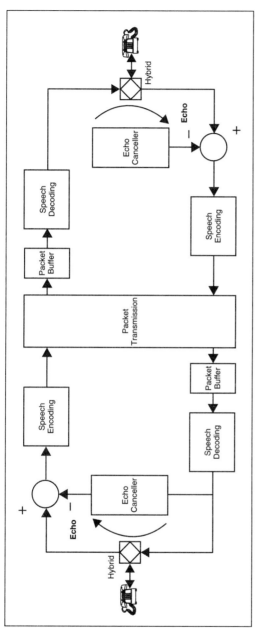

Figure 7-8 Full-duplex Hardware Implementation
(Courtesy of the IMTC)

7.4.4 Sources of Network Delays

Three of the above transmission impairments – packet loss, packet delay, and packet jitter – impact the quality of the received signal. Since a common theme among all three of these issues is delay, or latency, this component is worthy of further exploration.

There are a number of factors that affect the application performance, as perceived by the end users. Perhaps the most significant of these is the end-to-end delay. The maximum recommended one-way delay for most user applications, as specified in ITU-T G.114, is 150 milliseconds, or a round-trip delay of 300 milliseconds [7-19]. However, since voice quality is a very subjective measurement, some end users find variations above and below these standard specifications to be acceptable; therefore, round-trip objectives between 200–400 milliseconds are often quoted.

Reviewing Figure 7-8, note that the delays from a client implementation can come from several sources. The speech encoder incurs delays based on the algorithm used [7-20]. This encoding delay may consist of two components: a processing delay necessary to run the algorithm on the current frame of voice information, and a lookahead delay that occurs while the algorithm is looking at the next frame for correlation purposes. For example, the G.723.1 algorithm (which operates at 5.3 or 6.4 Kbps) has a processing delay of 30 milliseconds and a lookahead delay of 7.5 milliseconds, for a total coding delay of 37.5 milliseconds. In contrast, the G.729 and G.729A algorithms (which operate at 8 Kbps) have a processing delay of 10 milliseconds and a lookahead delay of 5 milliseconds, for a total coding delay of 15 milliseconds. Note the tradeoff between bit rate and coding delay – the lowest bit rate coder (G.723.1) also has a higher coding delay (37.5 milliseconds). Thus, when selecting VoIP equipment such as gateways, it behooves the network manager to ask the vendor which algorithms are available and the delays that result from each one.

Other delays include switching, routing, and other packet processing delays (typically a few milliseconds); transmission delays (dependent on the speed of the transmission link, and typically less than 10 milliseconds); signal propagation delays (dependent on the physical length of transmission link); jitter buffer delays (typically a settable parameter between 20–40 milliseconds); and decoding delays (typically half of the encoding delay, as noted in Reference [7-20]).

An example of end-to-end network delay measurements, based on a study performed at Bell Atlantic [7-21], is illustrated in Figure 7-9 and Figure 7-10. Note that the round trip, end-to-end delay for a PC-telephone call is comprised of six delay components: the telephone client, the PSTN, the Gateway, the IP network, the dialup access network (PSTN and modems), and the PC Client. The delay objective for business customers was assumed to be 100 milliseconds (round-trip) and the delay objective for consumers was 300 milliseconds (also round-trip). Delay objectives are then allocated across the six network components. Neither the Telephone Client nor the PSTN (on the left side of Figure 7-9) contribute a significant amount of delay. The column titled "Today" represents the results of Bell Atlantic testing. Note that these actual values are substantially higher than the theoretical figures. Also note that the PC Client and the Gateway have theoretical minimum values of 67.5 milliseconds, as it is assumed that two frames (at 30 milliseconds per frame of encoding delay, plus 7.5 milliseconds of lookahead delay) are encoded in each IP datagram. This is done to conserve some additional bandwidth. Recall from our discussion in Chapter 4 that the IP, UDP, and RTP headers add 40 octets of overhead to each IP datagram. By putting two voice frames inside each IP datagram, the expense of this overhead is somewhat mitigated.

Significant amounts of the total delays come from the Access portion (which includes modem delays), the PC Client, and the Gateway. Reducing these two components through advances in their respective technologies will improve the overall delay characteristics of VoIP networks.

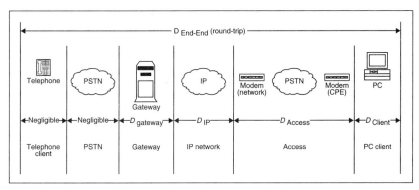

Figure 7-9 Sources of Network Delay
(Source: *IEEE Network*, May/June 1999)

Cisco Systems, Inc.'s *Voice over IP Design Implementation Guide* [7-22] presents additional examples of network delay calculations and discusses configuration options for their premises equipment. References [7-23] and [7-24] also discuss QoS issues from various perspectives.

Delay component	Consumer (objective)	Business (objective)	Today (actual)	Theoretical minimum	Milliseconds above minimum
PC client (D $_{Client}$)	100 milliseconds	30 milliseconds	150 milliseconds	67.5 milliseconds	82.5 milliseconds
Access (D $_{Access}$)	70 milliseconds	10 milliseconds	150 milliseconds	44 milliseconds	106 milliseconds
IP network (D $_{IP}$)	50 milliseconds	30 milliseconds	96 milliseconds	40 milliseconds	56 milliseconds
Gateway POP (D $_{Gateway}$)	80 milliseconds	30 milliseconds	160 milliseconds	67.5 milliseconds	92.5 milliseconds
PSTN/phone (D $_{Client}$)	Negligible	Negligible	Negligible	Negligible	0
Total	300 milliseconds	100 milliseconds	556 milliseconds	159 milliseconds	337 milliseconds

Notes:

1. The consumer objective is intended to be at the upper bound of acceptable. The businesss objective is intended to match PSTN performance.

2. Today figures for PC client, access, and gateway point of presence (POP) are from internal Bell Atlantic testing. The IP network figure was developed from: Clear Ink, Internet Weather Report, http://www.internetweather.com

3. Theoretical minimum figures assume G.723 6.3 Kbps encoding at 2 frames/IP packet, algorithmic delay only. The access figure further assumes 33.6 Kbps modem connection. The IP network figure further assumes U.S. coast-coast transport at the speed of light in metal (~150,0000 Kilometers/second).

Figure 7-10 VoIP Round-trip Delay Allocation and Current Performance in Milliseconds (Source: IEEE Network, May/June 1999)

7.5 Implementing Quality of Service

Having discussed the various factors that affect QoS, such as latency within the network, packet delays and loss, and so on, the next question that must be addressed is the industry response – what steps are being taken to improve QoS within IP-based internetworks?

The traditional solution to improving service performance – throwing more bandwidth at the problem – can be expensive, especially on the WAN side of the equation. As a result, net managers are looking for ways to optimize the performance of their network infrastructures. A number of alternatives have been proposed, but at the time of this writing there is not sufficient industry experience with any one of these alternatives to declare it the leading solution. This section presents a summary of the various proposals, along with sources for additional research.

7.5.1 Integrated Services

Integrated Services (int-serv) is a model developed by the IETF and characterized by the reservation of network resources prior to the transmission of any data. The Resource Reservation Protocol (RSVP), which is defined in RFC 2205 and discussed in Section 4.8, is the signaling protocol that is used to reserve the bandwidth on that transmission path. An end station that supports RSVP may request a particular level of network performance from the network, and at each downstream node the protocol attempts to reserve network resources on behalf of that end station. RSVP is designed to operate in conjunction with current routing protocols, such as the Open Shortest Path First (OSPF) and Border Gateway Protocols (BGP), and relies on these other protocols to determine where reservation requests should be sent. The int-serv model is implemented by four components: the Signaling Protocol (RSVP), an Admission Control Routine (which determines if network resources are available), a Classifier (which puts packets in specific queues), and a Packet Scheduler (which schedules packets to meet QoS Requirements). Details regarding int-serv are found in RFC 1633 [7-25].

7.5.2 Differentiated Services

Differentiated Services (diff-serv) was also developed by the IETF and it distinguishes packets that require different network services into different classes. In effect, diff-serv provides a relative priority scheme, whereby the packets are handled differently based on the values of an 8-bit Differentiated Services (DS) field. That DS field replaces the IPv4 Type of Service (TOS) field or the IPv6 Traffic Class field (these fields are fortunately also 8 bits in length). Packets are classified at the network ingress node according to some Service Level Agreement (SLA) criteria established between the Internet Service Provider (ISP) and the customer. It is assumed that the ISP would offer different levels of service, and also different cost structures, for the various options defined by the DS field. Details regarding diff-serv are found in RFC 2474 [7-26].

7.5.3 Multiprotocol Label Switching

Multiprotocol Label Switching (MPLS) is a forwarding scheme that was based on tag switching mechanisms developed by router vendors over the past few years. With MPLS, a 32-bit header (sometimes called the "tag") is placed between the local network and IP headers of the packet when it enters the MPLS domain. This header determines how that packet will be handled by the intervening routers. Because these routers must be able to interpret and act upon this new label, the MPLS-capable routers are called Label Switching Routers, or LSRs. The packets are classified at the ingress LSR, and only that 32-bit header is examined to determine how the packet should be handled within the network. Since the LSR only examines the MPLS header and not the entire IP header, this QoS mechanism can operate independently of the Network Layer protocol (such as IP) that is currently in use. Hence the word "multiprotocol" in the term MPLS. Details regarding MPLS are found in RFC 2702 [7-27].

7.5.4 Queuing and Congestion Avoidance Mechanisms

Many router vendors have developed mechanisms to improve QoS for time-sensitive applications such as voice and video. Most of these techniques fall into two general categories: priority queuing and congestion avoidance mechanisms.

Queuing mechanisms create multiple signal queues within the router, and allocate the available bandwidth to these queues according to some algorithm and/or network administrator-supplied rules. Cisco Systems' technique, called Weighted Fair Queuing (WFQ), classifies various incoming data flows according to source/destination address, protocol in use, or application/port, and then grants each one of these flows a specific amount of outgoing bandwidth based on some fairness criteria.

Congestion avoidance mechanisms augment the flow control properties that exist within protocols. With many of these protocols, such as TCP, data flows are retarded only after the network becomes congested, which causes packets to be dropped. The Random Early Detection (RED) and Weighted Random Early Detection (WRED) mechanisms attempt to anticipate when these congestion points will occur, and discard packets based on criteria such as buffer length or the Precedence bits within the IP header. Thus, RED or WRED minimizes the likelihood of large numbers of packets being sent to already congested queues, which would only result in further packet discard. Details regarding Cisco's use of the WFQ and RED mechanisms are found in Reference [7-22].

At the present time, the jury is still out on which of these alternatives, or combination of alternatives, will be most widely implemented. A trade organization, known as the QoS Forum [7-27], has been established as a central point for information exchange, interoperability testing, and education. References [7-29] through [7-32] provide additional information on QoS-related issues and implementations.

7.6 Deploying the Converged Network

Looking to implement Voice over IP? Better look before you leap – this marketplace is exploding with new vendors, products, and services. Some are ready for prime time, and some may need a little more experience. Here are some tips to get you started [7-33].

Do your homework: For most network managers, the voice world, with its own applications and standards, is new territory. For example, are you familiar with analog and digital trunk circuits, traffic measurements, Erlang tables, and the like? If not, start learning. Many VoIP vendors and trade groups have Web sites with a wealth of information, including white papers, case studies, primers on standards, newsletters, evaluation copies of client software, and so on.

Tap your existing resources: In many cases, the voice communication and data/networking responsibilities are handled by separate departments. Each may have a separate budget, and an empire to match. But there are likely two areas of expertise as well: circuit switching and traffic analysis for the voice side, and packet switching and IP knowledge on the networking side. Both of these skill sets are required for a successful VoIP implementation – force these two groups to collaborate, and tap into your existing resources.

Intranet vs. Internet: Voice over your corporate intranet and voice over the worldwide Internet is not the same. In the case of your intranet, you, as the network manager, can exert some control over the number of hops between two points, and the ensuing latencies. In contrast, the Internet was not designed for time-sensitive traffic that demands low delays. As a result, traffic that traverses the Internet must take whatever capacity available at the time. Therefore, get a good handle on your objectives. Are you willing to spend the effort to redesign your intranet as required to support voice, or are you simply looking for a lower-cost alternative for voice transport? Understand the various tradeoffs between intranet and Internet transport before you begin.

Know your traffic: Make sure that your data network can handle the increased amount of traffic before you add voice traffic to the mix. Many net managers are surprised to learn that the slow, steady growth of a few percent per month of network traffic can lead to a substantial increase when considered on an annualized basis. In other words, that T-3 circuit that you put in just last year may be getting close to its capacity during peak traffic periods. Make sure you really have the excess capacity that you think is available. The VoIP equipment should have mechanisms to meter the available end-to-end bandwidth, and to reject additional calls when insufficient bandwidth is available. In addition, get a handle on the number of hops between selected destinations and the resulting network latency, as these delays will dramatically affect the quality of the packetized voice and video service.

Most telephone traffic is characterized using statistical models called the Erlang tables, which were named after A.K. Erlang, a Danish scientist who was an early pioneer in the study of telephone network design. These models are used for traffic engineering studies, and can be applied to a variety of voice-based applications, including PBXs, voicemail, and interactive voice response systems. Typical applications of Erlang analysis would be to calculate the number of lines required for a particular grade of service, the number of call agents that are needed for a given call volume, and so on. An inexpensive software package, called the Westbay Traffic Calculators from Westbay Engineers, Ltd. (West Sussex, U.K.), is available to ease these calculations. (A demo version of this software is available on the CD that accompanies this text.)

Measuring performance: Your end users will likely judge the success or failure of the converged network implementation based, in part, on their current perception of the telephone industry, which is known for high-quality, reliable service. (The number of 99.999 percent – or "five nines" – of reliability is an often quoted statistic.) Thus, in addition to managing the hardware and the software elements of the network, the net architect must also consider the clients' expectations of service and reliability. To do this effectively, performance details regarding the various VoIP network elements should be measured, such as packet delay and packet loss, signal/noise ratios, and other statistics that affect voice and data transmission quality. The ability to baseline the network and identify service-affecting trends as they develop are also key ingredients for optimum performance tuning. Do you have performance tools, such as network monitors, analyzers, and management consoles, available that can give you an objective window into the operation of your converged network?

Watch your existing carrier contracts: Many net managers have existing service contracts with their carriers that should be reviewed prior to jumping into VoIP service. A significant number of minutes may need to be diverted from existing carrier commitments to new IP services in order for the economics of the new hardware investments to be favorable. And when that diversion occurs, you may end up paying more for your existing voice services.

For example, assume that your existing service agreement specifies a rate of $0.05 per minute if you use one million minutes per month, and $0.03 per minute if you use two million minutes per month. Assume that you have recently used over 2 million minutes per month (at $0.03), but you estimate that you will drop substantially below this amount when you divert some of your voice traffic to data transport. In this new scenario, the existing (non-IP) voice traffic will cost you $0.05 per minute because you have dropped below a price point. In other words, while reducing costs with new IP services, you may increase costs for the remaining voice services. A word to the wise: look at the inter-related economics before you commit. In addition, a Service Level Agreement (SLA) that specifies uptime, throughput, and point-to-point latency objectives should be included in that carrier commitment.

International vs. domestic long distance: One of the early driving factors in the VoIP marketplace has been the promise of "free" or very low cost long distance service. But before you take this promise at face value, get a good handle on your calling patterns, and determine what percentage of your traffic is international versus domestic. With international rates in excess of $1.00 per minute to some destinations, VoIP rates that are only a few cents per minute look very favorable and make some compromises in quality worth it. The domestic story may paint a completely different picture, as most managers of enterprise networks are able to negotiate voice contracts that are comparable to the VoIP quotes. Clearly understand your traffic destinations so that your economic model is not unfairly biased.

Proprietary or not? Be aware that the ink is just drying on some of the recently released standards, such as the ITU-T's Recommendation H.323 version 2, *Packet-*

Based Multimedia Communication Systems. As a result, several generations of products are available: vendor-proprietary solutions; vendor-proprietary solutions that have been tested with other vendors for interoperability; products that claim to be compliant with standards, such as T.120 and H.323; and products that have been tested for interoperability. The International Multimedia Teleconferencing Consortium (IMTC), a nonprofit organization with 140 members, conducts periodic interoperability tests of vendors' equipment. Become familiar with these testing efforts.

Selecting a voice codec: The analog voice must be converted to a digital pulse stream before it can be placed in packets and sent over a corporate intranet or the Internet. A codec (short for coder/decoder) is the device that performs these voice processing functions. A variety of standards are available, including the ITU-T G.711 (64 Kbps voice), G.729 (8 Kbps), and G.723.1 (5.3–6.4 Kbps). In addition, a number of vendors have developed their own proprietary schemes. Each one of these alternatives has unique characteristics, including the quality and delay associated with the coding algorithm, which vary with the amount of voice information that is being crammed into the packet. It is therefore important to understand the characteristics of the voice to be transmitted, as well as the expectations of the end users. Do the network requirements include the ability to pass fax traffic or music-on-hold over IP? Or is voice traffic the sole need? Does the gateway product allow for multiple codec options, or is it locked into only one standard and/or algorithm? Ask some questions about the codecs to better match your network requirements.

Application priorities: Real-time traffic, such as voice and video, should be given priority over more routine transmissions such as file transfers and email. Several methods are possible: setting a priority by IP address, by protocol, or by using a reservation protocol, such as the Resource Reservation Protocol (RSVP). However, not all routers are configurable to support one or all of the above schemes. Check your existing routing infrastructure to see if prioritization capabilities exist.

Ease of use: Remember the early days of alternative carriers, when you had to remember to dial an extra dozen access digits and accounts codes to complete a long distance call? Users have higher expectations now – voice gateways must be easy for the end users to operate and must work within existing dialing plans if they are going to be accepted. As you research various products, ask for a demonstration of the dialing sequence that is required to access the VoIP network, and verify that it is compatible both technically and procedurally with your existing methods of establishing, transferring, and otherwise managing voice calls.

Interoperability with existing voice systems: What's your application? The VoIP gateway may need to interoperate with a number of existing and future voice processing systems such as your private branch exchange (PBX), automatic call director (ACD), interactive voice response (IVR) system, and others. Do the trunk circuit port types on your PBX match those that are available from your gateway vendors? Are the signaling protocols between switches compatible with the new VoIP gear? Are you planning any future expansion or applications, such as a migration to ISDN or the installation of a Web-enabled call center? Make sure that the new VoIP hardware is compatible with all other voice systems.

Another related issue to examine is the number of signal processing steps from the source to the destination. In general, the voice quality degrades in proportion to the number of signal compression/decompression segments that occur on an end-to-end basis. Therefore, if such processing occurs in each of the PBX, voice mail, and VoIP gateway systems, voice quality is likely to suffer. Consider whether any of these steps can be combined, such as being integrated within the PBX system, to reduce the number of end-to-end signal processing functions.

References [7-34] through [7-37] provide additional implementation suggestions.

7.7 Looking Back

This volume of the *IP Library* has taken us on a new journey, which you have hopefully found interesting. We have examined converged networks, where both voice and data applications coexist over a common, IP-based infrastructure. We have also explored some of the business, technical, and implementation aspects of these networks, and have looked at some of the current research, such as that being done by the IETF [7-38].

Now the rest is up to you. If you feel that the concepts presented here might benefit your organization, then jump in and give converged networks a try. But remember the admonitions of the previous sections: start small, preferably with a lab environment, and thoroughly test your applications under as controlled conditions as possible before moving these applications into a production environment. As you test, remember that you are trying to *marry* two vastly different architectures – connection-oriented applications with a connectionless network infrastructure – and that some professional counseling may be in order to keep that marriage running smoothly.

You will become the *network marriage counselor*, looking at design tradeoffs and making various adjustments so that the combined voice and data networks can live together in harmony and satisfy the toughest critics of all, the end users.

May all of your clients live happily ever after!

7.8 References

[7-1]   Information regarding the work of the International Multimedia Teleconferencing Consortium can be found at `http://www.imtc.org`.

[7-2]   The International Multimedia Teleconferencing Consortium. IMTC Voice over IP Forum Service Interoperability Agreement 1.0, December 1, 1997. Available at `ftp://ftp.imtc-files.org/imtc-site/VoIP-AG/incoming/VoIPIA1.doc`.

[7-3]   The International Multimedia Teleconferencing Consortium. iNOW! Standards–Based IP Telephony Interoperability Profile, February 23, 1999. Available at `http://www.imtc.org/act_inow.htm` or `http://www.inowprofile.com`.

[7-4]   RADVision, Inc. "H.323 Gatekeepers." The RADVision H.3232 Handbook Library, Volume 1, Issue 1, 1998. Available at `http://www.radvision.com`.

[7-5]   Handley, M., et al. "SIP: Session Initiation Protocol." RFC 2543, March 1999.

[7-6]   A number of resources regarding SIP can be found at: `http://www.cs.columbia.edu/sip/`.

[7-7]   Schulzrinne, Henning, and Jonathan Rosenberg. "The Session Initiation Protocol: Providing Advanced Telephony Services Across the Internet." *Bell Labs Technical Journal* (November/December 1998): 144–160.

[7-8]   deCarmo, Linden. "Internet Telephony Protocols." *Dr. Dobb's Journal* (July 1999): 30–41.

[7-9]   Schulzrinne, Henning. "Comparison of H.323 and SIP," September, 1999. Available at `http://www.cs.columbia.edu/sip/h323-comparison.html`.

[7-10]   Arango, Mauricio, et al. "Media Gateway Control Protocol (MGCP)." Work in Progress, August 17, 1999.

[7-11]   Information regarding the IETF Media Gateway Control Working Group (MEGACO) is available at `http://www.ietf.org/html.charters/megaco-charter.html`.The MEGACO Working Group archives are available at `http://standards.nortelnetworks.com/archives/megaco.html`.

[7-12]   Keating, Tom. "An API Refresher Course." *CTI* (August 1998): 46–52.

[7-13] Microsoft Corporation. "IP Telephony with TAPI 3.0," 1999.
Available at http://www.microsoft.com/windows/server/
technical/networking/iptelephony.asp.

[7-14] Quinton, Michelle. "Windows NT 5.0 Brings You New Telephony
Development Features with TAPI 3.0." *Microsoft Systems Journal*
(November 1998): 37–54.

[7-15] International Telecommunications Union – Telecommunication
Standardization Sector. Terms and Definitions Relating to Quality
of Service and Network Performance Including Dependability.
ITU-T Recommendation E.800, August 1994.

[7-16] International Telecommunications Union – Telecommunication
Standardization Sector. Methods for Subjective Determination
of Transmission Quality. ITU-T Recommendation P.800,
August 1996.

[7-17] International Telecommunications Union – Telecommunication
Standardization Sector. Objective Measurements of Telephone-
band (300-3,400 Hz) Speech Codecs. ITU-T Recommendation
P.861, February 1998.

[7-18] Jackson, Edward R., and Andrew M. Schroepfer. *IP Telephony:
Driving the Open Communications Revolution.* Piper Jaffray
Equity Research Report, February 1999.

[7-19] International Telecommunications Union – Telecommunication
Standardization Sector. General Characteristics of International
Telephone Connections and International Telephone Circuits –
One-Way Transmission Time. ITU-T Recommendation G.114,
February 1996.

[7-20] Kostas, Thomas J., et al. "Real Time Voice over Packet Switched
Networks." *IEEE Network* (January/February 1998): 18–27.

[7-21] Goodman, Bill. "Internet Telephony and Modem Delay." *IEEE
Network* (May/June 1999): 8–16.

[7-22] Cisco Systems, Inc. *Voice Over IP Design Implementation Guide.*
Document 9511930, February 1999.

[7-23] Larson, Eric, and Steve Nikola. "Voice Technologies for IP and
Frame Relay Networks." Motorola, Inc. Network Systems Division
White Paper, April 1998.

[7-24] Kavi, Prabhu. "Achieving Toll-Quality Voice over IP." *Internet
Telephony* (Second Quarter 1998): 90–91.

[7-25]   Braden, R., et al. "Integrated Services in the Internet
           Architecture: An Overview." RFC 1633, June 1994.

[7-26]   Nichols, K., et al. "Definition of the Differentiated Services
           Field (DS Field) in the IPv4 and IPv6 Headers." RFC 2474,
           December 1998.

[7-27]   Awduche, D., et al. "Requirements for Traffic Engineering Over
           MPLS." RFC 2702, September 1999.

[7-28]   Information regarding The QoS Forum is available at
           http://www.qosforum.com.

[7-29]   Duquet, Barbara. "Quality of Service Testing in the VoIP
           Environment: A Primer." *Internet Telephony* (October 1998):
           68–73.

[7-30]   Verscheure Olivier, et al. "User-Oriented QoS in Packet Video
           Delivery." *IEEE Network* (November/December 1998): 12–21.

[7-31]   Xiao, Xipeng, and Lionel M. Ni. "Internet QoS: A Big Picture."
           IEEE Network (March/April 1999): 8–18.

[7-32]   Stenson, Tom. "The QoS Quagmire." *Network World*
           (September 6, 1999): 53–57.

[7-33]   Miller, Mark A. "Getting There from Here – Tips for Planning
           Your Voice over IP Migration." *Network World* (August 10,
           1998): 61.

[7-34]   Larson, Eric. "Voice and Multimedia over Corporate Intranets."
           Motorola, Inc. Network Systems Division White Paper,
           April 1998.

[7-35]   Willis, David. "Voice over IP, The Way it Should Be." *Network
           Computing* (January 11, 1999): 96–99.

[7-36]   Haramaty, Lior. "VoIP Part II: The Technical Deployment."
           Internet Telephony (August 1999): 30–32.

[7-37]   Reimers, Barbara DePompa. "The Bumpy Road to IP."
           InternetWeek (August 16, 1999): 38–41.

[7-38]   The Internet Engineering Task Force has a number of working
           groups that are devoted to the research of Internet Telephony and
           multimedia networking. For information on the various IETF
           workgroups, see http://www.ietf.org/html.charters.

Appendix A

About the CD-ROM

The CD-ROM that accompanies this book contains the following information:

Folder RFC

This folder includes a number of Request For Comments (RFC) documents that relate to IP-based multimedia networks. These documents are published by various Working Groups of the Internet Engineering Task Force (IETF). In addition, there are four key documents in this subdirectory:

- ◆ RFC-RETRIEVAL.TXT, the file *ftp://ftp.isi.edu/in-notes/rfc-retrieval.txt*, which provides instructions on ways to retrieve RFC documents from the Internet. (Also see Appendix F for details on this subject.)

- ◆ RFC-INDEX.TXT, the file *ftp://ftp.isi.edu/in-notes/rfc-index.txt*, which is an index to the currently available RFCs. This file is updated periodically, and is also available from the RFC repository sites.

- ◆ RFC1700.TXT, the Assigned Numbers document, *ftp://ftp.isi.edu/in-notes/rfc1700.txt*, which lists Internet-related Parameters. This file is also available from the other RFC repository sites.

- ◆ RFC2200.TXT, the Internet Official Protocol Standards document, *ftp://ftp.isi.edu/in-notes/rfc2200.txt*.

Each RFC document published at the present time carries the following notice: Copyright (c) The Internet Society (1999). All Rights Reserved.

This document and translations of it may be copied and furnished to others, and derivative works that comment on or otherwise explain it or assist in its implementation may be prepared, copied, published and distributed, in whole or in part, without restriction of any kind, provided that above copyright notice and this paragraph are included on all such copies and derivative works. However, this document itself may not be modified in any way, such as by removing the copyright notice or references to the Internet Society or other Internet organizations, except as needed for the purpose of developing Internet standards in which case the procedures for copyrights defined in the Internet Standards process must be followed, or as required to translate it into languages other than English.

The limited permissions granted above are perpetual and will not be revoked by the Internet Society or its successors or assigns.

Folder eRing

Voice over IP client software (Windows 95, 98, NT-compatible) from:

eRing Solutions, Inc.
62 Somerville
Westmount, Quebec
CANADA H3Z 1J5
Tel: 514.481.8324
www.ering.net

See the README file in this folder for more information.

Folder MessageClick

Fax over IP client software (Windows 95, 98, NT 4.0-compatible) from:

MessageClick, Inc.
90 John Street, Suite 310
New York, NY 10038
Tel: 212.385.5351
www.messageclick.com

See the README file in this folder for more information.

Folder Westbay

Traffic analysis software (Windows compatible) from:

Westbay Engineers Ltd.
11 Langstone Close
Crawley
West Sussex
RH10 7JR
UNITED KINGDOM
Tel: +44 1293 888500
www.erlang.com

See the README file in this folder for more information.

Appendix B

Addresses of Standards Bodies

ANSI STANDARDS
American National Standards Institute
11 West 42nd Street, 13th Floor
New York, NY 10036
Tel: (212) 642-4900 or
    (888) 267-4783
Sales Department: (212) 642-4980
www.ansi.org

ATIS PUBLICATIONS
Alliance for Telecommunications
Industry Solutions
(Formerly the Exchange Carriers
Standards Association)
1200 G Street NW, Suite 500
Washington, DC 20005
Tel: (202) 628-6380
Fax: (202) 393-5453
www.atis.org

AT&T PUBLICATIONS
Lucent Technologies
P.O. Box 19901
Indianapolis, IN 46219
Tel: (317) 322-6557 or
    (888) 582-3688
Fax: (800) 566-9568
www.lucentdocs.com

CSA INTERNATIONAL
Canadian Standards Association
178 Rexdale Boulevard
Etobicoke, ONT M9W 1R3
Canada

Tel: (416) 747-4000 or
    (800) 463-6727
Fax: (416) 747-4149
www.csa-international.org

DISA STANDARDS
Defense Information Systems Agency
www.itsi.disa.mil

DOD STANDARDS
DoD Network Information Center
Boeing Corporation
7990 Boeing Court, M/S CV-50
Vienna, VA 22183-7000
Tel: (703) 821-6266 or
    (800) 365-3642
Fax: (703) 821-6161
www.nic.mil

ECMA STANDARDS
European Computer Manufacturers
Association
114 Rue de Rhone
CH-1204 Geneva
Switzerland
Tel: 41 22 849 60 00
Fax: 41 22 849 60 01
Email: helpdesk@ecma.ch
www.ecma.ch

EIA STANDARDS
Electronic Industries Association
2500 Wilson Boulevard
Arlington, VA 22201
Tel: (703) 907-7500
Fax: (703) 907-7501
www.eia.org

ETSI STANDARDS
European Telecommunications
Standards Institute
ETSI Publications Office
650 route des Lucioles
06921 Sophia Antipolis Cedex
France
Tel: 33 (0)4 92 94 43 95/43 64
Fax: 33 (0)4 93 65 47 16
Email: membership@etsi.fr
www.etsi.org

**FEDERAL INFORMATION
PROCESSING STANDARDS (FIPS)**
U.S. Department of Commerce
National Technical Information
Service (NTIS)
5285 Port Royal Road
Springfield, VA 22161
Tel: (703) 605-6000 or
    (800) 553-6847
Fax: (703) 605-6900
www.ntis.gov

IEC STANDARDS
International Electrotechnical
Commission
IEC Central Office
3, rue de Verenbe
P.O. Box 131
1211 Geneva 20
Switzerland
Tel: 41 22 919 0211
Fax: 41 22 919 0300
Email: dn@iec.ch
www.hike.te.chiba-u.ac.jp/
ikeda/IEC

IEEE STANDARDS
Institute of Electrical and Electronics
Engineers
445 Hoes Lane
P.O. Box 1331
Piscataway, NJ 08855-1331
Tel: (732) 981-0060 or
    (800) 678-4333
Fax: (732) 981-0538
www.ieee.org

INTERNET STANDARDS
Internet Society International
11150 Sunset Hill Road, Suite 100
Reston, VA 20190-5321
Tel: (703) 326-9880 or
    (800) 468-9507
Fax: (703) 326-9881
Email: isoc@isoc.org
www.isoc.org

ISO STANDARDS
International Organization for
Standardization
1, Rue de Varembé
Case postale 56
CH-1211 Geneva 20
Switzerland
Tel: 41 22 749 01 11
Fax: 41 22 733 34 30
Email: central@isocs.iso.ch
www.iso.ch

ITU STANDARDS
International Telecommunications
Union
Information Services Department
Place des Nations
CH-1211 Geneva 20
Switzerland
Tel: 41 22 730 5111
Fax: 41 22 733 7256
Email: itumail@itu.int
www.itu.ch

NATIONAL INSTITUTE OF
STANDARDS AND TECHNOLOGY
Technology Building 820
NIST N, Room B-562
Gaithersburg, MD 20899
Tel: (301) 975-2000
Fax: (301) 948-6213
www.nist.gov

TELCORDIA TECHNOLOGIES
(Formerly Bell Communications
Research)
Information Management Services
8 Corporate Place, Room 3A-184
Piscataway, NJ 08854-4156
Tel: (732) 699-5800 or
     (800) 521-2673
Fax: (732) 336-2559
www.telcordia.com

WWW STANDARDS
World Wide Web Consortium
Massachusetts Institute of Technology
Laboratory for Computer Science
545 Technology Square Bldg. NE 43,
Room 358
Cambridge, MA 02139
Tel: (617) 253-5851
Fax: (617) 258-5999
Email: www-request@w3.org
www.w3.org

Many of the above standards may be
purchased from:

Global Engineering Documents
15 Inverness Way East
Englewood, CO 80112
Tel: (303) 790-0600 or
     (800) 854-7179
Fax: (303) 397-2740
www.global.ihs.com

Phillips Business Information, Inc.
1201 Seven Locks Road, Suite #300
Potomac, MD 20854-2958
Tel: (301) 340-1520 or
     (800) 777-5006
Fax: (301) 309-3847
Email: clientservices.pbi@
       phillips.com
www.phillips.com

Appendix C

Forums, Consortiums, and IETF Working Groups

FORUMS

ADSL Forum
39355 California Street, Suite 307
Fremont, CA 94538
Tel: (510) 608-5905
Fax: (510) 608-5917
Email: adslforum@adsl.com
www.adsl.com

ATM Forum
Worldwide Headquarters
2570 W. El Camino Rio, Suite 304
Mountain View, CA 94040
Tel: (650) 949-6700
Fax: (650) 949-6705
Email: info@atmforum.com
www.atmforum.com

ATM Forum
European Office
Boulevard Saint Michel 78
1040 Brussels, Belgium
Tel: 32 2 732 8505
Fax: 32 2 732 8408

Frame Relay Forum
North American Office
39355 California Street, Suite 307
Fremont, CA 94538
Tel: (510) 608-5920
Fax: (510) 608-5917

Email: frf@frforum.com
ftp://frforum.com
www.frforum.com

Frame Relay Forum
Asia/Pacific Office
Bldg. Hamamatsucho
Suzuki Bldg. 3F
1-2-11, Hamamatsucho
Minato-ku Tokyo, 105, Japan
Tel: 81 3 3438 3694
Fax: 81 3 3438 3698

Frame Relay Forum
European Office
c/o OST, BP 158
Z1 Sud Est rue du bas Village
35510 Cesson Sevigne Cedex
France
Tel: 33 99 51 76 55
Fax: 33 99 41 71 75

ISDN Users Group
c/o NIST
100 Bureau Drive, Stop 8920
Gaithersburg, MD 20899-8920
Tel: (301) 975-2937
Fax: (301) 926-9675
Email: niuf@nist.gov
www.niuf.nist.gov

CONSORTIUMS

ATM Local Telephony Alliance (ALTA)
www.altainfo.org
Enterprise Computer Telephony
Forum (ECTF)
39355 California Street
Fremont, CA 94536
Tel: (510) 608-5915
Fax: (510) 608-5917
www.ectf.org

International Multimedia Teleconferencing Consortium (IMTC)
Bishop Ranch 2
2694 Bishop Drive, Suite 275
San Ramon, CA 94583
Tel: (925) 277-1320
Fax: (925) 277-8111
www.imtc.org

The IP Multicast Initiative (IPMI)
4400 Bayou Boulevard, Suite 18
Pensacola, FL 32503-1908
Tel: (850) 476-1156
Fax: (850) 476-1548
www.ipmi.org

Multimedia Services Affiliate Forum (MSAF)
P.O. Box 60835
Santa Barbara, CA 93160
Tel: (805) 964-0240
Fax: (805) 692-1905
www.msaf.org

IETF WORKING GROUPS

Audio Video Transport (avt)
Mailing List: rem-conf@cs.net
Subscriptions: rem-conf-request@
cs.net

Multiparty Multimedia Session Control (mmusic)
Mailing List: confctrl@isi.edu
Subscriptions: confctrl-request@
isi.edu

PSTN and Internet Internetworking (pint)
Mailing List: pint@lists.research.
bell-labs.com
Subscriptions: pint-request@lists.
research.bell-labs.
com
www.bell-labs.com/
mailing-lists/pint

IP Telephony (iptel)
Mailing List: iptel@lists.
research.bell-labs.
com
Subscriptions: iptel-request@
lists.research.
bell-labs.com
www.bell-labs.com/
mailing-lists/iptel

Appendix D

Multimedia Standards from the ITU-T

G.Series: Transmission Systems and Media; Digital Systems and Networks

G.114	One-way transmission time
G.165	Echo cancellers
G.168	Digital network echo cancellers
G.711	Pulse code modulation (PCM) of voice frequencies
G.722	7 KHz audio-coding within 64 Kbit/s
G.723	Speech coders
G.723.1	Dual rate speech coder for multimedia communications transmitting at 5.3 and 6.3 Kbit/s
G.724	Characteristics of a 48-channel low bit rate-encoding primary multiplex operating at 1544 Kbit/s
G.725	System aspects for the use of the 7 KHz audio codec within 64 Kbit/s
G.726	40, 32, 24, 16 Kbit/s adaptive differential pulse code modulation (ADPCM)
G.727	5-, 4-, 3- and 2-bits/sample embedded adaptive differential pulse code modulation (ADPCM)
G.728	Coding of speech at 16 Kbit/s using low-delay code excited linear prediction
G.729	Coding of speech at 8 Kbit/s using conjugate-structure algebraic-code-excited linear-prediction
G.729A	Annex A Reduced complexity 8 Kbit/s CS-ACELP speech codec

H. Series: Transmission of Non-telephone Signals

H.100	Visual telephone systems
H.225.0	Call signaling protocols and media stream packetization for packet-based multimedia communication systems
H.225.0v1	Media stream packetization and synchronization for visual telephone on nonguaranteed quality of service LANs
H.235	Message Integrity for the H.225 RAS Channel
H.245	Control protocol for multimedia communication
H.246	Line Transmission of Non-Telephone Signals – Interworking of H.Series multimedia terminals with H.Series multimedia terminals and voice/voiceband terminals on GSTN and ISDN
H.261	Video codec for audiovisual services at p x 64 Kbit/s
H.263	Video coding for low bit rate communication
H.320	Narrowband visual telephone systems and terminal equipment
H.321	Adaptation of H.320 visual telephone terminals to B-ISDN environments
H.322	Visual telephone systems and terminal equipment for local area networks that provide a guaranteed quality of service
H.323	Packet-based multimedia communications systems
H.323v1	Visual telephone systems and equipment for local area networks that provide a nonguaranteed quality of service
H.324	Terminal for low bit-rate multimedia communication
H.450.1	Generic functional protocol for the support of supplementary services in H.323
H.450.2	Call transfer supplementary service for H.323
H.450.3	Call diversion supplementary service for H.323

Q.Series: Switching and Signaling

Q.931   Digital Subscriber Signaling System No.1 ISDN User-Network
                 Interface Layer 3 Specification for Basic Call Control

T. Series: Terminal Equipment and Protocols for Telematic Services

T.4   Standardization of Group 3 facsimile terminals for document
                transmission

T.6   Facsimile coding schemes and coding control functions for
                Group 4 facsimile apparatus

T.30   Procedures for document facsimile transmission in the general
                switched telephone network

T.37   Procedures for the transfer of facsimile data via store and
                forward on the internet series T terminals for telematic services
                Study Group 8

T.38   Procedures for real time group 3 facsimile communications over
                IP Networks series T terminals for telematic services Study
                Group 8

T.120   Data protocols for multimedia conferencing

T.121   Generic application template

T.122   Multipoint communication service – Service definition

T.123   Network specific data protocol stacks for multimedia
                conferencing

T.124   Generic Conference Control

T.125   Multipoint communication service protocol specification

T.126   Multipoint still image and annotation protocol

T.127   Multipoint binary file transfer protocol

T.128   Multipoint application sharing

V.Series: Data Communication over the Telephone Network

V.17	A 2-wire modem for facsimile applications with rates up to 14,400 bps
V.21	300 bits per second duplex modem standardized for use in the General Switched Telephone Network and on point-to-point 2-wire leased telephone-type circuits
V.27ter	4800/2400 bits per second modem standardized for use in the General Switched Telephone Network
V.29	9600 bits per second modem standardized for use on point-to-point 4-wire leased telephone-type circuits

Appendix E

Multimedia- and IP-related Documents from the IETF

RFC 768	User Datagram Protocol
RFC 783	The TFTP Protocol (Revision 2)
RFC 791	Internet Protocol
RFC 792	Internet Control Message Protocol
RFC 793	Transmission Control Protocol
RFC 821	Simple Mail Transfer Protocol
RFC 826	An Ethernet Address Resolution Protocol
RFC 854	Telnet Protocol Specification
RFC 877	A Standard for the Transmission of IP Datagrams Over Public Data Networks
RFC 894	A Standard for the Transmission of IP Datagrams over Ethernet Networks
RFC 903	A Reverse Address Resolution Protocol
RFC 904	Exterior Gateway Protocol Formal Specification
RFC 951	Bootstrap Protocol (BOOTP)
RFC 959	File Transfer Protocol (FTP)
RFC 1034	Domain Names – Concepts and Facilities
RFC 1035	Domain Names – Implementation and Specification
RFC 1042	A Standard for the Transmission of IP Datagrams over IEEE 802 Networks
RFC 1055	A Nonstandard for Transmission of IP Datagrams over Serial Lines: SLIP

RFC 1058   Routing Information Protocol

RFC 1103   A Proposed Standard for the Transmission of IP Datagrams over
              FDDI Networks

RFC 1112   Host Extensions for IP Multicasting

RFC 1157   A Simple Network Management Protocol (SNMP)

RFC 1201   Transmitting IP Traffic over ARCNET Networks

RFC 1209   The Transmission of IP Datagrams over the SMDS Service

RFC 1293   Inverse Address Resolution Protocol

RFC 1438   Internet Engineering Task Force Statements Of Boredom (SOBs)

RFC 1490   Multiprotocol Interconnect over Frame Relay

RFC 1577   Classical IP and ARP over ATM

RFC 1723   RIP Version 2 Carrying Additional Information

RFC 1771   A Border Gateway Protocol 4 (BGP-4)

RFC 1901   Introduction to Community-based SNMPv2

RFC 2068   Hypertext Transfer Protocol – HTTP/1.1

RFC 2131   Dynamic Host Configuration Protocol

RFC 2178   OSPF Version 2

RFC 2201   Core Based Trees (CBT) Multicast Routing Architecture

RFC 2205   Resource Reservation Protocol (RSVP)

RFC 2236   Internet Group Management Protocol, Version 2

RFC 2271   An Architecture for SNMP Management Frameworks (SNMPv3)

RFC 2326   Real-time Streaming Protocol (RTSP)

RFC 2327   Session Description Protocol

RFC 2543   Session Initiation Protocol

Appendix F

Obtaining Internet Documents

Registration Services

Many of the administrative functions for the Internet are handled by the InterNIC, which is operated by Network Solutions, Inc.:

Network Solutions, Inc.
Attn: InterNIC Registration Services
505 Huntmar Park Drive
Herndon, VA 22070
Tel: (703) 742-0400
Fax: (703) 742-8449
www.networksolutions.com

Internet Organizations

A number of groups contribute to the management, operation, and proliferation of the Internet. These include (in alphabetical order):

CommerceNet
4005 Miranda Avenue, Suite 175
Palo Alto, CA 94304
Tel: (650) 858-1930
Fax: (650) 858-1936
Email: info@commerce.net
www.commerce.net

Commercial Internet Exchange Association
1301 Connecticut Avenue, Northwest, 5th Floor
Washington, DC 20036
Tel: (703) 709-8200
Fax: (703) 709-5249
Email: admin@cix.org
www.cix.org

Internet Architecture Board
Email: iab @isi.edu
www.iab.org

Internet Assigned Numbers Authority
P.O. Box 12607
Marina del Rey, CA 90292-3607
Tel: (310) 822-1511
Fax: (310) 823-6714
Email: iana@iana.org
www.iana.org

Internet Engineering Task Force
IETF Secretariat
c/o Corporation for National Research Initiatives
1895 Preston White Drive, Suite 100
Reston, VA 20191-5434
Tel: (703) 620-8990
Fax: (703) 620-9071
Email: ietf-info@ietf.org
www.ietf.org

Internet Service Providers' Consortium
646A Venice Boulevard
Venice, CA 90291
Tel: (310) 827-8466
Fax: (310) 827-8434
www.ispc.org

Internet Society
c/o International Secretariat
11150 Sunset Hills Road, Suite 100
Reston, VA 20190-5321
Tel: (703) 326-9880
Fax: (703) 326-9881
Email: isoc@isoc.org
www.isoc.org

North American Network Operators Group
c/o Merit Network
4251 Plymouth Road, Suite C
Ann Arbor, MI 48105-2785
Tel: (734) 764-9430
Fax: (734) 647-3185
Email: info@merit.edu
www.nanog.org

World Wide Web Consortium
c/o MIT Laboratory for Computer Science
545 Technology Square
Cambridge, MA 02139
Tel: (617) 253-2613
Fax: (617) 258-5999
Email: admin@w3.org
www.w3.org

Obtaining RFCs

The following is an excerpt from the file *http://isi.edu/rfc-retrieval.txt*, or *ftp://ftp.isi.edu/in-notes/rfc-retrieval.txt*, which is available from many of the RFC repositories listed below. This information is subject to change; therefore, obtain the current version of this file if problems occur. Also note that each RFC site may have instructions for file retrieval (such as a particular subdirectory) that are unique to that location.

RFCs may be obtained via email or FTP from many RFC repositories. The Primary Repositories will have the RFC available when it is first announced, as will many Secondary Repositories. Some Secondary Repositories may take a few days to make available the most recent RFCs.

Many of these repositories also now have World Wide Web servers. Try the following URL as a starting point:

http://www.isi.edu/rfc-editor.org/

Primary Repositories

RFCs can be obtained via FTP from NIS.NSF.NET, NISC.JVNC.NET, FTP.ISI.EDU, WUARCHIVE.WUSTL.EDU, SRC.DOC.IC.AC.UK, FTP.NCREN.NET, FTP.SESQUI.NET, FTP.NIC.IT, FTP.IMAG.FR, FTP.IETF.RNP.BR, or WWW.NORMOS.ORG.

1. NIS.NSF.NET

To obtain RFCs from NIS.NSF.NET via FTP, login with username "anonymous" and password "name@host.domain"; then connect to the directory of RFCs with cd /internet/documents/rfc. The file name is of the form rfcnnnn.txt (where "nnnn" refers to the RFC number).

For sites without FTP capability, electronic mail query is available from NIS.NSF.NET. Address the request to NIS-INFO@NIS.NSF.NET and leave the subject field of the message blank. The first text line of the message must be "send rfc-nnnn.txt" with nnnn the RFC number.

Contact: rfc-mgr@merit.edu

2. NISC.JVNC.NET

RFCs can also be obtained via FTP from NISC.JVNC.NET, with the pathname rfc/rfcNNNN.txt (where "NNNN" refers to the number of the RFC). An index can be obtained with the pathname rfc/rfc-index.txt.

JvNCnet also provides a mail service for those sites that cannot use FTP. Address the request to "SENDRFC@NISC.JVNC.NET" and in the "Subject:" field of the message indicate the RFC number, as in "Subject: rfcNNNN" (where NNNN is the RFC number). Please note that RFCs whose numbers are less than 1000 need not place a leading "0". (For example, RFC932 is fine.) For a complete index to the RFC library, enter "rfc-index" in the "Subject:" field, as in "Subject: rfc-index". No text in the body of the message is needed.

Contact: rfc-admin@nisc.jvnc.net

3. FTP.ISI.EDU

RFCs can be obtained via FTP from FTP.ISI.EDU, with the pathname in-notes/rfc-nnnn.txt (where "nnnn" refers to the number of the RFC). Login with FTP username "anonymous" and password "name@host.domain".

RFCs can also be obtained via electronic mail from ISI.EDU by using the RFC-INFO service. Address the request to "rfc-info@isi.edu" with a message body of:

```
Retrieve: RFC
Doc-ID: RFCnnnn
```

(Where "nnnn" refers to the number of the RFC (always use 4 digits – the DOC-ID of RFC 822 is "RFC0822").) The RFC-INFO@ISI.EDU server provides other ways of selecting RFCs based on keywords and such; for more information send a message to "rfc-info@isi.edu" with the message body "help: help".

Contact: RFC-Manager@ISI.EDU

4. WUARCHIVE.WUSTL.EDU

RFCs can also be obtained via FTP from WUARCHIVE.WUSTL.EDU, with the pathname info/rfc/rfcnnnn.txt.Z (where "nnnn" refers to the number of the RFC and "Z" indicates that the document is in compressed form).

At WUARCHIVE.WUSTL.EDU the RFCs are in an "archive" file system and various archives can be mounted as part of an NFS file system. Please contact Chris Myers (chris@wugate.wustl.edu) if you want to mount this file system in your NFS.

WUArchive now keeps RFCs and STDs under

```
ftp://wuarchive.wustl.edu./doc/
or http://wuarchive.wustl.edu./doc/
```

Contact: chris@wugate.wustl.edu

5. SRC.DOC.IC.AC.UK

RFCs can be obtained via FTP from SRC.DOC.IC.AC.UK with the pathname rfc/rfc-nnnn.txt.gz or rfc/rfcnnnn.ps.gz (where "nnnn" refers to the number of the RFC). Login with FTP username "anonymous" and password "your-email-address". To obtain the RFC Index, use the pathname rfc/rfc-index.txt.gz. (The trailing .gz indicates that the document is in compressed form.)

SRC.DOC.IC.AC.UK also provides an automatic mail service for those sites in the UK that cannot use FTP. Address the request to info-server@doc.ic.ac.uk with a Subject: line of "wanted" and a message body of:

```
request sources
topic path rfc/rfcnnnn.txt.gz
request end
```

(where "nnnn" refers to the number of the RFC.) Multiple requests may be included in the same message by giving multiple "topic path" commands on separate lines. To request the RFC Index, the command should read: topic path rfc/rfc-index.txt.gz.

They are also available by HTTP in http://sunsite.doc.ic.ac.uk/rfc/
The archive is available using NIFTP and the ISO FTAM system.
Contact: ukuug-soft@doc.ic.ac.uk

6. FTP.NCREN.NET

To obtain RFCs from FTP.NCREN.NET via FTP, login with username "anonymous" and your internet email address as password. The RFCs can be found in the directory /rfc, with file names of the form:

```
rfcNNNN.txt or rfcNNNN.ps
```

where NNNN refers to the RFC number.
This repository is also accessible via WAIS and the Internet Gopher.
Contact: rfc-mgr@ncren.net

7. FTP.SESQUI.NET

RFCs can be obtained via FTP from FTP.SESQUI.NET, with the pathname pub/rfc/rfcnnnn.xxx (where "nnnn" refers to the number of the RFC and xxx indicates the document form, txt for ASCII and ps for Postscript).

At FTP.SESQUI.NET the RFCs are in an "archive" file system and various archives can be mounted as part of an NFS file system. Please contact RFC-maintainer (rfc-aint@sesqui.net) if you want to mount this file system in your NFS.

Contact: rfc-maint@sesqui.net

8. FTP.NIC.IT

RFCs can be obtained from the ftp.nic.it FTP archive with the pathname rfc/rfc-nnnn.txt (where "nnnn" refers to the number of the RFC). Login with FTP, username "anonymous" and password "name@host.domain".

The summary of ways to get RFCs from the Italian Network Information Center is the following:

Via ftp: `ftp.nic.it directory rfc`
Via WWW: `http://www.nic.it/mirrors/rfc`
Via email: send a message to listserv@nic.it whose body contains "get RFC/rfc<number>.[txt,ps]".

For receiving a full list of the existing RFCs include in the body the command "index RFC/rfc".

Contact: D.Vannozzi@cnuce.cnr.it

9. FTP.IMAG.FR

RFCs can be obtained via FTP from ftp.imag.fr with the pathname /pub/archive/IETF/rfc/rfcnnnn.txt (where "nnnn" refers to the number of the RFC).

Login with FTP username "anonymous" and password "your-email-address". To obtain the RFC Index, use the pathname /pub/archive/IETF/rfc/rfc-index.txt.

Internet drafts and other IETF related documents are also mirrored in the /pub/archive/IETF directory.

Contact: `rfc-adm@imag.fr`

10. WWW.NORMOS.ORG

RFCs, STD, BCP, FYI, RTR, IEN, Internet-Drafts, RIPE, and other Internet engineering documents can be found at `http://www.normos.org` and `ftp://ftp.normos.org`.

The RFCs are available as:

```
http://www.normos.org/ietf/rfc/rfcXXXX.txt
ftp://ftp.normos.org/ietf/rfc/rfcXXXX.txt
```

STD, BCP, FYI, RTR, IEN documents are available as:

```
http://www.normos.org/ietf/[std,bcp,fyi,rtr,ien]/[std,bcp,fyi,rtr,ie
n]XXXX.txt
ftp://ftp.normos.org/ietf/[std,bcp,fyi,rtr,ien]/[std,bcp,fyi,rtr,ien
]XXXX.txt
```

Internet-drafts are available as:

```
http://www.normos.org/ietf/internet-drafts/draft-....txt
ftp://ftp.normos.org/ietf/internet-drafts/draft-....txt
```

Full-text search and database queries are available from the Web interface. Please send questions, comments, suggestions to info@normos.org.

11. MIRRORS.RCN.COM

RFCs can be obtained via FTP from MIRRORS.RCN.COM. Log in with the username 'anonymous' and the password 'name@host.domain', then change your directory to /pub/in-notes. The file name is of the form rfcnnnn.txt (where 'nnnn' is the RFC number without leading zeros).

Contact: mirror-staff@lists.rcn.net

12. FTP.IETF.RNP.BR

RFCs can be obtained via FTP from FTP.IETF.RNP.BR with the pathname rfc/rfc-nnnn.txt (where "nnnn" refers to the number of the RFC). Login with FTP username "anonymous" and password "your-email-address". To obtain the RFC Index, use the pathname rfc/rfc-index.txt. Internet-Drafts and other IETF related documents are also mirrored.

Contact: rfc-admin@ietf.rnp.br

Secondary Repositories

AUSTRALIA AND PACIFIC RIM

Site:	munnari
Contact:	Robert Elz <kre@cs.mu.OZ.AU>
Host:	munnari.oz.au
Directory:	rfc
Notes:	RFCs in compressed format rfcNNNN.Z postscript RFCs rfcNNNN.ps.Z

Site:	The Programmers' Society
	University of Technology, Sydney
Contact:	ftp@progsoc.uts.edu.au
Host:	ftp.progsoc.uts.edu.au
Directory:	rfc (or std).
Notes:	Both are stored uncompressed.

DENMARK

Site:	University of Copenhagen
Host:	ftp.denet.dk
Directory:	rfc

FINLAND

Site:	FUNET
Host:	nic.funet.fi
Directory:	index/RFC
Directory:	/pub/netinfo/rfc
Notes:	RFCs in compressed format. Also provides email access by sending mail to archive-server@nic.funet.fi.

FRANCE

Site:	Centre d'Informatique Scientifique et Medicale (CISM)
Contact:	ftpmaint@univ-lyon1.fr
Host:	ftp.univ-lyon1.fr
Directories:	pub/rfc/* Classified by hundreds pub/mirrors/rfc Mirror of Internic
Notes:	Files compressed with gzip. Online decompression done by the FTP server.

Site:	Institut National de la Recherche en Informatique et Automatique (INRIA)
Address:	info-server@inria.fr
Notes:	RFCs are available via email to the above address. Info Server manager is Mireille Yamajako (yamajako@inria.fr).

GERMANY

Site:	EUnet Germany
Host:	ftp.Germany.EU.net
Directory:	pub/documents/rfc

NETHERLANDS

Site:	EUnet
Host:	mcsun.eu.net
Directory:	rfc
Notes:	RFCs in compressed format.

NORWAY

Host:	ugle.unit.no
Directory:	pub/rfc

ROMANIA

Site:	SunSITE Romania at the Politehnica University of Bucharest
Contact:	space@sunsite.pub.ro
Host:	sunsite.pub.ro/pub/rfc
	or via httpsunsite.pub.ro/pub/mirrors/ds.internic.net

SOUTH AFRICA

Site:	The Internet Solution
Contact:	ftp-admin@is.co.za
Host:	ftp.is.co.za
Directory:	internet/in-notes/rfc

SWEDEN

Host:	sunic.sunet.se
Directory:	rfc
Host:	chalmers.se
Directory:	rfc

UNITED STATES

Site:	cerfnet
Contact:	help@cerf.net
Host:	nic.cerf.net
Directory:	netinfo/rfc

Site:	NIC.DDN.MIL (DOD users only)
Contact:	NIC@nic.ddn.mil
Host:	NIC.DDN.MIL
Directory:	rfc/rfcnnnn.txt
Note:	DOD users only may obtain RFCs via FTP from NIC.DDN. MIL. Internet users should NOT use this source due to inadequate connectivity.

Site:	uunet
Contact:	James Revell <revell@uunet.uu.net>
Host:	ftp.uu.net
Directory:	inet/rfc

UUNET Archive

UUNET archive, which includes the RFCs, various IETF documents, and other information regarding the Internet, is available to the public via anonymous ftp (to ftp.uu.net) and anonymous uucp, and will be available via an anonymous kermit server soon. Get the file

```
/archive/inet/ls-1R.Z
```

for a listing of these documents.

Any site in the US running UUCP may call +1 900 GOT SRCS and use the login "uucp". There is no password. The phone company will bill you at $0.50 per minute for the call. The 900 number only works from within the US.

Requests for special distribution of RFCs should be addressed to either the author of the RFC in question or to RFC-Manager@ISI.EDU.

Submissions for Requests for Comments should be sent to RFC-EDITOR@ISI.EDU. Please consult "Instructions to RFC Authors," RFC 2223, for further information.

Requests to be added to or deleted from the RFC distribution list should be sent to RFC-REQUEST@ISI.EDU.

Users with .MIL addresses may send a request to MAJORDOMO@NIC.DDN.MIL with an empty Subject: line and a message: subscribe rfc [your email address].

Changes to this file "rfc-retrieval.txt" should be sent to RFC-MANAGER@ISI.EDU.

The RFC-Info Service

The following describes the RFC-Info Service, which is an Internet document and information retrieval service. The text that follows describes in detail the service, which was obtained by using "Help:Help" as discussed below.

RFC-Info is an email based service to help in locating and retrieving RFCs, FYIs, STDs, and IMRs. Users can ask for "lists" of all RFCs, FYIs, STDs, and IMRs having certain attributes such as their ID number, keywords, title, author, issuing organization, and date.

To use the service send email to RFC-INFO@ISI.EDU with your requests in the body of the message. Feel free to put anything in the SUBJECT; the system ignores it. The body of the message is processed with case independence.

To get started you may send a message to RFC-INFO@ISI.EDU with requests such as in the following examples (without the explanation between):

Help: Help	[to get this information page]
List: FYI	[list the FYI notes]
List: RFC	[list RFCs with window as keyword or in title] Keywords: window
List: FYI	[list FYIs about windows] Keywords: window
List: *	[list all documents by Cooper] Author: Cooper
List: RFC	[list RFCs about ARPANET, ARPA NETWORK, etc.] Title: ARPA*NET
List: RFC	[list RFCs issued by MITRE, dated 7+8/1991] Organization: MITRE Dated-after: Jul-01-1991 Dated-before: Aug-31-1991
List: RFC	[list RFCs obsoleting a given RFC] Obsoletes: RFC0010
List: RFC	[list RFCs by authors starting with "Bracken"] Author: Bracken* [* is a wild card matching all endings]
List: IMR	[list the IMRs for the first 6 months of 92] Dated-after: Dec-31-1991 Dated-before: Jul-01-1992
Retrieve: RFC	[retrieve RFC 822] Doc-ID: RFC0822 [note, always 4 digits in RFC#]
Retrieve: FYI	[retrieve FYI 4] Doc-ID: FYI0004 [note, always 4 digits in FYI#]
Retrieve: STD	[retrieve STD 1] Doc-ID: STD0001 [note, always 4 digits in STD#]
Retrieve: IMR	[retrieve May 1992 Internet Monthly Report] Doc-ID: IMR9205 [note, always 4 digits = YYMM]
Help: Manual	[to retrieve the long user manual, 30+ pages]

Help: List	[how to use the LIST request]
Help: Retrieve	[how to use the RETRIEVE request]
Help: Topics	[list topics for which help is available]
Help: Dates	["Dates" is such a topic]
List: keywords	[list the keywords in use]
List: organizations	[list the organizations known to the system]

A useful way to test this service is to retrieve the file *Where and how to get new RFCs* (which is also the file rfc-retrieval.txt noted above in the section "Obtaining RFCs"). Place the following in the message body:

```
Help: ways_to_get_rfcs
```

Internet Engineering Standards Repository

A search engine, called NORMOS, is available to retrieve information about IETF, RIPE, W3C, and IANA documents. To use the search engine, contact:

```
http://www.normos.org
```

Internet Mailing Lists

A number of mailing lists are maintained on the Internet for the purposes of soliciting information and discussions on specific subjects. In addition, a number of the Internet Engineering Task Force (IETF) working groups maintain a list for the exchange of information that is specific to that group.

For example, the IETF maintains two lists: the IETF General Discussion list and the IETF Announcement list. To join the IETF Announcement list, send a request to:

```
ietf-announce-request@ietf.org
```

To join the IETF General Discussion, send a request to:

```
ietf-request@ietf.org
```

A number of other mailing lists are available. To join a mailing list, send a message to the associated request list:

```
listname-request@listhost (for example, snmp-request@psi.com)
```

with the following as the message body:

```
subscribe listname (for example, subscribe snmp)
```

A complete listing of the current IETF working groups and their respective mailing lists is available at:

```
http://www.ietf.org/maillist.html
```

Appendix G

Acronyms and Abbreviations

A

A	ampere
AARP	AppleTalk Address Resolution Protocol
ABP	alternate bipolar
ACC	audio codec capabilities
ACD/PBX	Automatic Call Distributor
ACELP	Algebraic-Code-Excited-Linear-Prediction
ACF	Admission Confirmation message
ACK	acknowledgment
ACS	asynchronous communication server
ACTLU	activate logical unit
ACTPU	activate physical unit
ADPCM	Adaptive Differential Pulse Code Modulation
ADSP	AppleTalk Data Stream Protocol
AEP	AppleTalk Echo Protocol
AFI	authority and format identifier
AFP	AppleTalk Filing Protocol
AFRP	ARCNET Fragmentation Protocol
AGS	asynchronous gateway server
AH	authentication header
AI	artificial intelligence
AMI	alternate mark inversion

AMT	address mapping table
ANSI	American National Standards Institute
API	applications program interface
APPC	Advanced Program-to-Program Communication
ARE	all routes explorer
ARI	address recognized indicator bit
ARJ	Admission Reject message
ARM	administrative runtime module
ARP	Address Resolution Protocol
ARPA	Advanced Research Projects Agency
ARPANET	Advanced Research Projects Agency Network
ASCE	Association Control Service Element
ASCII	American Standard Code for Information Interchange
ASIC	application-specific integrated circuits
ASN.1	Abstract Syntax Notation One
ASP	AppleTalk Session Protocol
ATM	Asynchronous Transfer Mode
ATP	AppleTalk Transaction Protocol
AUP	acceptable use policy
AUTHU	authentication option
AVM	administrative view module
AVO	audiovisual object
AVT	Audio-video Transport

B

B8ZS	bipolar with 8 ZERO substitution
BC	block check
BER	Basic Encoding Rules
BIOS	Basic Input/Output System

BITNET	Because It's Time NETwork
BIU	basic information unit
BOC	Bell Operating Company
BOF	Birds of a Feather
BOFL	Breath of Life
BOOTP	Bootstrap Protocol
BPDU	bridge protocol data unit
bps	bits per second
BPV	bipolar violations
BRI	Basic Rate Interface
BSAC	bit-sliced arithmetic coding
BSC	binary synchronous communication
BSD	Berkeley Software Distribution
BTU	basic transmission unit
BUI	browser user interface
BW	Bandwidth

C

CAS	Channel Associated Signaling
CATNIP	Common Architecture for Next Generation Internet Protocol
CATS	Consortium for Audiographics Teleconferencing Standards
CBR	Constant Bit Rate
CCIS	common channel interoffice signaling
CCITT	International Telegraph and Telephone Consultative Committee
CCR	commitment, concurrency, and recovery
CCS	Common Channel Signaling
CD	Compact disc
CDPD	Cellular Digital Packet Data
CDR	Call Detail Records

CDV	constant delay value
CELP	Codebook excited predictive linear coding
CICS	customer information communication system
CIDR	Classless Interdomain Routing
CIF	Common Intermediate Format
CIR	Committed Information Rate
CLNP	Connectionless Layer Network Protocol
CLNS	Connectionless-mode Network Services
CLTP	Connectionless Transport Protocol
CMIP	Common Management Information Protocol
CMIS	Common Management Information Service
CMISE	Common Management Information Service Element
CMOL	CMIP on IEEE 802.2 Logical Link Control
CMOT	Common Management Information Protocol over TCP/IP
Codec	coder-decoder
CONS	Connection-mode Network Services
CORBA	Common Object Request Broker Architecture
COS	Corporation for Open Systems
CO Switch	Central Office Switch
CPE	customer premises equipment
CPU	Central Processing Unit
CRC	cyclic redundancy check
CREN	The Corporation for Research and Educational Networking
CRS	configuration report server
CS ACELP	Conjugate-Structure Algebraic-Code-Excited-Linear-Prediction
CSMA/CD	Carrier Sense Multiple Access with Collision Detection
CSNET	computer+science network
CSU	Channel Service Unit
CT	Computer telephony
CTERM	Command Terminal Protocol

CTI Interface   Computer Telephony Integration

D

DA	destination address
DAP	Data Access Protocol
DARPA	Defense Advanced Research Projects Agency
DAT	duplicate address test
DCA	Defense Communications Agency
DCC	Data Country Code
DCE	data circuit-terminating equipment
DDCMP	Digital Data Communications Message Protocol
DDN	Defense Data Network
DDP	Datagram Delivery Protocol
DECmcc	DEC Management Control Center
DEMPR	DEC multiport repeater
DES	Data Encryption Standard
DFT	discrete Fourier transform
DHCP	Dynamic Host Configuration Protocol
DIX	DEC, Intel, and Xerox
DL	data link
DLC	data link control
DLCI	data link connection identifier
DMA	direct memory access
DMI	Desktop Management Interface
DMTF	Desktop Management Task Force
DNIC	Data Network Identification Code
DNS	Domain Name System
DOD	Department of Defense
DPA	demand protocol architecture

DPCM	differential pulse code modulation
DRP	DECnet Routing Protocol
DSAP	destination service access point
DSI	digital speech interpolation
DSP	digital signal processing
DSU	Data Service Unit
DSU/CSU	Data service unit/channel service unit
DTE	data terminal equipment
DTMF	Dual Tone Multifrequency
DTR	data terminal ready
DTV	digital television
DVC	desktop videoconferencing

E

E and M	Ear and Mouth
EBCDIC	Extended Binary Coded Decimal Interchange Code
ECL	End Communication layer
ECSA	Exchange Carriers Standards Association
EDI	electronic data interchange
EGA	enhanced graphics array
EGP	Exterior Gateway Protocol
EIA	Electronic Industries Association
ELAP	EtherTalk Link Access Protocol
EOT	end-of-transmission
ESF	extended superframe format
ES-IS	End System to Intermediate System Protocol
ESP	encapsulating security payload
ETSI	European Telecommunications Standards Institute

F

FAL	file access listener
FAS	frame alignment signal
FAT	file access table
FCC	Federal Communications Commission
FCI	frame copied indicator bit
FCS	frame check sequence
FDDI	fiber distributed data interface
FDM	frequency division multiplexing
FEC	forward error correction
FECN	forward explicit congestion notification
FID	format identifier
FIPS	Federal Information Processing Standard
FM	function management
FMD	function management data
FoIP	Fax over Internet Protocol
FT1	fractional T1
FTAM	File Transfer Access and Management
FTP	File Transfer Protocol
FXO	Foreign exchange office

G

G	giga-
GB	gigabyte
GCC	Generic Conference Control
GCF	Gatekeeper Confirmation message
GHz	gigahertz
GOSIP	Government OSI profile

GRJ	Gatekeeper Reject message
GRQ	Gatekeeper Request message
GSTN	general switched telephone network
GUI	graphical user interface

H

HA	hardware address
HDLC	High-Level Data Link Control
HDTV	high-definition TV
HEMS	high-level entity management system
HLLAPI	High-level language API
HMMO	Hypermedia Managed Object
HMMP	Hypermedia Management Protocol
HMMS	Hypermedia Management Schema
HMOM	Hypermedia Object Manager
HTML	Hypertext Markup Language
HTTP	Hypertext Transfer Protocol
Hz	hertz

I

IAB	Internet Activities Board
IANA	Internet Assigned Numbers Authority
ICD	international code designator
ICMP	Internet Control Message Protocol
ICP	Internet Control Protocol
IDI	initial domain indicator
IDP	Internetwork Datagram Protocol
IDRP	Interdomain Routing Protocol

IEEE	Institute of Electrical and Electronics Engineers
IETF	Internet Engineering Task Force
I/G	individual/group
IGMP	Internet Group Management Protocol
IGP	Interior Gateway Protocol
IGRP	Internet Gateway Routing Protocol
IMPS	interface message processors
IMTC	International Multimedia Teleconferencing Consortium
I/O	input/output
IOC	interoffice channel
IP	Internet Protocol
Ipng	Internet Protocol, next generation
IPv6	Internet Protocol, version 6
IPv6CP	Internet Protocol version 6 Control Protocol
IPC	Interprocess Communications Protocol
IP sec	Internet Protocol security
IPX	Internetwork Packet Exchange Protocol
IR	Internet router
IRTF	Internet Research Task Force
ISAKMP	Internet Secure Association Key Management Protocol
ISDN	Integrated Services Digital Network
IS-IS	Intermediate System to Intermediate System Protocol
ISN	initial sequence number
ISO	International Organization for Standardization
ISOC	Internet Society
ISODE	ISO Development Environment
ISP	Internet Service Provider
ITSP	Internet Telephony Service Provider
ITU	International Telecommunication Union
ITU-D	International Telecommunication Union Development Sector

ITU-R	International Telecommunication Union Radiocommunications Sector
ITU-T	International Telecommunication Union Standardization Sector
IVR	Interactive Voice Response
IWU	internetworking unit
IXC	inter-exchange carrier

J

JDBC	Java Database Connectivity
JMAPI	Java Management Application Programming Interface
JPEG	Joint Photographic Experts Group

K

Kbps	kilo bits per second
kHz	kilohertz
KLT	Karhunen-Loeve transform
LAA	locally administered address
LAN	local area network
LANE	LAN Emulation
LAP	link access procedure
LAPB	Link Access Procedure Balanced
LAPD	Link Access Procedure D Channel
LAT	Local Area Transport
LATA	local access transport area
LAVC	local area VAX cluster
LCP	Link Control Protocol
LDAP	Lightweight Directory Access Protocol
LD-CELP	Low delay code excited linear prediction
LEC	local exchange carrier

LEN	length
LF	largest frame
LLAP	LocalTalk Link Access Protocol
LLC	Logical Link Control
LME	layer management entity
LMI	layer management interface
LMMP	LAN/MAN Management Protocol
LMMPE	LAN/MAN Management Protocol Entity
LMMS	LAN/MAN Management Service
LMMU	LAN/MAN Management User
LPAS	Linear prediction analysis-by-synthesis
LPC	linear predictive coding
LPP	Lightweight Presentation Protocol
LRQ	Location Request
LSB	least significant bit
LSL	Link Support layer

M

MAC	medium access control
MAE	Metropolitan Area Exchanges
MAN	metropolitan area network
MBONE	Multicasting backbone
Mbps	megabits per second
MC	Multipoint controller
MCS	Multipoint Communication Service
MCU	Multipoint Control Unit
MELP	mixed-excitation LPC
MGCP	Media Gateway Control Protocol
MHS	message handling service

MHz	megahertz
MIB	management information base
MILNET	Military Network
MILSTD	military standard
MIOX	Multiprotocol Interconnect over X.25
MIPS	millions instructions per second
MIS	management information systems
MLID	multiple link interface driver
MNP	Microcom Networking Protocol
MOP	Maintenance Operations Protocol
MOS	Mean Opinion Scores
MPEG	Motion Pictures Expert Group
MP-MLQ	Multipulse Maximum Likelihood Quantization
MPOA	Multiprotocol over ATM
MSAU	multistation access unit
MSB	most significant bit
MSS	maximum segment size
MTA	message transfer agent
MTBF	mean time between failures
MTTR	mean time to repair
MTU	maximum transmission unit
MUX	multiplex, multiplexor

N

NACS	NetWare Asynchronous Communications Server
NAK	negative acknowledgment
NAPs	Network Access Points
NASI	NetWare Asynchronous Service Interface
NAU	network addressable unit

NAUN	nearest active upstream neighbor
NBP	Name Binding Protocol
NCP	Network Control Program
NCP	Network Control Protocol
NCSI	network communications services interface
NDIS	Network Driver Interface Standard
NetBEUI	NetBIOS Extended User Interface
NetBIOS	Network Basic Input/Output System
NFS	Network File System
NIC	network information center
NICE	network information and control exchange
NIS	names information socket
N ISDN	narrowband-ISDN
NIST	National Institute of Standards and Technology
NLA	next-level aggregation identifier
NLM	netware loadable module
NMS	network management station
NOC	network operations center
NOS	network operating system
NSAP	Network Service Access Point
NSF	National Science Foundation
NSP	Network Services Protocol
NT	network termination
NTSC	National Television Standards Committee

O

OBASC	object-based analysis-synthesis coding
OBC	object-based coding
OC1	optical carrier, level 1

ODI	Open Data Link Interface
OID	object identifier
OIM	OSI Internet management
OSF	Open Software Foundation
OSI	Open Systems Interconnection
OSI-RM	Open Systems Interconnection Reference Model
OSPF	Open Shortest Path First

P

PA	protocol address
PABX	private automatic branch exchange
PAD	packet assembler and disassembler
PAL	Phased Alternating Line
PAP	Printer Access Protocol
PBX	Private Branch Exchange
PC	personal computer
PCI	protocol control information
PCM	pulse code modulation
PDN	public data network
PDU	protocol data unit
Pel	Picture element
PEP	Packet Exchange Protocol
PIC	Primary interexchange carrier
pixel	Picture element
PLEN	protocol length
PMTU	path maximum transmission unit
POP	point of presence
POSIX	Portable Operating System Interface – UNIX
POTS	plain old telephone service

PPP	Point-to-Point Protocol
PRI	Primary Rate Interface
PSDN	packet-switched data network
PSN	packet switch node
PSP	presentation services process
PSPDN	packet switched public data network
PSTN	Public Switched Telephone Network
PTP	point-to-point
PUC	Public Utility Commission

Q

| QCIF | Quarter Common Intermediate Format |
| QoS | Quality of Service |

R

RARP	Reverse Address Resolution Protocol
RAS	Registration Admissions Status
RBOC	Regional Bell Operating Company
RC	routing control
RD	route descriptor
RED	Random Early Detection
RFCs	Request for Comments
RFS	remote file system
RGB	red-green-blue
RH	request/response header
RI	routing information
RII	route information indicator
RIP	Routing Information Protocol

RISV	Reference Impairment System for Video
RJE	remote job entry
RMI	Remote Method Invocation
RMON	remote monitoring
ROSE	Remote Operations Service Element
RPC	Remote Procedure Call
RPS	ring parameter server
RRJ	Registration Reject message
RRQ	Registration Request message
RSVP	Resource Reservation Protocol
RSX	Real-time Resource-Sharing Executive
RT	routing type
RTCP	Real-time Control Protocol
RTP	Real Time protocol
RTSP	Real Time Stream Protocol
RTT	round trip time
RU	request/response unit

S

SA	source address
SABME	set asynchronous balanced mode extended
SAP	service access point
SB-ADPCM	subband adaptive differential pulse code modulation
SCS	system communication services
SDLC	Synchronous Data Link Control
SDN	software defined network
SECAM	Sequentiel Couleur Avec Memoire (French), Sequential Color with Memory
SEQ	sequence

SG	Study Group
SGCP	Simple Gateway Control Protocol
SGMP	Simple Gateway Management Protocol
SIPP	Simple Internet Protocol Plus
SKIP	Simple Key Management for the Internet Protocol
S/L	strict/loose bits
SLA	site-level aggregation identifier
SLIP	Serial Line IP
SMB	server message block
SMDS	Switched Multimegabit Data Service
SMI	structure of management information
SMPTE	Society of Motion Picture and Television Engineers
SMTP	Simple Mail Transfer Protocol
SNA	System Network Architecture
SNADS	Systems Network Architecture Distribution Services
SNAP	subnetwork access protocol
SNMP	Simple Network Management Protocol
SOH	start of header
SONET	Synchronous Optical Network
SPI	Security Parameters Index
SPP	Sequenced Packet Protocol
SPX	Sequenced Packet Exchange protocol
SQEG	speech quality experts group
SR	source routing
SRF	specifically routed frame
SRI	Stanford Research Institute
SRT	source routing transparent
SRTS	synchronous residual time stamp
SSAP	source service access point
STE	spanning tree explorer

SUA	stored upstream address
SVC	switched virtual circuit
SVGA	Super visual graphics array

T

TAPI	Telephony Application Programming Interface
TASI	Time Assignment Speech Interpolation
TB	terabyte
TCP	Transmission Control Protocol
TCP/IP	Transmission Control Protocol/Internet Protocol
TDM	Time Division Multiplexing
TELNET	Telecommunications Network Protocol
TFTP	Trivial File Transfer Protocol
TH	transmission header
TLA	top-level aggregation identifier
TLAP	TokenTalk Link Access Protocol
TLI	Transport Layer Interface
TLV	Type-Length-Value encoding
TOS	Type of Service
TP	Transport Protocol
TSAG	Telecommunication Standardization Advisory Group
TSI	time slot interchange
TSR	terminate-and-stay resident
TTL	time to live
TTS	text-to-speech
TVML	television modeling language
TUBA	TCP/UDP with Bigger Addresses

U

UA	user agent
UDP	User Datagram Protocol
U/L	universal/local
ULP	Upper Layer Protocols
UNMA	unified network management architecture
URJ	Unregister Reject message
URQ	Unregister Request message
UT	universal time
UTP	unshielded twisted pair
UUCP	UNIX to UNIX copy program

V

V	volt
VAN	value-added network
VAP	value-added process
VARP	VINES Address Resolution Protocol
VBR	Variable Bit Rate
VC	virtual circuit
VFRP	VINES Fragmentation Protocol
VGA	video graphics array
VICP	VINES Internet Control Protocol
VINES	Virtual Networking System
VIP	VINES Internet Protocol
VIPC	VINES Interprocess Communications
VLBV	very low bit-rate video
VLC	variable length code
VLSI	very large-scale integration

VLSM	variable length submask
VMS	virtual memory system
VoIP	Voice over IP
VPI/VCI	virtual channel identifier/virtual path identifier
VPN	Virtual Private Network
VRTP	VINES Routing Update Protocol
VSPP	VINES Sequenced Packet Protocol
VT	virtual terminal

W

WAN	wide area network
WBEM	Web-based Enterprise Management
WFQ	Weighted Fair Queuing
WIN	window
WRED	Weighted RED

X

XDR	External data representation
XID	exchange identification
XMP	X/Open Management Protocol
XNS	Xerox Network System

Z

ZIP	Zone Information Protocol
ZIS	Zone Information Socket
ZIT	Zone Information Table

Appendix H

Trademarks

Access Power Advanced Communications is a trademark of Access Power Gateway Network, Inc.

PostScript is a trademark of Adobe Systems.

Apple, the Apple logo, AppleTalk, EtherTalk, LocalTalk, Macintosh, and TokenTalk are registered trademarks of Apple Computer, Inc.

.comfax is a trademark of .comfax, Inc.

DEC, DECmcc, DECnet, Digital, LAT, LAVC, Micro-VAX, MOP, POLYCENTER, ThinWire, Ultrix, VAX, and VAX Cluster are trademarks, and Ethernet is a registered trademark of Compaq Computer Corporation.

Concentric Network is a trademark of Concentric Network Corporation.

IP Library and IP Technologies Library are trademarks, and DigiNet is a registered trademark of Digital Network Corporation.

eFusion, the Push-to-Talk button, and the eFusion logo are registered trademarks of eFusion, Inc. Push-to-Talk (PtT), eBridge, eStream, Hop On, Hop Off, TeamBrowse, and MultiHold are trademarks of eFusion, Inc.

GRIC is a registered trademark of GRIC Communications, Inc.

iBasis Network is a trademark of iBasis, Inc.

Net2Phone is a registered servicemark of IDT Corporation.

Ethernet, Intel and Video Phone are registered trademarks of Intel Corporation.

IBM PC LAN, PC/AT, PC/XT, SNA, System/370, MicroChannel, NetBIOS, SAA, and System View are trademarks of International Business Machines Corporation; and AIX, AT, IBM, NetView, and PS/2 are registered trademarks of International Business Machines Corporation.

IRIS Phone is a registered trademark of IRIS Systems.

ITXC is a trademark of ITXC Corporation.

Level 3 Communications is a trademark of Level 3 Communications, Inc.

MediaRing and MediaRing Talk are trademarks of MediaRing Inc.

Microsoft, Microsoft NetMeeting, MS-DOS, LAN Manager, Windows and Windows NT are registered trademarks of Microsoft Corporation.

NCI Global Multi Media Network is a trademark of NCI Communications, Inc.

CoolTalk is a trademark of Netscape Communications Corporation.

WebPhone is a registered trademark of NetSpeak Corporation used under license by Creative Technology, Ltd.

NetVoice is a trademark of NetVoice Technologies Corporation.

Networks Telephony is a trademark of Networks Telephony Corporation.

IPX, ManageWise, NetWare, NetWare 386, Novell, and SPX are trademarks, and Novell is a registered trademark of Novell, Inc.

OnLive is a trademark of OnLive, Inc.

Qwest is a registered trademark of Qwest Communications.

BSD is a trademark of the Regents of the University of California.

Java, Network File System, NFS, Sun, Sun Microsystems Inc., Sun Microsystems, SunNet, SunOS and SunSoft are trademarks or registered trademarks of Sun Microsystems, Inc. SPARC is a registered trademark of SPARC International, Inc., licensed to Sun Microsystems, Inc.

Internet Phone is a trademark of VocalTec Communications.

DigiPhone is a trademark of Wincroft, Inc.

UNIX is a registered trademark of X/Open Company Ltd.

Ethernet and Xerox are registered trademarks of Xerox Corporation.

All other trademarks are the property of their respective owners.

Index

IDG Books Worldwide, Inc.
End-User License Agreement

READ THIS. You should carefully read these terms and conditions before opening the software packet(s) included with this book ("Book"). This is a license agreement ("Agreement") between you and IDG Books Worldwide, Inc. ("IDGB"). By opening the accompanying software packet(s), you acknowledge that you have read and accept the following terms and conditions. If you do not agree and do not want to be bound by such terms and conditions, promptly return the Book and the unopened software packet(s) to the place you obtained them for a full refund.

1. <u>License Grant</u>. IDGB grants to you (either an individual or entity) a nonexclusive license to use one copy of the enclosed software program(s) (collectively, the "Software") solely for your own personal or business
   purposes on a single computer (whether a standard computer or a workstation component of a multiuser network). The Software is in use on a computer when it is loaded into temporary memory (RAM) or installed into permanent memory (hard disk, CD-ROM, or other storage device). IDGB reserves all rights not expressly granted herein.

2. <u>Ownership</u>. IDGB is the owner of all right, title, and interest, including copyright, in and to the compilation of the Software recorded on the disk(s) or CD-ROM ("Software Media"). Copyright to the individual programs recorded on the Software Media is owned by the author or other authorized copyright owner of each program. Ownership of the Software and all proprietary rights relating thereto remain with IDGB and its licensers.

3. <u>Restrictions On Use and Transfer</u>.

   (a) You may only (i) make one copy of the Software for backup or archival purposes, or (ii) transfer the Software to a single hard disk, provided that you keep the original for backup or archival purposes. You may not (i) rent or lease the Software, (ii) copy or reproduce the Software through a LAN or other network system or through any computer subscriber system or bulletin@@hyboard system, or (iii) modify, adapt, or create derivative works based on the Software.

   (b) You may not reverse engineer, decompile, or disassemble the Software. You may transfer the Software and user documentation on a permanent basis, provided that the transferee agrees to accept the terms and conditions of this Agreement and you retain no copies. If the Software is an update or has been updated, any transfer must include the most recent update and all prior versions.

4. <u>Restrictions on Use of Individual Programs</u>. You must follow the individual requirements and restrictions detailed for each individual program in Appendix A of this Book. These limitations are also contained in the individual license agreements recorded on the Software Media. These limitations may include a requirement that after using the program for a specified period of time, the user must pay a registration fee or discontinue use. By opening the Software packet(s), you will be agreeing to abide by the licenses and restrictions for these individual programs that are detailed in Appendix A and on the Software Media. None of the material on this Software Media or listed in this Book may ever be redistributed, in original or modified form, for commercial purposes.

5. Limited Warranty.

(a) IDGB warrants that the Software and Software Media are free from defects in materials and workmanship under normal use for a period of sixty (60) days from the date of purchase of this Book. If IDGB receives notification within the warranty period of defects in materials or workmanship, IDGB will replace the defective Software Media.

(b) IDGB AND THE AUTHOR OF THE BOOK DISCLAIM ALL OTHER WARRANTIES, EXPRESS OR IMPLIED, INCLUDING WITHOUT LIMITATION IMPLIED WARRANTIES OF MERCHANTABILITY AND FITNESS FOR A PARTICULAR PURPOSE, WITH RESPECT TO THE SOFTWARE, THE PROGRAMS, THE SOURCE CODE CONTAINED THEREIN, AND/OR THE TECHNIQUES DESCRIBED IN THIS BOOK. IDGB DOES NOT WARRANT THAT THE FUNCTIONS CONTAINED IN THE SOFTWARE WILL MEET YOUR REQUIREMENTS OR THAT THE OPERATION OF THE SOFTWARE WILL BE ERROR FREE.

(c) This limited warranty gives you specific legal rights, and you may have other rights that vary from jurisdiction to jurisdiction.

6. Remedies.

(a) IDGB's entire liability and your exclusive remedy for defects in materials and workmanship shall be limited to replacement of the Software Media, which may be returned to IDGB with a copy of your receipt at the following address: Software Media Fulfillment Department, Attn.: Voice over IP: Strategies for the Converged Network, IDG Books Worldwide, Inc., 10475 Crosspoint Blvd., Indianapolis, IN 46256, or call 1-800-762-2974. Please allow three to four weeks for delivery. This Limited Warranty is void if failure of the Software Media has resulted from accident, abuse, or misapplication. Any replacement Software Media will be warranted for the remainder of the original warranty period or thirty (30) days, whichever is longer.

(b) In no event shall IDGB or the author be liable for any damages what-soever (including without limitation damages for loss of business profits, business interruption, loss of business information, or any other pecuniary loss) arising from the use of or inability to use the Book or the Software, even if IDGB has been advised of the possibility of such damages.

(c) Because some jurisdictions do not allow the exclusion or limitation of liability for consequential or incidental damages, the above limitation or exclusion may not apply to you.

7. U.S. Government Restricted Rights. Use, duplication, or disclosure of the Software by the U.S. Government is subject to restrictions stated in paragraph (c)(1)(ii) of the Rights in Technical Data and Computer Software clause of DFARS 252.227-7013, and in subparagraphs (a) through (d) of the Commercial Computer – Restricted Rights clause at FAR 52.227-19, and in similar clauses in the NASA FAR supplement, when applicable.

8. General. This Agreement constitutes the entire understanding of the parties and revokes and supersedes all prior agreements, oral or written, between them and may not be modified or amended except in a writing signed by both parties hereto that specifically refers to this Agreement. This Agreement shall take precedence over any other documents that may be in conflict herewith. If any one or more provisions contained in this Agreement are held by any court or tribunal to be invalid, illegal, or otherwise unenforceable, each and every other provision shall remain in full force and effect.

my2cents.idgbooks.com

Register This Book — And Win!

Visit **http://my2cents.idgbooks.com** to register this book and we'll automatically enter you in our fantastic monthly prize giveaway. It's also your opportunity to give us feedback: let us know what you thought of this book and how you would like to see other topics covered.

Discover IDG Books Online!

The IDG Books Online Web site is your online resource for tackling technology — at home and at the office. Frequently updated, the IDG Books Online Web site features exclusive software, insider information, online books, and live events!

10 Productive & Career-Enhancing Things You Can Do at www.idgbooks.com

- Nab source code for your own programming projects.

- Download software.

- Read Web exclusives: special articles and book excerpts by IDG Books Worldwide authors.

- Take advantage of resources to help you advance your career as a Novell or Microsoft professional.

- Buy IDG Books Worldwide titles or find a convenient bookstore that carries them.

- Register your book and win a prize.

- Chat live online with authors.

- Sign up for regular e-mail updates about our latest books.

- Suggest a book you'd like to read or write.

- Give us your 2¢ about our books and about our Web site.

You say you're not on the Web yet? It's easy to get started with IDG Books' *Discover the Internet,* available at local retailers everywhere.

CD-ROM INSTALLATION INSTRUCTIONS

To install the CD-ROM, insert the disk into the CD-ROM drive on your computer. You can access the contents of the CD-ROM through Windows Explorer, or by opening My Computer on the desktop.

The CD-ROM contains a collection of public domain Internet documents, from the Internet Architecture Board (IAB), Internet Engineering Task Force (IETF), Internet Research Group (IRG), and other Internet-related organizations. For a list of categories and subdirectories, please see Appendix A.